Transition from School to Work

Transition from School to Work

New Challenges for Youth with Severe Disabilities

Paul Wehman, Ph.D.
M. Sherril Moon, Ed.D.
Jane M. Everson, M.S.
Wendy Wood, M.S.
J. Michael Barcus, M.S.

School of Education
Virginia Commonwealth University

·P·A·U·L·H·
BROOKES
PUBLISHING CO.

Baltimore • London • Toronto • Sydney

Paul H. Brookes Publishing Co.
Post Office Box 10624
Baltimore, Maryland 21285-0624

Typeset by Brushwood Graphics Inc., Baltimore, Maryland.
Manufactured in the United States of America by
The Maple Press Company, York, Pennsylvania.

Library of Congress Cataloging-in-Publication Data
Transition from school to work.
   Bibliography: p.
   Includes index.
   1. Vocational guidance for the handicapped—United
States.   2. Handicapped—Employment—United States.
I. Wehman, Paul.
HV1568.5.T72   1987   362.4'088055   87-15137
ISBN 0-933716-92-3 (soft)

Contents

The Authors ix
Foreword   *Susan Brody Hasazi* xi
Preface xiii
Acknowledgments xv

Chapter 1   **Transition from School to Work**   1
   What is Transition?   2
   Factors Influencing Transition during Past Decades   4
   A Model for Vocational Transition of
   Handicapped Youth   7
   Public School: The Foundation of Effective
   Transition   7
   Planning for Vocational Transition: The Process   11
   Formal Individualized Student Plans   12
   Problems Involved in Implementing Effective
   Employment Programs in School Settings   14
   Summary   27

Chapter 2   **What Happens to Youth with Disabilities
               after They Grow Up?**   29
   Why Conduct Follow-Up Surveys of Special
   Education Graduates?   30
   Studies Related to Postsecondary Vocational
   Adjustment   32
   Methodological and Logistical Difficulties in
   Conducting Post-21 Follow-Up Surveys   38
   Conclusions About Post-21 Studies   40
   Surveying for Postsecondary Adjustment: A Sample   41
   Summary   41
   Appendix: Adjustment of Mentally Retarded Persons   42

Chapter 3   **Planning for Transition from School to Work**   49
   Elements of the Transition Process   50
   Summary   68

Chapter 4   **Individualized Transition Planning** 69
Implementing an Individualized Transition Planning
Procedure 71
Communication with Parents 96
Summary 96

Chapter 5   **Interagency Cooperation** 97
Interagency Cooperation at the State Level 98
The Local Level 101
Models of Interagency Interaction 113
A Three-Way Interagency Agreement for Transition
Planning and Supported Employment Service:
Mission Statement 116
Cooperating Agency Liaisons 118
Individualized Transition Meetings 119
Supported Employment Services 122
Exchange of Information 126
Expected Outcomes 127
Administrative Considerations 128
Summary 129

Chapter 6   **School-Based Vocational Preparation** 131
School Vocational Preparation: A Historical
Perspective 131
Underlying Assumptions of an Individualized Education
Program: What to Teach 138
Systematic, Behavioral Instruction in Natural
Settings: How to Teach 145
Summary 163
Appendix 163

Chapter 7   **Adult Service Alternatives: Day Care or
Employment?** 165
Employment for Individuals with Disabilities:
A Rationale 166
The Costs of Unemployment for Persons with
Disabilities 168
Major Vocational Alternatives for Adults with
Disabilities 171
Supported Employment 179
The Supported Competitive Employment Model 182
Mobile Work Crews and Enclaves 187
The Small Business Option 192
Deciding Which Option to Choose 192

Chapter 8   **Defining Professional and Parent Roles and
Responsibilities** 195
Defining Roles and Responsibilities 197
Characteristics of Effective Interagency and

Transdisciplinary Teams 210
Strategies for Changing Roles and Team Building 212
Summary 215

Chapter 9   Transition: Local and State Initiatives in
            Action 217
Factors Associated with Promoting Transition
Planning at the Local or State Level 217
Transition Into Supported Competitive Employment:
Five School Systems Making It Work 219
Transition Initiatives at the State Level 229
Transition Activities in Selected States 248
Some Concluding Thoughts 250
Summary 251

Appendix A   Guidelines for Parent Involvement in
             Vocational Training 253
Appendix B   Knowing Work and Residential Options 257
Appendix C   Federal Initiatives, Legislative Mandates,
             and Employment Incentive Programs 259
Appendix D   Employment Information Resources 271
Appendix E   Annotated Bibliography on Supported
             Employment and Transition 275

References 301

Index 311

The Authors

Paul Wehman, Ph.D.
Professor of Special Education and
    Director
Rehabilitation Research and
    Training Center
Virginia Commonwealth University
1314 West Main Street
Richmond, Virginia 23284-0001

M. Sherril Moon, Ed.D.
Assistant Professor of Special
    Education and Director of
    Training
Rehabilitation Research and
    Training Center
Virginia Commonwealth University
1314 West Main Street
Richmond, Virginia 23284-0001

Jane Everson, M.S.
Project Coordinator, Transition Into
    Employment
Rehabilitation Research and
    Training Center
Virginia Commonwealth University
1314 West Main Street
Richmond, Virginia 23284-0001

Wendy Wood, M.S.
Director of Head Injury Project
Rehabilitation Research and
    Training Center
Virginia Commonwealth University
1314 West Main Street
Richmond, Virginia 23284-0001

J. Michael Barcus, M.S.
Assistant Director of Training
Rehabilitation Research and
    Training Center
Virginia Commonwealth University
1314 West Main Street
Richmond, Virginia 23284-0001

Foreword

THE TRANSITION FROM SCHOOL TO WORK FOR YOUTH WITH SEVERE DISABILITIES HAS become a major issue of concern for parents, professionals, and policymakers. Recent follow-up studies of young people with disabilities who left or graduated from high school over the past 5 years reveal not only high unemployment rates, but disproportionate numbers of young women with disabilities unemployed as compared to their male counterparts. In addition, there are few opportunities for community integration. In spite of the relatively bleak picture painted by those and other accounts of "life after graduation," there is reason for hope. Current literature reveals a growing body of experience and knowledge elucidating strategies and practices that facilitate employment, independence, and integration for persons with disabilities. Recent research and practice have identified a number of school-based variables which, when incorporated into transition programs, appear to improve success rates for client placement. These variables include: the development of transition plans as a component of the IEP, interagency involvement in the planning and implementation of transition plans, introduction of vocational training (as early as elementary school), paid work during the high school years, integrated vocational education programs, community-based training, and utilization of the family-friend network for locating and obtaining employment. While some of these practices are not new to the field, others present unique challenges to educators and adult services professionals. In this book, Paul Wehman and his colleagues at Virginia Commonwealth University have identified strategies for implementing the promising practices described above. These strategies promise to advance the planning of positive futures for young people with severe disabilities.

The book is unique because it outlines a systematic approach to effecting change in work and school environments. Strategies for developing policies and for planning activities at both the state and local levels are described in detail, as are methods for achieving interagency collaboration in the delivery of transition services. Case studies of local school districts and state level initiatives are provided, and common elements among these model programs are identified. Thus the reader is invited to contemplate a variety of approaches that have proven to be successful.

In addition to addressing the large systems issues, such as policy development, the book provides a comprehensive description of the Individualized Transition Planning (ITP) process. Issues related to determining who should participate in the ITP process, identification of appropriate outcomes and teaching strategies, and the roles and responsibilities of school, adult services professionals, and parents are described in detail. For educators who may not be familiar with postsecondary services, the chapter on supported employment alternatives to traditional, nonvocational day programs may be helpful. Familiarity with these new and promising employment models will help professionals to expand secondary school curricula and programs to include transition planning, and will improve the process of individualized transition planning for persons with disabilities.

Wehman and his colleagues have demonstrated through their work in Virginia that young people with severe disabilities can make the transition smoothly from school to employment in the community. The information articulated in this book will allow educators, parents, and human services professionals to initiate and carry out local blueprints for change that will ultimately result in positive employment outcomes for youth with disabilities. Finally and perhaps most importantly, the book demonstrates that for individuals with severe disabilities, what is perhaps the last barrier to societal integration, that of employment, is finally being seriously and systematically addressed.

Susan Brody Hasazi, Ed.D.
University of Vermont

Preface

THE PAST 5 YEARS HAVE REVEALED TREMENDOUS INTEREST ON THE PART OF PROFESsionals and parents in helping adolescents with disabilities prepare for adulthood. One such step toward adulthood takes place when students leave school. Leaving school is a major life-style change for all students, whether or not they have disabilities. Once young people no longer attend school, they are expected to assume greater responsibilities and to meet the increased expectations of society. It is usually expected, for example, that upon graduation, one will begin full-time employment and begin to live independently. The opportunities to take on these employment and residential responsibilities should be as available for young adults with severe disabilities as they are for nondisabled persons.

The *Wall Street Journal* devoted a major article to the troubling fact that disabled youth are leaving school and are encountering long waiting lists for services, or are finding there are no adult services available at all. It is noteworthy that a leading national newspaper like the *Wall Street Journal* has drawn attention to the challenge of transition. The *Journal* observes:

> . . . About 50,000 mentally impaired students—those with IQs 30 or more points below the 100 norm—now graduate each year from public high schools. Special educators consider this generation unique. Because of parental pressure in the 1960s and federal legislation 12 years ago, public schools were forced to begin educating these children through age 21, thus marking them as the first such generation to escape institutionalization en masse. Most of them have, along with their parents, heightened expectations that they needn't lead limited lives. . . .
> . . . Many, however, are emerging from school without direction. While nearly all require additional help to develop job skills, the roughly 5,000 training and support programs nationwide, many of them underfunded, are unable to handle even the people on waiting lists. As a result, these young adults are typically forced to move into adult facilities or stay at home, where they often become depressed and lose the work, living and social skills they acquired in the outside world. (January 16, 1987)

The implementation of Public Law 94-142 was a significant achievement because it paved the way for an era of expanding transition from school to adulthood planning. Federal and state statutes requiring school for all handicapped children have created a covenant between parents and professionals to provide these children with educational services. The logical outgrowth of this covenant is the necessity for planning and implementing *meaningful* movement of the student from school to employment and community living in adulthood.

What is clear to those closely involved with effective transition programs is that for a program to be successful, there must be a reliance on individualized program planning, service delivery, and interagency coordination. These elements are the backbone of any effective transition programming. The recent federal initiatives concerning transition have helped professionals focus their attention on the importance of individualized programmatic and transitional planning, on community- and industry-referenced service delivery in local programs, and on the necessity of interagency coordination. While there can be little doubt that these concepts have been with us for a long time, there is room for professionals and parents to greatly improve the quality of these elements. The sustained federal focus on transition can be the vehicle for such improvements by promoting local and statewide systems through legislative resolutions, changes in state laws, and special project funding.

This book is a comprehensive look at the transition movement, with special attention devoted to service provision for students with severe disabilities. The text focuses upon sustained employment as the primary goal rather than community and personal adjustment. This approach is not intended to minimize the importance of community living competence but rather to emphasize the substantial influence that employment can have on all dimensions of one's life. It is the authors' goal to show that when professionals and parents work closely together on a single goal, significant outcomes can accrue. This book is for professionals, parents, advocates, and students who are interested in seeing how all aspects of transition can be pulled together into a coherent blueprint for change.

Acknowledgments

THE COMPLETION OF THIS BOOK COULD NOT HAVE BEEN ACCOMPLISHED WITHOUT THE aid of the many people with whom we work closely, or without the cooperation of our colleagues in the field. With their help, we have endeavored to write a book that is based upon actual community services and shaped by our working relationships with many local and state agency personnel. To these professionals we owe a debt of gratitude. Jean Rollin in Florida, Bill Rosenberg and Larry Naeve in California, Paul Bates, Adelle Renzaglia, Frank Rusch, and Sharon Freagon in Illinois, Timm Vogelsberg in Pennsylvania, Linda Goodman in Connecticut, and Pat McCarthy in South Carolina have consistently given us feedback and provided models that have provided direction and guidance in the development of our thinking about transition.

The expertise made available by a number of professionals within the state of Virginia has given us the opportunity to learn optimal ways to plan and implement meaningful transition. JoAnn Marchant, Harold Burke, Sue McClennon, Roslyn Walker, Kathy Sadler, Mike Hill, Pat Poplin, Al Dickerson, Jim Rothrock, Linda Veldheer, Tom Bass, Les Jones, Jody Sands, Stephen Conley, Fred Orelove, Howard Garner, and Grant Revell are persons intimately involved as local and state leaders in transition. Their work and thoughts have shaped our thinking.

Within our own research center at Virginia Commonwealth University, the list of people who have given generously of their time is almost endless. We acknowledge the help of Patricia Goodall, John Kregel, Vicki Brooke, Wendy Parent, Mark Hill, Katty Inge, Paul Sale, M. V. Morton, Monique Wiggins, David Pitonyak, Steve Hall, Elizabeth Getzel, Grace Reyes, Carole Jesiolowski, Donna Allemani, Kelly Ibbotson, and Pam Sherron.

Some of our work has been supported by state and federal grant funds. The encouragement and leadership of federal officials at the U.S. Department of Education have given the transition movement a place of importance that could not have existed earlier. Specifically, we wish to thank Madeleine Will, G. Thomas Bellamy, Michael Herrell, Richard Melia, Carol Inman, Paul Thompson, Michael Ward, Delores Watkins, Betty Baker, and William Halloran for their guidance and support. Our book is developed as a source of information for people who wish to learn more about transition. Such a demand for this information could have never occurred without a federal initiative from the U.S. Department of Education.

Finally, but by no means least of all, we deeply appreciate the excellent typing and manuscript preparation provided by Jan Smith, Dawn Lorinser, Brenda M. Robinson, Rachel Conrad, and Melissa Robinson. Persons with such skills are the unsung heroes of any project like this. We are sincerely grateful for the effort they put into making this project a success.

Chapter 1

Transition from School to Work

LARRY EDWARDS[1] IS IN THE FINAL YEAR OF HIS SPECIAL EDUCATION program. He has been receiving special education since 1975 when President Ford signed the Education for All Handicapped Children Act (PL 94-142). Larry has been labeled as autistic. He cannot speak and often engages in disruptive behavior. Susan Wilson is also in her final year of school. She has been placed for several years in a class for children with multiple handicaps. Susan cannot see or walk. Martha Roberts was born with Down syndrome in 1965. She began school in 1976, and after 10 years of special education will be leaving school this year. John Salisbury, who is completely hearing impaired and was born with cerebral palsy, has just reached his 21st birthday.

What do these four young adults have in common with over 250,000 special education students each year? Each will be looking to find meaningful employment and some degree of residential independence. The four students above will also require coordinated transition planning from one major service system—public schools—to another major service system—adult services. In the cases of students who are graduating from special education programs, they all have another major feature in common. They are leaving one service system that mandates free and appropriate educational services under federal law and moving to another service system that is not under mandate to provide adult services for all disabled adults. Thus, many of these students will not receive services, either because of a lack of funds or due to perceived severity of disability. In many ways it has been this law, the Education for All Handicapped Children Act, which has stimulated significant pressure on adult service programs to respond to increased numbers of exiting students. Furthermore, all of these students are subject to the capabilities and willingness of lo-

---

[1]This name and the names that follow in this section are completely fictitious.

1

cal and state professionals across many agencies and disciplines to work together. Harmonious coordination of vocational, residential, transportation, case management, and other key services for the period from school to adulthood will need to be planned. Special education teachers, vocational education personnel, administrators, rehabilitation counselors, adult service program personnel, and case managers can either facilitate or impede the smoothness of transition from school to work.

This book outlines how to make such coordination happen. It also addresses how to design effective school programs for transition and how to recognize and develop meaningful employment programs. Above all, this book is for service professionals and students in the many disciplines that directly affect the viability of transition. The need for transition planning is not one that will shortly fade away. It has been estimated that over 60% of all special education students currently are between 14 and 21 years of age (Elder, 1984). By 1995, the first full generation of handicapped children will have completed special education. The purpose of this book is to provide several answers as to how to best effect this transition from school to the workplace.

WHAT IS TRANSITION?

Transition is a term that has been used frequently in professional circles (Brown et al., 1981; Rusch & Chadsey-Rusch, 1985). The U.S. Department of Education's Office of Special Education and Rehabilitative Services (OSERS) has made transition a major priority. The Assistant Secretary of this office, Madeleine Will, and her staff developed a conceptual transition model (1984a) that is characterized by an emphasis on quality secondary programs, a description of generic employment services, time-limited employment services, ongoing employment services, and an array of adult employment alternatives. Each of these three employment services is viewed as a bridge from school to work. *Generic services* are those already available to nonhandicapped people in the community (e.g., personnel agencies) and that probably would be used by mildly handicapped consumers. *Time-limited services,* on the other hand, are specialized rehabilitation or other adult services that are uniquely suited to help a handicapped person gain employment. These services come to an end once the individual succeeds in finding work. *Ongoing vocational services* (also called supported employment services) have not been available in most communities but would be aimed at hard-to-place severely handicapped people.

Wehman, Kregel, and Barcus (1985) have described vocational transition in the following definition:

> Vocational transition is a carefully planned process, which may be initiated either by school personnel or by adult service providers, to establish and implement a plan for either employment or additional vocational training of a handicapped student who will graduate or leave school in three to five years; such a process must involve special educators, vocational educators, parents and/or the student, an adult service system representative, and possibly an employer.

The key aspects of this definition are that: 1) members of multiple disciplines and service delivery systems must participate, 2) parental involvement is essential, 3) vocational transition planning must occur well before 21 years of age, 4) the process must be planned and systematic, and 5) the vocational service must be of a quality nature. A young student with autism making the transition from a school program that provides instruction in learning the letters of the alphabet, the days of the week, the seasons of the year, coloring skills, and other preschool developmental activities into a different setting (such as an adult activity center) with the same training objectives is being placed in a program that accomplishes little and distorts the purpose of the transition initiative. The Wehman model (Wehman, Kregel, & Barcus, 1985) is discussed in greater detail later in this chapter.

Halpern (1985) broadened the OSERS emphasis from primary vocational training to *community adjustment*. Community adjustment requires competence in social and interpersonal skills, home living, and employment. Halpern believes that social and interpersonal skills may be the most important element of all in the transition process. Halpern's model has been very useful in focusing the attention of professionals on *all* aspects of transition, not only employment.

It is the authors' belief that both employment and independent living are critically important elements of the change from school to adulthood for all students, not only for those with severe handicaps. Therefore, this book focuses not only on vocational alternatives for students over the age of 21, but community living and residential opportunities as well.

The U.S. Department of Education Transition Model

As noted above, the Office of Special Education and Rehabilitative Services has made transition a major federal priority. The OSERS model accommodates many exiting students with mild handicaps who will need no special services. This, of course, will be the majority of handicapped youth. Next, there is a group of students who will require time-limited services, assistance that is only provided for a limited length of time, usually until the person's needs have been met. Vocational rehabilitation services are a good example of this type of service. Ongoing service is the last bridge for employment described in the OSERS model. This level reflects the need of individuals with the most severe handicaps who cannot work without permanent follow-along assistance and support. Table 1.1 shows this model graphically.

FACTORS INFLUENCING
TRANSITION DURING PAST DECADES

As has been already noted, transition of youth from school to adulthood is a topic that is gaining much interest among professionals in special education, developmental disabilities, and rehabilitation. The expanding literature in this area includes descriptive case studies (Zetlin & Turner, 1985), vocational transitional models (Wehman, Kregel, & Barcus, 1985), community integration transition models (Halpern, 1985), and process related articles (McCarthy, Everson, Inge, & Barcus, 1985). It is noteworthy that the perspectives contributed by many professionals from different disciplines have stimulated national interest in transition planning programs.

Role of the Federal Government

The federal government has been influential in several ways. The Education for Handicapped Children Amendments of 1983 (PL 98-199), for example, included a Secondary Education and Transition Services Section. Section 626 authorizes funds to be spent on research, training, and demonstration in the transition area. This section has been recently further renewed by the 1986 Education Amendments. Another key manifestation of involvement by the federal government has been the leadership of the U.S. Department of Education, Office of Special Education and Rehabilitative Services, under Assistant Secretary Madeleine Will and Dr. Jean Elder, former Commissioner of the Administration of Developmental Disabilities. Their policies, combined with an orchestrated use of federal discretionary money, have had far-reaching consequences. The focused communication between these two offices has had the dramatic effect of riveting the attention of service providers, educators, legislators, university personnel, and even the media on the subject of transition. This increased public awareness is timely. Large numbers of previously unserved or underserved handicapped children are beginning to near the end of their special education. These young adults and their families want to know what services will be available for them after schooling has ended. Many of the parents of these children are highly informed and are not

Table 1.1.   Bridges to employment: The U.S. Department of Education's view of transition

High school	Employment
Regular jobs	1. No special services—typical routes taken by non-disabled persons; families and individuals find work or training without agency support. Vocational and technical schools and colleges are important to this kind of transition, as are family contacts, volunteer jobs, and neighborhood networks. Numbers of disabled persons working to employment through this route are unknown, but potential for development especially in community colleges and vocational-technical schools is great for mildly disabled citizens.
Regular jobs with modifications, when necessary	2. Time-limited services—usually must have some sort of disability to qualify for service, but generally restricted to those thought capable of succeeding in a regular job after services are withdrawn; most vocational rehabilitation services, federal and state funded job training programs, and postsecondary vocational education programs are time-limited in nature. In the past, almost all transitional programs have been time-limited and have not included young people with severe disabilities.
Regular jobs and special employment options providing decent wages	3. Ongoing services—will provide training and employment for citizens with more severe disabilities and will ensure support on a lifelong basis if necessary; represents a fundamental change in current agency practices and will require policy and funding revamping for mental retardation agencies, welfare organizations, and rehabilitation service providers. This transition process calls for the creation of several *supported employment* options, such as specialized training programs in industry, work crews and enclaves, and competitive jobs with continuous, public supported supervision. Such options would replace traditional, nonvocational adult activity programs.

willing to settle for just any type of adult services. The advocacy role of these parents is placing enormous pressure on vocational rehabilitation and adult service agencies to expand present employment alternatives and to develop new ones as well. It is fair to say that parents of younger children still in the special education system will have elevated expectations and will not tolerate inferior post-21 outcomes for their children.

Role of Vocational Training Technology

In addition to the substantial role the federal government has played in promoting transition, a large amount of new information is becoming available on the demonstrated vocational competencies of persons with severe handicaps. The past 15 years have seen an explosion of articles that illustrate and describe vocational and independent living competence by persons with severe handicaps. This increased competence has led to greater employment opportunities and improved expectations on the part of candidates, parents, and some professionals. The realization that many more persons with severe handicaps can perform real jobs has made transition a highly visible and meaningful topic, and one of serious urgency.

From the research of Marc Gold in 1972 showing how persons with severe retardation could put together bicycle brakes to the initial demonstration that people with similar labels could become competitively employed less than 10 years later (Wehman, 1981), it is evident that the increase in knowledge about transition has been incredible. Exclusionary practices based on assumptions of lack of employment potential are increasingly being questioned because of the expanding research data on vocational training and employment programs.

Role of the Media

A third influence that is increasing public awareness of the importance of transition planning is the media. Both the electronic and print media demonstrate a growing interest and awareness that persons with severe handicaps can work and live in the community. Articles such as those by Drogin (*Los Angeles Times,* March 16, 1985), Klinger (Alexandria, *Virginia Gazette,* May, 1985) and McLeod (*Psychology Today,* March, 1985) are becoming increasingly common. As the media become more involved, skeptical professionals and uninformed parents, as well as the community at large, will begin to develop more responsive attitudes.

Perhaps one of the leading articles in this vein was published by Roger Ricklefs in the *Wall Street Journal* (October 21, 1986). Information from this article such as in the following two excerpts reached millions of people in the United States:

> The older man can print his name only if you print it first. The younger man can do nothing more demanding intellectually than tell time. But together they have made a once-filthy shopping mall in Jersey City, N.J., spotless.
>
> "It is 100% better since they took over the job," says a liquor-store manager in the mall. "Before, it was so dirty we had to go out and clean it ourselves."

or

> The Association for Retarded Citizens spent three weeks teaching a New Jersey man with an IQ of 28 how to pack bags at a supermarket. "Every few months, we get a call that David is once again putting the bread at the

bottom and the milk on top . . . So we send a job coach to work side by side with him for two or three days, and he gets back in the right habits."

An article like this one that is specific in focus and that highlights people with such severe impairments reveals the public attention that competent handicapped workers are receiving. Adult day programs that are not oriented toward employment will need to increasingly re-examine their goals.

A MODEL FOR VOCATIONAL
TRANSITION OF HANDICAPPED YOUTH

Facilitating transition from school to the workplace is not a one-step process. It requires movement through the three stages of *school instruction, planning for the transition process,* and *placement into meaningful employment.* It is essential that service providers and agencies consider all available services, including the foundation services offered by public schools and the range of vocational alternatives offered by community agencies. Previous efforts at interagency agreements that purported to ameliorate transition problems actually resulted, in all too many cases, in movement of a student from one inadequate school program to another equally inadequate program.

Figure 1.1 presents a model that the authors feel overcomes the shortcomings of earlier attempts at transition and builds upon efforts that have previously succeeded. As illustrated in the figure, an appropriate special education program is characterized by functional curriculum (Wehman, Renzaglia, & Bates, 1985) in a school setting that reflects integration with nonhandicapped peers (Certo, Haring, & York, 1983; Stainback & Stainback, 1984), and that provides for a community-based instructional model of school services (Falvey, 1986; Wehman & Hill, 1982). These secondary program characteristics are fundamental to vocational transition. The actual transition process includes a formal individualized transition plan that features substantial parental input and cooperation from key agencies such as rehabilitation. Finally, neither the school program nor the planning process is sufficient without a range of varied work or employment options available to students after graduation.

PUBLIC SCHOOL: THE
FOUNDATION OF EFFECTIVE TRANSITION

Preparing students to be independent in their living skills and employable in the marketplace should be the major goals for the educational system. Without careful planning and preparation for post-

III.
Employment
Outcome
	Vocational outcome
	1. Competitive
	    employment
	2. Work crews/
	    enclaves
	3. Specialized shel-
	    tered work
	    arrangements
		Follow-up
		1–2 years later

II. **Process**	Individualized program plan 1. Formalize transi- tion responsibilities 2. Early planning	

	Consumer input 1. Parent 2. Student	Interagency cooperation 1. School 2. Rehabilitation 3. Adult day program 4. Voc-technical center

I.
Input and
Foundation
	Secondary and voca-
	tional special education
	program
	1. Functional
	    curriculum
	2. Integrated school
	    environment
	3. Community-based
	    service delivery	

Figure 1.1.   Three stage vocational transition model for handicapped youth, input and foundation; process; employment outcome.

school placement, these goals are seldom achieved by handicapped youth. However, over the past few years, critical program characteristics that contribute to effective programming have been identified (Bates, Renzaglia, & Wehman, 1981). These characteristics provide the foundation for meaningful transition from school to the workplace; therefore, it is of little value to discuss transition planning without crystallizing several key programming components. Critical characteristics of an appropriate secondary program include: 1) functional curriculum, 2) integrated schools, and 3) community-based service delivery.

Functional Curriculum

Training activities must be designed to prepare persons for vocational opportunities that are actually available in their community. To ensure this outcome, school personnel must continuously assess available community employment and analyze the specific skills required for successful job performance. As a result of this activity, the vocational curriculum for specific students can then be identified. In designing functional secondary programs, selection of vocational skills must not be based on convenience and should not be based on such criteria as what kind of equipment has been donated to the school or on stereotypic views of what people believe handicapped youth should do when they grow up. Instead, the functional curriculum reflects skills required in actual local employment situations. Usually, developmental curriculum materials and guides will not provide the most direct and efficient approach. The functional curriculum will ensure that the skills being trained are generalizable to potential jobs, thus facilitating eventual movement into the labor force.

All too often, vocational training for handicapped youth has not begun until the student is approximately 15–16 years of age. Since many handicapped youth learn very slowly, common sense dictates that vocational experiences should begin early and should continue through the student's school years. Early vocational emphasis does not mean that 5-year-old children are put on job-sites for training. It does mean that appropriate vocational objectives for training are selected at each age level (Wehman, 1983). The objectives should reflect behaviors that are important to community functioning and employment, that are useful for the student, and that are consistent with the expectations of nonhandicapped peers in similar age groups. Appropriate vocational training means that the feasibility of employment and the importance of work for a normalized existence are instilled early in children and their parents.

Hence, the functional approach to vocational training is also longitudinal. Students begin developing skills early with increasing involvement as they become older. These longitudinal activities should result in gains in vocational skills (e.g., attending to task, competitive production rate, broadened range of jobs a student can perform, production quality) and in job related skill areas (e.g., independent mobility, appropriate selection of clothing, ability to interact socially with co-workers). As a result, students will graduate with an increased chance of either already being employed or of rapidly gaining employment.

A new text by Wilcox and Bellamy (1987) addresses the need for life-centered activities to be selected from a catalog format. Once goals such as shopping or eating in a restaurant have been selected, the appropriate functional skills are identified for instruction.

Educational and Community Integration

A major weakness in many vocational programs is that handicapped students are often placed in programs separate from those for nonhandicapped students. This arrangement gives rise to a situation where an individual can do the job, but cannot relate to his or her co-workers, most of whom may be nonhandicapped. Such a situation of social isolation should be avoided, because the social aspects of a job may contribute enormously to the sense of satisfaction derived from it. This is especially true in settings such as entry-level service occupations, where many individual tasks in themselves may not be particularly rewarding. Many substantially handicapped workers often find jobs in these settings; it is therefore crucial that during training, handicapped workers learn to interact appropriately with their nonhandicapped peers. The reverse of this is equally true. Normal workers who are accustomed to and comfortable with handicapped persons can be invaluable in making placements successful. The most natural means to this end is to integrate all students in vocational training as much as possible.

A second benefit of increased integration in training is that it ensures that handicapped youth are held to realistic goals and skill levels. It may be too easy to modify or eliminate an objective that all members of a special population find difficult when they are the only ones in the program. If, however, they are trained alongside students who do succeed, for example, at using a time clock, there is increased motivation to both teachers and slower students to find a way for the students to adapt, or to practice until the skill is learned. Quite often, there are significant gaps in the job skills that handicapped persons bring with them on referral, and each missing link seriously undermines their perceived value in the eyes of many employers. For example, an employee who, on the one hand, is able to operate an automated dish machine, empty and reline trash cans, and sweep effectively may, on the other hand, have poor mopping skills. If his job description requires that he performs all these tasks, his employer may say, "He can't do the job at all." Holding handicapped students to the same standards in training as their nonhandicapped peers would help reduce this problem.

One final organizational point deals with the question of keeping students in a secondary training program as long as legally allowed (generally, until age 22). There are occasionally handicapped students who are ready to apply their vocational training in real jobs before their formal graduation date has arrived. They should be encouraged to do so. In situations where a certificate of attendance will be granted rather than a genuine high school diploma, there is very little for a well-prepared student to lose by leaving early. Sadly however, there is often a de facto assumption that even fully trained students will stay to the end of training. This can be counterproductive, wasting some students' time and preventing certain opportunities for good placements from being seized.

Community-Based Instruction

Students over the age of 12 should participate for progressively extended periods of time in community-based sites away from school (Falvey, 1986). Job training sites should be established in vocations where there is a potential market for employment. Staff must be provided to conduct job-site training, and systematic instruction should be conducted at these community sites. Behaviors that should be targeted include acquisition of specific job skills, production rates, mobility, and interpersonal skills.

The necessity for community-based instruction is related to the two previously mentioned components of functional curriculum and integrated services. It should be clear that the best curriculum in the most integrated school will still not effect job placement unless steady practice and community work experiences are made available for students. In the authors' experience, a principal reason for vocational failure on the part of significantly handicapped people is that persons with disabilities lack exposure to natural job environments like hospitals, fast food restaurants, and offices.

In sum, life skill–oriented curriculum goals prepare students to learn appropriate skills, an integrated training environment enhances interpersonal skills with nonhandicapped workers and other peers, and community training enhances each of these components by allowing students an opportunity to practice in real situations. Educational programming which reflects these tenets will help students prepare for the next phase in the model.

Chapter 6, which is devoted to school programming and community-based instruction, explores each of the above described components in more detail. Also, a major section later in this chapter addresses ways of overcoming curriculum deficiencies in programs.

PLANNING FOR VOCATIONAL TRANSITION: THE PROCESS

As has already been observed, unless specific and formalized planning for vocational transition occurs, students will not receive a quality postsecondary program nor will they enter the labor force. Therefore, even an excellent secondary program offering good adult service alternatives cannot benefit handicapped youth without planning and coordination of services. Referral back to Figure 1.1, the Three Stage Transitional Model described earlier, indicates the necessity of having a formal transition plan and of delineating responsibilities of staff and participating agencies. Input from parents and students, as well as interagency coordination, are essential. This process is briefly described below.

FORMAL INDIVIDUALIZED STUDENT PLANS

The focal point of the vocational transition process is the development of a formal, individualized transition plan for every handicapped student. Without a written plan specifying the skills to be acquired by the student and the transition services to be received prior to and following graduation, the other major elements of the transition model will have little impact. The plan should include annual goals and short-term objectives that reflect skills required to function on the job, at home, and in the community. Transition services should also be specified, including referral to appropriate agencies, job placement, and on-the-job follow-up.

Transition plans should be comprehensive in scope. Working in the community requires many different skills. In addition to specific job skill training, students must also be prepared to effectively use community services, manage their money, travel to and from work independently, and interact socially with other individuals. Plans must address all these skill areas to meet the comprehensive needs of handicapped students. Plans should also be individualized. Not every individual will be prepared for the same postschool environment. Similarly, each individual will require a different set of postschool services. Plans must focus on the needs of specific persons, rather than on the general needs of the classroom or the categories of disability. In addition, transition plans should identify who is responsible for initiating and following through on each specified activity.

Finally, transition plans must be longitudinal in nature. This requires the participation of all individuals and agencies involved in the transition process during the initial development of the plan. The plan should first be developed 4 years prior to an individual's graduation and then modified at least once a year until the individual has successfully adjusted to a postschool vocational placement. While in school, the transition plan should be considered a section of the student's Individualized Education Program (IEP). After leaving school, the plan can be a component of a client's Individual Written Rehabilitation Plan (IWRP), if he or she is served by vocational rehabilitation, or part of the individualized service plan of a community service agency. While the agency assuming major responsibilities for services will change over time, the participants involved in developing and modifying the plan should remain the same during the course of vocational transition, thereby assuring continuity of goals and services.

Parental Input

The informed participation of parents and guardians is a critical component of the vocational transition process. Parents should be made aware of the employment alternative available to their son or daughter upon graduation. Parents and guardians must be provided an opportunity to acquire the knowledge and skills needed to effectively participate in transition planning. Public schools should initiate parent education activities to provide consumers with background information. Systematically planned parent education programs will improve the effectiveness and durability of parent involvement in the vocational transition process.

Parent education activities should begin at least by the time the student reaches the age of 16. Content should be based on problems and concerns identified through needs assessment activities. Horton and her colleagues (Horton, Maddox, & Edgar, 1983) have developed a parent questionnaire needs assessment that can be used to identify the needs of students and parents. The major areas of concern identified by the assessment process can then be addressed through parent meetings and program visitations.

Parent education meetings sponsored by public schools or advocacy groups are an effective method of training parents to represent their child's vocational interests. Meetings should: 1) orient parents to the community agencies providing postschool services to handicapped individuals; 2) familiarize parents with the specific responsibilities of special education, vocational education, vocational rehabilitation, and adult service programs in the vocational transition process; and 3) prepare parents to work with various agencies to develop transition plans and to apply for future services. Parental visits to local adult service facilities are also useful. School systems may be able to assist in arranging visitations. They may also provide parents with information about what to look for during a visitation and about ways to compare different service programs. This firsthand information should help alleviate parental concerns and fears about their child's future, and should enable them to knowledgeably participate in transition planning.

Interagency Cooperation

Interagency cooperation refers to coordinated efforts among agencies such as public schools, rehabilitation services, adult day programs, and vocational-technical training centers to ensure the delivery of appropriate, nonduplicated services to each handicapped student (Horton et al., 1983). This concept has been widely advocated (Greenan, 1980; Lacour, 1982) as an effective management tool that will aid the development of fiscally accountable human service systems. Federal legislative mandates actively promote cooperative activities as a means of conserving resources and reducing inefficiency. The varied service needs of handicapped individuals demand the development of an array of available programs to meet the full service provisions of PL 98-199 and Section 504 of the Rehabilitation Act.

Unfortunately, efforts to encourage interagency cooperation have had little impact on the design and delivery of services. Although approximately 35 states have developed formal interagency agreements, and many communities have implemented local agreements, numerous problems persist. Agencies differ widely in their diagnostic terminology and eligibility criteria. Services continue to be duplicated, while communities fail to initiate programs (e.g., supported work placement) that are needed to complete a local continuum of services. Political and attitudinal barriers also inhibit interagency cooperation. Administrators often enter collaborative efforts suspicious of the intentions of other agencies, defensive of their own "turf," and fearful that interagency cooperation may lead to budget cuts and termination of programs.

A number of specific steps can be taken to overcome the obstacles cited above and to increase the likelihood of cooperation. Information exchange must occur to identify the legislative mandates, types of services provided, eligibility requirements, and individual planning procedures of each of the participating agencies. Intensive staff development activities must then occur to enable administrators and direct service personnel to develop an understanding of the regulations and potential contributions of other agencies. This investigation should result in a restructuring of services in order to eliminate duplication and to guarantee that options are available to meet the service needs of all handicapped individuals. Finally, the process must result in the involvement of appropriate agencies in joint planning activities.

PROBLEMS INVOLVED IN IMPLEMENTING
EFFECTIVE EMPLOYMENT PROGRAMS IN SCHOOL SETTINGS

The previous model sets the stage for much of the philosophy and practices discussed in this book. However, there remain several problems that need to be addressed. For example: how effectively can employment programs for people with severe disabilities be generated while these students are still in school? What are the different models and options available? Should employment wait until students leave school? Is job placement primarily the responsibility of vocational rehabilitation? These problems are identified and discussed here. Discussion of the vocational options for students over the age of 21 described in Figure 1.1 is found in Chapter 7.

The problems identified below are based on a review of the appropriate literature and on the authors' experiences with competitive employment programs. These problems are recurring and seem to continually interfere with or impair job placements for individuals with competitive employment potential. The importance of circumventing these problems—ideally, while the student is still in school—is paramount to effecting meaningful transition, as adult programs are often underdeveloped and have substantial waiting lists for services.

Inadequacy of Current Curriculum

As was observed in the previous section, a major problem in linking secondary programs with placement into competitive employment is the inadequacy of the current special education curriculum. Teachers and other support personnel do not systematically evaluate vocational environments in which students will ultimately work. There is an extensive reliance on curriculum guides that all too often do not reflect the competencies necessary for vocational independence. Not infrequently, Individualized Education Program objectives only reflect content that the teacher feels comfortable with, or that has been dictated by a state Department of Education curriculum, rather than objectives that are crucial for eventual placement into nonsheltered employment.

A major reason for the continued teaching of nonfunctional skills probably stems from the fact that teachers do not usually participate in job placement or job-site training. Therefore, they do not know what skills are high in utility in the workplace. When teachers examine relevant work environments carefully for curriculum selection they are engaging in ecological analysis. An inventory (Belmore & Brown, 1978; Falvey, 1986) can be completed of behaviors necessary for success in a dishwasher's job, a landscaper's job, a farmer's job, a clerical assistant's job, and so forth. However, one must actually go to the job-sites to carefully analyze the behaviors that are required for job completion. These behaviors must then be formulated into objectives that are taught to students in preparation for eventual job placements. Until this approach is adopted more widely, adult service providers will continue to face serious difficulties in finding job placements for persons with handicaps.

It would be useful if several curricula that do provide functional skills could be recommended. Finding task analyses of vocational skills (e.g., Wehman & McLaughlin, 1980) should be no problem for the teacher; the difficulty is in identifying *which* skills are the most marketable in the student's community and which should therefore be taught.

Administrative Organization

Programs to help handicapped youth within public schools are usually composed of a network of disciplines established to meet the various educational needs of handicapped students. Generally, each discipline—vocational education, special education, or occupational therapy, for example—is mandated to provide specific services. Often these disciplines experience difficulty in providing their service without infringing on the services provided by others. Many times, communication between disciplines is difficult to initiate or maintain. In addition, program decisions for the disabled lie in the hands of persons far removed from day-to-day instruction. Often, decisions to implement program changes such as community-based training and job placement are based on administrative convenience rather than on the needs of the students. The result is a fragmentation of service delivery, with each discipline frequently implementing instructional objectives in isolation. The Individualized Education Program of each student becomes fragmented, without a longitudinal goal, such as employment, in evidence.

Intraagency coordination of services is a critical first step in providing appropriate services. The utilization of a team approach that systematically combines the thinking of various school personnel to develop comprehensive longitudinal individualized programs is necessary. Leadership and organizational roles need to be designated for the efficient administration of teams. Major tasks of the team include gathering comprehensive information about a student, analyzing and synthesizing these findings into goals and objectives, and ultimately designing a longitudinal educational plan. Team planning can result in the fullest and most efficient utilization of all school resources available.

Obviously, other resources in the community should be utilized. Unfortunately, many special education administrators are not fully aware of what services are available to students upon graduation. Similarly, many graduates leave school with no idea of where or how to obtain services. They join the ranks of the unemployed and continue to be a liability to the community rather than a contributor to the tax base. Awareness of where graduates go upon completion of public school programs has direct bearing on curricular content and service delivery strategies of the programs. Knowledge of what services are available in the community, of how these services are provided, of who is eligible, of how many individuals can be served, and of what happens to individuals not included in the services is critical in the management of educational programs for persons with disabilities. Establishment of formal relationships between public school systems and postschool service providers is imperative. The agencies should then identify a contact person within each system. Information exchange must occur to identify the legislative mandates, types of services provided, eligibility requirements, and individual planning procedures of each agency. In addition, intensive staff development should be conducted to enable administrators and direct service personnel to develop an understanding of the contributions and limitations of other agencies. This should result in a restructuring of overall service delivery to eliminate duplication of services and ensure that options are available to meet the service needs of disabled individuals. The final result is involvement of appropriate agencies in joint planning activities in order to ensure appropriate service delivery to the disabled citizens within the community.

Limited Communication between Vocational and Special Educators

Another major problem is that many vocational educators who know their area of speciality do not know how to effectively teach persons with handicaps. What they know but cannot communicate is not going to help their students. This leads to students not developing their full potential, which is especially unfortunate in the special population classroom. Special education teachers must act as consultants to vocational teachers in order to maximize communication between vocational teachers and their students.

There are a number of ways in which special education teachers can assist those teaching vocational skills. First of all, it is necessary to make the time to be in touch. The special educator may then suggest ways, for example, to break a difficult task down into component steps that can then be learned one by one. The special education teacher may also advise on reasonable ways to adapt class activities and homework assignments so that handicapped students may be better able to participate. Besides these points, a special educator can share his or her experiences with particular students and their successes in other areas, as well as suggest successful ways of relating to students. This can serve to encourage vocational educators, to whom handicapped students may be new and overwhelming, as well as help them to generalize skills into vocational settings. In-service training is mandated by PL 94-142 for all those who work with exceptional children, and is a useful resource if conducted properly.

Successful implementation of a supported work program requires innovative organization and management of personnel. The first step is the commitment to a philosophy of preparing students to be productive members of the adult community. It is generally accepted that in order to prepare persons for life and work, it is necessary to expose them to the real world. Thus, it is crucial that the students train and work in the community whenever possible.

Administration policies should be outlined for the implementation of all activities. Specific policies regarding liability and transportation must be clearly established. General guidelines for service delivery should be stated. The authors suggest that all students ages 12–15 should receive a minimum of 2 hours per day in organized vocational training. Individuals ages 16–18 should receive a minimum of 3 hours per day in job training sites. Students over the age of 18 should be placed in a competitive job or on training sites for the majority of the school day. Related community-based training should be implemented concomitant to the vocational training and should be scheduled before in-school activities. All scheduling should reflect class and individual instructional priorities. In addition, teams should be formed, and specific times should be established for exchange of information between staff members such as teachers, aides, or therapists.

Related service personnel such as speech therapists, occupational therapists, or physical therapists, should provide their services during community-based training. These professionals should teach the skills most likely to permit individuals to obtain and hold a competitive job. Training should be implemented within the community or specific job-site. Speech therapists can work on improving socialization skills with co-workers, or on the ability to make needs known in grocery stores, and so forth. The occupational and/or physical therapist should improve the strength and stamina of individuals seeking employment. In addition, these professionals can be involved in the follow-up or monitoring of activities of competitively employed individuals.

Staff should be hired and given job placement and training responsibility. These individuals should focus on job identification, job training and follow-up on a full-time basis. Each trainer should attempt to place one person per month in a competitive employment position. The maximum placement and follow-up caseload for an effective trainer should be 15. The trainer should have responsibility for coordination of services for these individuals.

Unfortunately, economic times are such that many systems are unable to hire new personnel to do job placement. This should not prevent them from implementing the supported work model on a small scale. Schedules can be designed so that teachers can be freed from classroom responsibility. By scheduling activities such as music and art back-to-back, a teacher can make available as much as a half day for job-site training. Utilization of related service personnel, para-professionals, and administrators can provide additional personnel for training and follow-up in competitive employment sites. Systems utilizing this approach should initially identify one classroom of individuals for job-site training and placement. The system may only be able to focus on part-time work in the beginning, but eventually a full-time placement should be made available.

Failure to Attain Full Parental Support

Another frequent obstacle to the job placement of the disabled youth is lack of parental support. This is the result in most cases of parents' concern for the welfare of their offspring, rather than resistance to personal convenience (Moon & Beale, 1985). The authors have found such concern to be based on legitimate fears and doubts that have been held too long without benefit of offsetting information. These fears and doubts can result when qualified persons are denied employment or receive only lukewarm support—discouragement that may in fact increase the youth's chance of failure.

It is important to appreciate parents' fears and doubts, and to be sensitive to them in order to help set these concerns in their proper perspective. Parents know their children best, and they may seek reassurance that educators and professionals are always bearing the child's best interests in mind. All too often, well-intentioned professionals have been unable to deliver on promises to help, for example, in those instances when handicapped workers are abused or embarrassed on the job. On these occasions, parents will of course be concerned. Also, given the number of regulations governing Supplemental Security Income payments, there is need for caution to avoid disqualifying a person prematurely: fiscal responsibility is always in order. Other factors such as the trouble involved in helping a person prepare for a job, and the big letdown for all concerned when the job does not work out, are legitimate concerns. Parents may adopt a "show-me" attitude with respect to the question of whether their handicapped offspring should plan on being competitively employed. Only information that specifically addresses these questions may be expected to allay the uneasiness they generate. If parents received more ongoing positive input regarding the work potential of their retarded children, from an earlier time than is now the case, more healthy attitudes and expectations would result. Secondary level vocational educators can do much to help in this regard.

Vocational and special educators can help develop family support by making certain that they themselves are well-informed on the points at issue. There are increasingly numerous examples in professional literature of successful placement of severely handicapped workers (see Chapter 7). Being familiar with these examples will enable educators to speak with authority when advising parents and students on realistic expectations. If educators will take every opportunity to convey their own positive feelings about students' vocational potential, they will do much to overcome parents' hesitation and misgivings. One effective way to communicate the importance of planning for employment to students and families is by including vocational objectives in IEP's. In some situations, students are spending time in school-simulated workshops without there being any related objective in their educational plan. For this reason, it is important to formalize the role of vocational education in the student's program.

Any activity that can serve to demonstrate learned job skills to family members will increase their belief in the student's potential. Inviting the family to visit technical centers and other training sites would be helpful in this regard. Further visibility for students could be created through competition between students in training, or by having students volunteer to apply their developing skills in certain community settings. One excellent function that teachers might perform is to put the parents of successful program graduates in touch with other parents who are uneasy about their own children's futures. Such mutual support might be the best single means of raising parents' expectations regarding the work potential of their handicapped sons and daughters.

Ignorance and Resistance by the Public and by Employers

In seeking to place handicapped workers into competitive community employment, one major obstacle that may be encountered is resistance by the public and by employers. There is a law prohibiting discrimination against the handicapped, but it is of little practical day-to-day help. Some jobs such as busing tables in a restaurant have high visibility, and if customers are made uncomfortable by the appearance and behavior of the bus-person, a manager must take that into consideration for the sake of his business. It is a fact that many people are made uncomfortable by the sight of a handicapped worker. The authors feel that this is largely a result of ignorance and of the natural tendency to feel uneasy when reminded of anything one does not understand. In addition to these factors, many employers have legitimate doubts about handicapped workers' abilities and the adequacy of their training. These concerns are difficult to allay quickly, and such general misgivings often prevent specific applicants from receiving a chance to display their talents. Again, such misgivings are largely the result of ignorance. Secondary level vocational programs can and should assist in making the general public better informed of the truth about the employment potential of persons with disabilities.

Broadly speaking, more factual information is needed by the public at large about good training programs, proven success stories, and handicapped persons in general. To that end, mainstreaming and all other normalization efforts are the hope of the future. More immediately, other steps are needed and viable. Below are some ideas in this vein.

Having potential employers actually observe good training programs is one way of educating the employers. This could be done by approaching persons who manage large food service operations and asking them to observe and advise on possible ways of upgrading current programs. The hint of flattery involved may help create a positive attitude toward what they would see. These advisers would see a program with students already doing well enough, and would be impressed. Challenging the advisors to make suggestions would help reinforce the good image they might carry with them.

Staging competitions in which students use vocational skills they have learned, and inviting businessmen to serve as judges is another way of creating exposure. Such events could be within a school, between schools, or between school systems. Secondary benefits of such competitions would lie in providing students a good intermediate objective, and in possibly attracting media attention.

One way to broaden the general public's awareness of persons with handicaps and their abilities might be through arranging for students to volunteer their services for the sake of training opportunities. There are women's clubs, for example, that would be glad to have students serve at a luncheon where members would otherwise do it themselves. Other persons would welcome the practice of janitorial or grounds maintenance skills on their property by students seeking practical experience. Parents of students can be of great assistance in arranging such opportunities. More intellectually capable students may also be given supervisory responsibility on such field trips, thus avoiding a drain on teachers' time.

Transportation

Transportation is a critical issue that has a profound effect on the success of employment programs. This can be a major problem in schools that have limited vans for daily transportation other than from home to school. Financing transportation for community-based instruction can be a large barrier, but this does not have to be the case. Administrators should look at how they handle transportation for nonhandicapped students participating in similar vocational programs. The same transportation options utilized by nonhandicapped students should also be available to handicapped students.

In many communities, public transportation options such as the city bus system or taxi cabs are available. In some instances walking is another viable alternative. These transportation options should be encouraged because of their long-term availability. If an individual is unable to get to work, he or she is unemployable.

Unfortunately, not all programs have access to public transportation or are located within walking distance to potential jobs. In these situations, teachers might be utilized for initial transportation to the worksite. Efforts can then be exerted to get the individual worker into a car pool. The worker will have to pay for this option, but this is an expense which must be dealt with in order to remain employed. In other instances, parents or volunteers can provide transportation, although this is not the best solution. The use of public school vehicles, teachers, or family cars should only be used if normal community transportation options are not available.

Liability

A related obstacle to implementing employment programs is liability. School systems are skeptical of allowing training in the community due to the question of who is responsible if a student or teacher is injured. Thus, the initial administrative response is to deny community training on the premise that there are too many risks.

School systems have teacher liability insurance; however, this insurance usually covers instructional activities. These policies can provide effective reassurance to administrators. Additional coverage may be obtained through the insurance carrier if the district feels the need.

Students involved in community training should have written approval from their parent(s) or guardian. This should be an informed consent document. Only individuals with this form on file should be involved in job-site training. In addition, before training occurs the district should make certain that insurance coverage is available on all students. Often families are offered insurance coverage for their child during the school day for a nominal fee. This liability insurance covers all instructional activities. Such coverage should be a requirement for any student involved in community training.

Students that have been placed into a work position and are being paid a wage should be covered by the employer. The same coverage should be available to the student that is available to any other employee in that business. The trainers will be covered through the school system policy.

The issues described above, whether concerning liability or transportation or attitudes and curriculum, are substantial and should not be minimized. However, the problems of high unemployment are compelling as well, and it is reasonable to suggest that without a much more active role in employment-oriented programming by schools, students will continue without jobs. A major solution to solving many of these problems is through implementation of a systematic transition plan.

Public Awareness

Deloach, Wilkins, and Walker (1983) have explained that before a theory is adopted, it must pass through the stages of conceptualization, initial acceptance, legislative legitimization, and resource allocation before full integration into the system. Currently, the idea of supported employment and community living options for persons with severe disabilities is in the stage of legislative legitimization and resource allocation. For progression beyond this point, communities must actively pursue a public awareness program.

Transformation of ideas does not occur merely through modeling. Throughout the United States, several projects have demonstrated the success of community integration of persons with severe disabilities (Kusserow, 1984; Paine, Bellamy, & Wilcox, 1984). Yet, agencies continue to pour funds into service programs rather than employment outcomes, into segregated work and residential environments instead of integrated environments, and into vocational settings with substandard or no wages versus settings with minimum wages and benefits. An assertive effort must be made to educate the entrepreneur, the taxpayer, the potential worker with disabilities, human service agencies, and parents concerning the potential for improvement in the adult life-styles of individuals with severe disabilities.

Name: Bob	Age: 16	Date: April 20

I. **Employment goal:** To become employed in an enclave in May, 1990 (Age 20).

   A. Educational objectives:

      1. To receive training in a production job enclave within a local industry with minimal supervision on a daily basis by December, 1985.

Activities:	Person(s) responsible:
—Locate a job-site	Voc. Ed. teacher, Rehab. counselor
—Provide job-site training	Sp. Ed. teacher, Voc. Ed. teacher
—Provide transportation during training	Sp. Ed. teacher
—Evaluate skills as part of vocational assessment	Voc. Ed. teacher, Sp. Ed. teacher
—Develop behavioral interventions as necessary	School psychologist, Sp. Ed. teacher

      2. To receive training in a food service enclave with minimal supervision on a daily basis by May, 1985.

Activities:	Person(s) responsible:
Same as # 1	Same as # 1

      3. To receive training in a technological job such as micrographics or data entry with minimal supervision on a daily basis by December, 1985.

Activities:	Person(s) responsible:
Same as # 1	Same as # 1

      4. To receive training in a janitorial and/or grounds maintenance enclave for an office building with minimal supervision by a job coach by May, 1986.

Activities:	Person(s) responsible:
Same as # 1	Same as # 1

      5. To receive a completed vocational assessment and job identification based on skills and interests by September, 1986.

Activities:	Person(s) responsible:
—Collect and analyze vocational skills during job training	Voc. Ed. teacher, Sp. Ed. teacher, Rehab. counselor
—Determine appropriate job for Bob based on skills and interests demonstrated through job-site training	All ITP team members

      6. To receive intensive job-site training within the enclave type identified in # 5 by December, 1988.

Activities:	Person(s) responsible:
Same as # 1	Same as # 1

   B. Administrative objectives:

      1. To ensure the development of a nonprofit organization receiving state, federal, and/or local funds to provide enclave supervision by May, 1989.

Figure 1.2. Individualized transition plan.

Figure 1.2. *(continued)*

Activities:	Person(s) responsible:
—Meet with community service boards and local rehabilitation agency to discuss the need for enclaves	Sp. Ed. coordinator
—Lobby for funds to be allocated for an enclave	Parent

2. To develop personnel policies to accommodate job-site trainers by September, 1985.

Activities:	Person(s) responsible:
—Develop overtime pay or compensation	School superintendent
—Develop policy to allow teachers to have flexible hours based on enclave hours	School superintendent

II. **Community living goal:** To move into a semi-independent apartment with not more than two other residents with disabilities and one staff resident by May, 1990.

A. Educational objectives:

1. To perform the following domestic tasks with periodic checks by staff: housecleaning, grocery shopping, clothing list development, meal preparation, grooming, yard maintenance, and making necessary phone calls (doctor, MH/MR case manager, family) by May, 1989.

Activities:	Person(s) responsible:
—Train skills in home	Sp. Ed. teacher
—Locate apartment for training	Mental retardation case manager
—Develop necessary adaptations	Sp. Ed. teacher, Occ. therapist, Speech therapist

2. To initiate the performance of all routine home activities through use of a picture schedule for each day by May, 1989.

Activities:	Person(s) responsible:
—Train independence in following sequence of tasks	Sp. Ed. teacher
—Develop daily schedules	Sp. Ed. teacher

3. To respond to unusual situations in the manner outlined in the safety manual with no assistance from staff by May, 1989.

Activities:	Person(s) responsible:
—Identify situations to be dealt with	Mental retardation case manager, apartment staff member
—Develop safety procedures manual	Sp. Ed. teacher, apartment staff member
—Train skills to deal with situations	Sp. Ed. teacher

(continued)

Figure 1.2. *(continued)*

4. To use the city bus with another student to go to the shopping mall, park, and medical clinic by May, 1988.

Activities:	Person(s) responsible:
—Transportation training	Sp. Ed. teacher

5. To locate appropriate store and shop for groceries or supplies with another student by May, 1988.

Activities:	Person(s) responsible:
—Set up checking account	Parent, Bob
—Locate appropriate mall	Sp. Ed. teacher
—Train community skills	Sp. Ed. teacher, Parent

6. To initiate and independently perform at least one leisure skill in each of the following areas by May, 1989: solo activity such as needlework, solo outdoor activity such as bike riding; outdoor activity with another person such as Frisbee, and a community activity such as skating.

Activities:	Person(s) responsible:
—Select activity in each category	Bob
—Train leisure skills	Sp. Ed. teacher

B. Administrative objectives

1. To complete referral process to appropriate adult services by May, 1986.

Activities:	Person(s) responsible:
—Make referral to vocational rehabilitation	Rehab. counselor
—Make referral for supplemental security income and Medicaid	Sp. Ed. coordinator

2. To obtain insurance coverage for students and staff during training in the apartment by September, 1985.

Activities:	Person(s) responsible:
—Obtain insurance coverage	School superintendent

3. To ensure the availability of semi-independent homes in the community to accommodate students leaving schools by May, 1987.

Activities:	Person(s) responsible:
—Meet with local agency officials	Sp. Ed. coordinator

Individualized Transition Plan

As the Individualized Education Program became the catalyst to appropriate instruction for students with severe handicaps in areas such as self-help skills, the Individualized Transition Plan (ITP) is the key to successful transition of the student into work and community living by the time he or she leaves school. In states such as Florida, Illinois, and Massachusetts, the ITP is required by state law. Although the ITP may be part of the IEP, it must be addressed separately, with particular focus on the student's independent adult life. By the time a student reaches age 16, the first ITP should be developed. Generally, the special education teacher or other designated school employee (e.g., counselor, social worker, psychologist, or transition coordinator) takes the lead in contacting appropriate representatives for a planning team to attend transition meetings. Composition of the team depends on the unique needs of the student. An important element in team member selection is the joint involvement of school personnel responsible for training and job procurement, as well as human service providers who could offer support and follow-up during the student's adulthood.

These individuals should be involved in instruction that will increase the probability that individuals obtain and hold a competitive job. Figure 1.2 is an example of how an Individualized Transition Plan might be prepared for the 16-year-old with moderate or trainable level mental retardation.

SUMMARY

This book focuses upon transition from the viewpoint of school personnel, adult service personnel, vocational rehabilitation staff, parents, and advocates. The authors view transition as a multifaceted and changing process that must be interdependent to be successful. The purpose of this book is to train educators, rehabilitators, and community service personnel, on both an in-service and pre-service level, how to facilitate the transition process for the tens of thousands of handicapped youth who will eventually leave special education programs for employment and independent living.

Chapter 2

What Happens to Youth with Disabilities after They Grow Up?

IN THE BEGINNING OF THE PREVIOUS CHAPTER THE FUTURE OF SEVERAL fictitious students who had recently completed special education was discussed. What happens to Susan or John after they grow up has been a frequent topic in the professional literature, particularly in the early 1970s (Stanfield, 1973) and continuing up to as recently as last year (Halpern, Close, & Nelson, 1986). In fact, to a large extent the entire transition movement has been stimulated by the fact that tens of thousands of youth with handicaps are finally beginning to leave special education programs. Therefore, many educators have begun research to determine what really does happen to young adults with severe handicaps after school is over. The purpose of this chapter is to review this research.

It is clear from a review of the professional literature that special educators have a keen interest in the issue of postsecondary school adjustment (e.g., Titus & Travis, 1973). A careful examination of the studies in this area reveals two phases of articles on postsecondary school adjustment. The first phase of articles were published from the mid-to-late 1960s into the early 1970s. These papers focused upon the general aspects of adult adjustment after the end of schooling and were primarily limited to those persons with mental retardation. A second wave of similar studies was initiated in the mid-1970s and continues into the present. The purpose of those studies has been to evaluate the postsecondary employment and independent living status of handicapped individuals once they graduated from school. The findings of these post-21 surveys have been instrumental as catalysts behind the recent national drive to effect meaningful transition programs in all 50 states. The logic has been: *if we spend millions of dollars and other resources to educate handicapped youngsters, then we should also follow-up to see what types of adjustment and services* they are experiencing as young adults. The data associated with such follow-up efforts have not always been encouraging, hence, there has been a renewed emphasis on providing greater employment opportunities for those persons who have been considered unemployable. (See Chapter 7 for more information on employment alternatives for adults.)

Therefore, the purpose of this chapter is to address selected issues related to postsecondary adjustment of youth with disabilities. The authors provide a rationale for completing follow-up surveys and then selectively review recent literature in this area. Methodological problems inherent in some of these studies are discussed and overall conclusions are suggested. Finally, a sample follow-up survey and guidelines for implementation are presented.

WHY CONDUCT FOLLOW-UP SURVEYS OF SPECIAL EDUCATION GRADUATES?

There are a number of reasons why extensive follow-up surveys of special education graduates have been conducted. Table 2.1 summarizes each of these reasons briefly. The first reason is to see how many students are taking full advantage of the rights provided by law. There are very high dropout rates of mildly handicapped students in many states. For example, in Florida it is estimated (Rollin, 1986) that 25%–30% of all handicapped students drop out well before school is completed. A county-by-county survey in that state is currently being planned to assess the full extent of this dropout problem.

The determination of the number of students, on average, who leave at what age is helpful in budget planning for adult services in

Table 2.1.   Why complete follow-up surveys of special education graduates?

1. To see how many students complete 4 years of special education versus dropouts
2. To assess employment status
3. To assess adaptive behavior competence
4. To gain a benchmark of the local school program's effectiveness
5. To evaluate the degree of coordination of different agencies in the community and their effects on the adjustment of special education graduates

various localities. The 1983 Education for Handicapped Children Amendments required annual reporting of such data to state Departments of Education by the local education agencies. This amount of quantitative data coupled with qualitative information from follow-up surveys helps determine a clear profile of which students are receiving and benefiting from services and at what level.

A second reason for conducting such surveys is to assess the employment status of graduating students. Most surveys ask respondents whether they are now working, whether they are planning to work, the type of vocational experiences they had in school, how professionals have been helpful or not, and so forth. Employment data results from several states have been rather alarming. In Washington, Colorado, Vermont, Virginia, Nebraska, and Illinois, studies have shown 42%–88% unemployment depending on the functioning level and disability of the student. For example, in Virginia it was observed that 88% of the students labeled moderately, severely, or profoundly handicapped had never worked during the 5-year period since leaving school (Wehman, Kregel, & Seyfarth, 1985b).

Assessment of adaptive behavior competence is a third reason for surveying special education graduates. Halpern, Close, and Nelson (1986) have worked hard on this topic, as has Kregel (Wehman, Kregel, & Seyfarth, 1985b). The level of community integration, personal life-styles, and independent and residential living are barometers of how well young adults with disabilities are adjusting to adulthood. More work needs to be done in this area since most of the surveys have appeared to focus more on the employment dimension.

The successful adult adjustment of special education graduates is undoubtedly a reflection of how effective a special education program is in preparing students. While it can be very unfair to evaluate schools solely on the successful placement of graduates, the general public is increasingly making such judgments with regard to non-handicapped graduates. Witness an issue of *Forbes* (December, 1986) magazine that devoted the cover article to education. The lack of positive change in SAT scores over 20 years was contrasted with the ten-fold increase in cost of educational services and tuition. It may only be a matter of time before society "grades" the schools not on the perceived quality of their services but on the placement and adjustment outcomes of students. The past 10 years may in one way have been a honeymoon period as the special education law was being implemented. Schools are now faced not only with being responsible for service delivery for all handicapped students, but also for meaningful transition outcomes as well.

A final reason offered for regular and repeated surveys of special education graduates is to determine the amount of community adjustments made over time. Substance abuse, criminal behavior, and anti-social actions are negative examples of how students might not adjust in their community. Volunteerism, taking civic responsibility, and participation in community groups, however, are positive illustrations of how community integration might be determined.

This rationale varies from the previous one in that it is meant to evaluate the degree of coordination between multiple agencies in the community. The purpose of such a survey is to see if social services, vocational rehabilitation, mental health, and other contributing agencies are making a difference in the adjustment patterns of students in the community. All too often these agencies have enormous caseloads, and new cases from the schools are not always welcomed. Nevertheless, as the following chapters show, it is the collective strength of these different agencies that gives transition planning credibility and fuels the process of meaningful change.

STUDIES RELATED TO POSTSECONDARY VOCATIONAL ADJUSTMENT[1]

While it is impossible to review all of the postsecondary studies that have been completed, a selective overview of the purpose and results of many of these studies will be beneficial. The criteria for inclusion of most of those is twofold: first, they were conducted during or after the period of legal and/or statutory advocacy for children with handicaps (i.e., since 1970); second, the studies were data-based, that is, they generated survey data for analysis.

The 1970–1980 Time Period

The review of postsecondary studies is divided into two parts, the 1970–1980 period and 1980 to the present. What follows is a chronological report of a series of different studies that occurred during this time period.

One of the first studies done in the 1970s was by Halpern (1973). This study reports the results of two follow-up studies conducted in Oregon. The first report consisted of follow-up interviews with 49 students leaving school in 1969, 38 of whom were reinterviewed in 1970. The second report consisted of evaluating 43 cooperative workstudy projects that had been funded in Oregon. The results of both studies suggest that employment of new workers with retardation may be af-

---

[1]This review was adapted from the excellent bibliography development by Michael Shafer. We are indebted to him for this material.

fected by economic conditions, whereas established workers may not be affected. Additionally, Halpern presents information to suggest that projects coordinated by state rehabilitation agencies may be better prepared to place their clients into employment.

Similarly, Titus and Travis (1973) discuss the results of a follow-up survey interview conducted with 35 mildly retarded graduates, their parents and employers, from the LaGrange area of Illinois during the summer of 1969. At the time of the interview, all but one of the graduates were employed; 57% were still employed by their first employer. Median wages were reported at $2.08 per hour. Female graduates were employed most frequently in institutional services, while male graduates were most frequently employed in stock or warehouse positions. Employers indicated that students could have been better prepared to perform a wider variety of tasks and better able to deal with social interactions. This study was similar to studies conducted by Dinger (1973) and Colloster (1975) in Michigan and Seattle, respectively.

A long-standing major leader in the field, Donn Brolin (1973), also conducted one of the earlier studies with students labeled educable mentally retarded. In this article he reports the results of field interviews conducted with 80 former students who attended schools in Minneapolis between 1966–1972. The students' parents were also interviewed. A relatively large proportion of these individuals were labeled as mildly mentally retarded, with 79% of the students having reported IQs above 55. Overall, a 44% employment rate was reported, with better postschool vocational adjustment correlating with past enrollment in work-study programs. Brolin's results provide support for the establishment of career educational curriculum programs, additional postschool assistance services, interagency cooperation, and follow-up programs for exiting students who are mentally retarded.

One of the few studies that has ever looked at the parent expectations for children labeled severely and profoundly handicapped was conducted by Venn, Dubose, and Merbler (1977). Parents and teachers of 10 children were surveyed concerning their expectations for the adult lives of the children. The children ranged in chronological age from 3 to 16 years. All of the children were visually impaired with at least one additional handicapping condition. A total of 10 parents and 10 teachers were surveyed in five areas: 1) education, 2) vocation, 3) living arrangement, 4) social life, and 5) potential income. Significant differences in expectations for the education and income achievements of the children were observed between the parents and teachers, with the parents generally being more optimistic.

These papers were among the first that began to look closely at how disabled youth were adjusting into adulthood. However, the full force of Public Law 94-142 had not fully emerged until the 1980s. The following papers trace the impact that this law was beginning to have on policymakers, parents, educators, and the students themselves.

The 1980–1986 Time Period

Massachusetts was the first state to legislatively address the needs of the "after 22," transition age handicapped population (1982). An initial report was developed as a precursor to this legislation by sampling certain localities in Massachusetts. This technical report summarizes a statewide survey of service needs for a projected 3,625 residents of Massachusetts who will be turning 22 between 1983 and 1989 and who will be served by special education services. Approximately 445 students will leave school systems in Massachusetts each year and will require some form of adult services. *Most notably, over 90% of the sample reportedly will need some form of social services on a permanent, lifelong basis.* Additionally, 66% of the sample reported needing group residential services or other alternative living arrangements, while 83% reported training needs for improved independence and/or community living. With regard to employment training needs, only 28% reported needing competitive employment placements with or without subsidies, while 47% reported the need for sheltered employment, work activity, or day activity program services.

Brodsky (1983) developed a comprehensive survey for Oregon that she used as a doctoral dissertation. This dissertation reports the results of follow-up interviews and surveys of parents and case managers concerning the adjustment needs of Oregon graduates who were functioning in the trainable range of mental retardation. Approximately 56% of these students had never received any community-based vocational training during their school years, although 64% did report transition planning had occurred prior to leaving school. With regard to employment status, only 6% were involved in what the author entitles "community employment," and 57% were enrolled in work activity centers. Over 60% of the sample reported earning less than $1,000 per year, with 16% reporting no earned income whatsoever. With regard to residential services, 50% of the students were receiving no services at all despite the fact that the parents of 44% of the students had reported a residential service need at the time of graduation.

Another comprehensive survey was done by Crites, Smull, and Sachs (1984) at the University of Maryland School of Medicine. This report provides an extensive analysis of the service needs and characteristics of mentally retarded adults throughout the state of Maryland. This report provides information about 1,469 mentally retarded persons living at locations other than community group homes or state institutions. Thirty-nine percent of the sample is between the ages of 16 and 25. An unemployment rate found among the entire sample is 77%. The information also provided a profile of the care providers, who were found to be predominately female, the client's parent, and 51 years of age or older. This report also provides information regarding service needs, with 75% indicating some need for residential services and 95% indicating some need for day programming.

Another excellent paper was written by McDonnell, Wilcox, Boles, and Bellamy (1985). This article reports the results of a survey of parents of severely handicapped high school students residing in Oregon. The survey sought to identify the projected service needs of students after their departure from high school, the critical values held by parents in the selection of such services, and the extent and source of parental knowledge regarding adult services. The results reveal what services parents felt would be needed by their offspring. Interestingly, parents did not appear to value earned income in the selection of day program services, but instead selected services on the basis of the employment security and amount of training offered by the program. In the selection of residential services, parents appeared to most highly value the amount of training and privacy provided their daughter or son while showing little regard for contact with non-handicapped peers.

Two additional studies have been completed in different states: one in Colorado, and the other at four locations in Virginia. The study done by Mithaug, Horiuchi, and Fanning (1985) surveyed special education graduates in the state of Colorado. School information was collected and surveys were completed with a total 234 graduates from 26 school districts. These respondents consisted of persons with mental retardation (26%), perceptual or communication disorders (32%), emotional or behavior disorders (12%), or physical handicaps (19%), most of whom had received a regular high school diploma. The findings indicate most students were socially inactive and were still residing at home. Most had some employment experience. Sixty-three percent of the graduates were currently employed; (32% were full time), and 43% were earning less than $3.00 per hour.

In the second article, Wehman, Kregel, and Seyfarth (1985a) provide the results of a follow-up study of 300 school graduates in Virginia between the ages of 17 and 24. All of the respondents were characterized as mentally retarded, with approximately 60% of these individuals in the EMR range, while the others were moderately to profoundly retarded. The unemployment rate was estimated at 58%, with nearly three-quarters of the sample earning less than $500 per month. Additionally, the majority of respondents surveyed indicated that they had not utilized vocational rehabilitation nor local mental retardation services agencies.

Zetlin and Turner (1985) use a somewhat different approach to the study of transition. In this article the results of ethnographic field notes and life histories of adults who are mildly mentally retarded and their immediate family members are presented. Fifty-six percent of these individuals reported becoming aware of their handicap during their adolescent years. Additionally, many of these individuals reported extreme frustration when realizing that they would be unable to achieve normal goals, most specifically, employment. Social isolation was noted, as over half of the sample reported rejection by non-handicapped peers, and 23% of the repondents indicated having no boyfriend or girlfriend.

In terms of studies assessing special education graduates in follow-up surveys in rural environments, two papers emerge. First, Fardig, Alogozzine, Schwartz, Hensel, and Westling (1985) report Florida data. This article reports the results of a follow-up survey of 119 students (median age 19), who had separated from school and who were classified SLD (severe learning disability), EMR (educable mentally retarded), or EH (emotionally handicapped). Fifty-two percent of the students were currently employed (87% were full time), while 34% had no employment history at all since leaving school. Monthly wages ranged from $100–$1,000, with an average of $536. Recommendations of the study include the provision of vocational preparedness training in school, entry level skill training, and consistency of vocational instructor for students throughout high school.

The second article is actually part of a series of studies by Dr. Susan Brody Hasazi, who is perhaps the leading researcher for this specialty in the United States. Dr. Brody Hasazi and her colleagues (1985b) have been highly systematic in conducting comprehensive statewise follow-up surveys since the early 1980s. In the Brody Hasazi, Gordon, Roe, Finck et al. paper (1985) are results of a statewide follow-up survey in Vermont of 243 individuals with mental retardation who graduated during the period from 1981 to 1983. Utilizing school records, information was collected regarding school services, employment, and residential status. Major findings include: the majority of students found jobs thorugh the self-family-friend network; male and mildly retarded graduates show significantly higher employment rates; localities with interagency agreements between local education agencies (LEAs) and vocational rehabilitation agencies had higher employment rates, and significant correlations between actual work experience during school years and postschool employment.

The data in this paper are drawn from a larger study conducted in Vermont by Hasazi, Gordon, and Roe (1985). The results of this study, which included 462 handicapped young adults, indicated that 37% were unemployed. This cross-categorical sample was drawn from students who had left or graduated from school between 1979 and 1983.

Edgar and Levine (1986) also report a major effort at analyzing results from two follow-up studies being conducted within the state of Washington. Data are presented for 956 students who either graduated or left secondary school programs. These data are presented in both aggregate form as well as being separated, according to the type of disability experienced by the students. Additionally, normative data for all of the outcome measures are presented for a group of 103 students without handicaps. The overall employment rate for the handicapped sample was 55%, compared to 64% for the nonhandicapped sample. Additional information regarding weekly salary, agency utilization, employment history, and methods employed to obtain a job is also presented.

In Illinois, Freagon, Ahlgren, Smith, Costello, and Peters (1986) present follow-up data from 43 students who participated in the De-Kalb school system program during the past 5 years. These data reveal only a 7% competitive employment rate, with 17% unemployed and receiving no adult vocational services. Additionally, these authors report all wages to be less than $85 per month. These results are discussed in relevance to the need for interagency planning and cooperation between school agencies and adult service agencies.

Finally, McDonnell, Wilcox, and Boles (1986) ask an important question, that is, is enough known to plan for transition? In their article, results of a nationwide survey of educational, vocational, and residential administrators for individuals with severe handicaps are reported. The purposes of the study were to determine the types of services provided, the number of severely disabled clients served, and the projections for future service allocations. Results support previous research regarding the large number of students with severe handicaps "aging out" of high school. Furthermore, these results identify a prevalence of work activity and sheltered workshop provision with limited future growth projected. Similarly, limited future growth was projected for residential service where group home service options prevailed. Extensive waiting lists for both forms of services were also noted, emphasizing the massive need for, and critical shortage of, effective service options for the severely handicapped.

To date, the results of all of these studies seem to be among the best indications available as to what is happening to special education graduates after leaving school. What follows is a synopsis of the methodological problems inherent in these surveys plus several general conclusions.

METHODOLOGICAL AND LOGISTICAL DIFFICULTIES IN CONDUCTING POST-21 FOLLOW-UP SURVEYS

All survey research has some limitations, and the post-21 follow-up surveys of special education graduates are no different. Several of the studies—Hasazi et al. (1985), Edgar and Levine (1986), Brodsky (1983), and Mithaug et al., (1985)—were more comprehensive than others, and addressed many of the methodological pitfalls sample concerns that can occur in this type of research.

The first issue that necessarily arises in surveying the state of transition age young adults is: how was the sample drawn? Are the subjects in the study, in fact, a random sample, or do they represent the entire population of graduates in the state? If a sample is drawn, as the majority of studies did then, one must ask how representative the sample is of the population as a whole. Wehman, Kregel, and Seyfarth (1985a) developed a stratified sample across four major geographic areas and school localities. Data from this sample of 300 mentally retarded graduates appear to reflect the state as a whole for retarded young adults; however, this would only be confirmed by a survey of the entire state. Therefore, as a general rule those studies that pooled graduates from the entire state will be in a better position to extrapolate accurate conclusions than those that did not.

Reliability of Study

The second methodological concern that must be faced is the *reliability* of the collected data. There are many ways to capture data reliably. Unquestionably, anyone who reviews the previously described studies in great detail must examine how the data were collected. Below are a few of the ways it could be done:

1. Face-to-face interview with a student or parent
2. Phone interview with student or parent
3. Survey by mail
4. Review of records

These data collection techniques can be considered as generally the most reliable and probably the most expensive techniques. This list starts with the face-to-face interview as the most reliable and expensive and proceeds through increasingly unreliable and less expensive techniques down to the fourth method: the review of records. Wehman, Kregel, and Seyfarth (1985a) interviewed parents of 300 mentally retarded young adults. Each interview lasted 30–40 minutes. Because of the rural and sparsely populated nature of the state, Hasazi and her colleagues (1985) relied heavily on phone interviews and phone follow-up for their study in Vermont.

Relevance of Survey Items

The relevance of the items that are finally placed upon the survey is very important; relevancy determines the *validity* of the entire study. Therefore, the researcher or surveyor must decide which items are redundant, which are unnecessary, and which are less important than others. Since most surveys need to be relatively brief, it becomes essential to the success of the study that question design is judicious. The decision must be made whether to focus only on employment items or to investigate community living or personal life-style issues as well. The way in which data are to be collected will also influence the number of survey items included.

Access to Student Records and Location of Students

A logistical problem in doing this type of survey research is in gaining access to the names of students. This problem is complicated on several levels. First, there is the issue of confidentiality. Schools need to protect the names and files of current and past students. Second, some schools do not keep records for long periods of students no longer in school. Hence, locating these students becomes extremely difficult and time-consuming. This problem is further complicated when random samples are drawn and the subject cannot be located.

There are several possibilities for solving these problems. One way to protect confidentiality is to code by number each student who will be contacted. This can be done when the research is being performed by personnel outside the school system. In addition to such coding, researchers need to present their study to a local human rights committee for permission for the study to be completed.

Usually schools keep student records on hand for at least 3 years and sometimes 5–10 years. When this is the case, it makes good sense to start at the school system level for locating students. Often local mental health or mental retardation offices have comprehensive case management networks as well. Such offices, however, would not include the records of all disabled students.

Generally, much perseverance is necessary to locate a significant number of graduates. Families move away, change telephones, change names, and so forth. These factors can make this research difficult by slowing down the researcher's speed in assembling a viable sample.

CONCLUSIONS ABOUT POST-21 STUDIES

The myriad of studies completed are so different in terms of populations sampled, sampling techniques, size of area sampled, point in time the surveys were undertaken, and so on, that the task of drawing definitive conclusions is not an easy one. The authors are inclined to agree with leading researchers that the data reveal massive underemployment of workers with disabilities: Hasazi et al., (1985),

> More specifically, they suggest that mentally retarded young adults present markedly depressed work histories, are paid less than their handicapped colleagues, and typically are restricted to unskilled labor or service related occupations. (p. 223)

For the most part, the unemployment of individuals with severe handicaps has been a widespread national problem. As recently as February, 1986 a Louis Harris Poll indicated that two out of three disabled Americans were unemployed. What is especially interesting about this statistic is that most of these people say they would like to work if given an opportunity. In order to break this long-term cycle of structural unemployment, it is clear that youth need to develop meaningful employment histories even before they leave school.

The studies reviewed in the previous section generally reflect an unemployment rate across all levels and categories of handicapped youth of 5–10 times more than nonhandicapped persons. This is true regardless of the geographical location.

Such a level of unemployment is truly incredible given the abundance of funds, energy, and resources that go into special and vocational education, adult services, and vocational rehabilitation.

A second conclusion that can be drawn is that the role played by families and friends in helping identify jobs and employment opportunities is a major one. Those professionals in the helping professions play a less significant role than one might think. For example, in the Wehman, Kregel, and Seyfarth (1985a) study, almost 70% of the 300 young adults reported *never* having received any services from a local rehabilitation counselor.

Another major conclusion is that the disability level of those leaving special education seemed to be a factor in obtaining employment. Those with mild handicaps were more likely to be employed than those with moderate or severe handicaps. Such a conclusion is not surprising, yet it can also be misleading because it does not reflect the job turnover or job retention problems of individuals with mild handicaps. Furthermore, this conclusion does not address the under-employment problems that so many face.

A fourth conclusion is that excellent special education programs can make a difference in altering employment status. Those schools that provided community-based training, and those that were inte-grated, yielded better long-term job retention for graduates than those that did not (Wehman, Kregel, & Barcus, 1985).

Finally, it appears that community integration occurs more thor-oughly for those with mild handicaps than for those with severe handi-caps (Kregel, Wehman, Seyfarth, & Marshall, 1985). This finding is also not surprising; many youth with truly severely handicapping con-ditions are still in residential facilities. Nevertheless, more research is needed to fully ascertain the extent of community integration for per-sons with disabilities; many suspect it is still quite limited.

SURVEYING FOR POSTSECONDARY ADJUSTMENT: A SAMPLE

A chapter such as this one would not be complete without providing an illustration of the type of surveys that have been used to assess the follow-up status of graduating special education students. Therefore, the survey that was used in the Wehman, Kregel, and Seyfarth (1985a) studies is presented next. This survey took 5 months to develop and 2 months to field test before the actual surveying was completed. Ac-tual surveying of the 300 families took another 6 months. The survey is multifaceted in that it asked questions related to demographics, em-ployment, indpendent living, and life quality. To complete this survey takes approximately 45 minutes to an hour. Using the same interviews repeatedly will promote standardization of questions and uniformity of response to ambiguous questions. It is not necessary to administer the entire survey: parts of the survey can be utilized effectively.

SUMMARY

The purpose of this chapter has been to provide an in-depth look at the post-21 follow-up surveys of special education students once they leave school.

A literature review was provided along with an examination of the methodological problems of such studies. Major conclusions were drawn from these studies. Finally, the appendix at the end of this chapter provided a sample survey from one of the major studies that had been completed.

APPENDIX

Adjustment of Mentally Retarded Persons

Survey of Postsecondary Schools

Location _____   Interviewer _____

Date _____

I. Demographics
1. Name of respondent _____
2. Relationship of respondent to graduate
   a) Mother   b) Father   c) Legal guardian   d) Other _____
3. Respondent or respondent's spouse has been employed
   a) Consistently   b) Intermittently   c) Rarely
4. Combined income of respondent and/or respondent's spouse
   a) under $15,000   b) $15,000–$30,000   c) $31,000–$50,000
   d) Over $50,000
5. Name of graduate _____
6. a) Graduate's sex ___ M ___ F
   b) Date of birth ___ / ___ / ___
   c) Graduate's race ___ Caucasian ___ Black ___ Oriental
   ___ Other
7. Graduate's marital status a) Single   b) Married
   c) Separated/Divorced
8. Graduate's home location a) Rural   b) Urban   c) Suburban
9. School location a) Rural   b) Urban   c) Suburban
10. a) Year that graduate left school _____
    b) Age when graduate left school _____
11. Type of school program or arrangement graduate was in when left
    school:
    a) Resource room   c) Special class in regular school—trainable
    b) Special school   mentally retarded (TMR)/severely phys-
                           ically handicapped (SPH)
                        d) Special class in regular school—educable
                           mentally retarded (EMR)
                        e) Other _____
12. Does graduate have any medical problems that affect his or her
    daily life (heart conditions, seizures, etc.)? ___ Yes ___ No
    If so, what are they: _____

This survey was developed by Paul Wehman, John Kregel, and Kate Marshall at
The Rehabilitation Research and Training Center, Virginia Commonwealth University.
Any requests to use this survey should be directed to Dr. Paul Wehman.

II. Vocational

13. Is your son or daughter currently employed in a real job?
    ____ a) Full-time (32 hours per week or more)
    ____ b) Part-time
    ____ c) Not employed
    (IF *NOT* CURRENTLY EMPLOYED, SKIP TO QUESTION #21.
    QUESTIONS #15–20 APPLY *ONLY* TO CURRENTLY EM-
    PLOYED PERSONS.)

14. What is your son or daughter currently employed as?
    ____ a) Sheltered workshop   ____ e) Farm or agricultural
    employee   worker
    ____ b) Food service worker   ____ f) Office worker
    ____ c) Janitorial or cleaning   ____ g) Part of a crew of other
    worker   handicapped workers
    ____ h) Other _____

15. How does your son or daughter most frequently travel to and
    from his/her job?
    ____ a) On foot   ____ e) By facility bus
    ____ b) By car (parent drives)   ____ f) Carpool
    ____ c) By car (friend drives)   ____ g) Bicycle
    ____ d) By public bus   ____ h) Other

16. How long has your son or daughter been employed in his or her
    present job:
    ____ a) 0–6 months   ____ c) More than 1 year
    ____ b) 7 months to 1 year

17. What are your son's or daughter's current gross monthly wages?
    ____ a) 0–$50/month   ____ c) $201–$500/month
    ____ b) $51–$200/month   ____ d) $501–$700/month
    ____ e) Over $700/month

18. If your son or daughter is currently employed in regular or shel-
    tered employment, what benefits does he or she receive? (Check
    all that apply)
    ____ a) Meals   ____ d) Insurance benefits
    ____ b) Sick time   ____ e) Retirement
    ____ c) Vacation time   ____ f) Profit sharing
    ____ g) No fringe benefits

19. Does your son or daughter seem:
    ____ a) Extremely happy with his or her job
    ____ b) Satisfied with his or her job
    ____ c) Bored with his or her job but not planning to quit
    ____ d) He or she would like to or plans to quit his or her job

20. Did your son or daughter find his or her current job with the help
    of:
    ____ a) Rehabilitation   ____ e) A special outside
    counselor   program
    ____ b) A friend   ____ f) Your son/daughter found
    ____ c) A parent   the job independently
    ____ d) School counselor/   ____ g) Other
    teacher

21. If your son or daughter is not currently employed, has he or she ever: (Check all that apply)
(IF CURRENTLY EMPLOYED, SKIP TO QUESTION #23. QUESTIONS 21 AND 22 APPLY ONLY TO THOSE WHO ARE NOT CURRENTLY EMPLOYED.)
_____ a) Worked in a real job since leaving school and for at least 3 months
_____ b) Worked in a sheltered workshop
_____ c) Attended an adult activity or work activity center

22. If your son or daughter is not currently employed, is it because of any of the following reasons? (Check all that apply.)
_____ a) No job in the area that he or she can do
_____ b) No one to help him or her get a job
_____ c) No one to help provide training for a job
_____ d) Doesn't want to give up Social Security Disability Insurance
_____ e) No transportation available
_____ f) Other _____

23. How many jobs has your son or daughter held since leaving school?
_____ a) 0–1 jobs _____ b) 2–3 jobs _____ c) 4–5 jobs
_____ d) more than 5 jobs

24. What amount has your son or daughter earned since leaving school?
_____ a) 0–$999
_____ b) $1,000–$3,999
_____ c) $4,000–$7,999
_____ d) $8,000–$11,999
_____ e) $12,000–$14,999
_____ f) Over $15,000

25. What amount of services has your son or daughter received from the local rehabilitation counselor?
_____ a) Frequent training and job placement assistance
_____ b) Occasional visits to discuss job possibilities or other assistance
_____ c) No rehabilitative services have been provided

26. Can you name the rehabilitation counselor responsible for your son or daughter?
_____ Yes _____ No

27. What amount of services has your son or daughter received from local community mental retardation services (Chapter 10 or ARC)?
_____ a) Frequent training and job placement assistance
_____ b) Participation in day programs for learning self-care, social, recreation, and academic skills
_____ c) No community services have been provided

28. Has the Virginia Employment Commission been
_____ a) Helpful in job placement for your son or daughter
_____ b) Visited by your son or daughter but with no success
_____ c) Of no help to your son or daughter in job placement assistance
_____ d) Don't know

29. Has your son or daughter ever lost/resigned from his or her job(s) because of any of the following reasons? (Check all that apply.)

_____ a) Problem with his or
      her supervisor

_____ e) Work rate or ability
      lacking

_____ c) Lost transportation

_____ f) Job abolished

_____ d) Wanted Social
      Security payments
      instead of wages

_____ g) Never had job

_____ h) Other _____

30. What type of school vocational program did your son or daughter most frequently participate in?

    _____ a) A structured skill training program in a regular vocational class

    _____ b) A special class with some practice vocational training (primarily on school grounds)

    _____ c) A special vocational training program with practice of work skills (primarily off school grounds)

    _____ d) A CETA or Vocational Education subsidized work experience program, which included some wage payment

    _____ e) No vocational education program

III. Independent Living

31. Where does your son or daughter live?

    _____ a) At home

    _____ d) Supervised apartment

    _____ b) Group home

    _____ e) House or apartment without supervision

    _____ c) Residential facility

    _____ f) Other

32. Does your son or daughter do any of the following?

    _____ a) Walk about the community

    _____ d) Drive a car

    _____ e) Use public transportation

    _____ b) Ride a bicycle

    _____ c) Have a driver's license

33. Does your son or daughter do any of the following? (Check all that apply.)

    _____ a) Cook his or her own meals or snacks by him- or herself

    _____ e) Do household chores (dusting, vacuuming, etc.) by him- or herself

    _____ b) Do his or her own laundry

    _____ f) Clean entire house by him- or herself

    _____ c) Sew or mend his or her own clothes

34. Does your son or daughter do any of the following? (Check all that apply.)

    _____ a) Purchase food for him- or herself (from restaurants, grocery stores, or vending machines)

    _____ b) Purchase his or her own clothes for him- or herself

    _____ c) Select his or her own clothes for him- or herself

35. Which of the following community services does your son or daughter use regularly by him- or herself? (Check all that apply.)

    _____ a) Restaurants

    _____ d) Post offices

    _____ b) Stores

    _____ e) Hair stylists

    _____ c) Banks

36. Does your son or daughter do either of the following?

a) Attend church/synagogue services regularly ____ Yes ____ No
b) Participate in church/synagogue activities ____ Yes ____ No
(choir, clubs, etc.)

37. Does your son or daughter do any of the following? (Check all that apply.)
____ a) Toilet independently
____ b) Dress independently
____ c) Bathe and groom independently
____ d) Eat independently

38. Does your son or daughter do any of the following? (Check all that apply.)
____ a) Use money to make purchases
____ b) Make change by him- or herself
____ c) Write checks to make purchases by him- or herself
____ d) Balance his or her own checkbook by him- or herself
____ e) Pay his or her own bills
____ f) Have his or her own savings account

39. Does your son or daughter use the telephone for any of the following reasons? (Check all that apply.)
____ a) Call his or her family or friends
____ b) Call for community information (i.e., stores, movie theaters)
____ c) Does not use telephone

40. Does your son or daughter
a) Tell time ____ Yes ____ No   b) Set and use an alarm clock ____ Yes ____ No

41. Did your son or daughter
a) Take a minimum competency test in high school
____ Yes ____ No
b) Pass the minimum competency ____ Yes ____ No

42. At which of these facilities does your son or daughter spend 1 or more hours each week? (Check all that apply.)
____ a) Shopping facilities
____ b) Homes of friends
____ c) Outdoor recreation facilities (swimming, pool, parks, etc.)
____ d) Indoor recreation facilities (movies, video arcades, etc.)

43. Which of these activities does your son or daughter regularly enjoy at home? (Check all that apply.)
____ a) Watching TV
____ b) Listening to records or tapes
____ c) Playing card games
____ d) Playing table games
____ e) Crafts
____ f) Playing video games
____ g) Other _____
_____

44. In which of these activities does your son or daughter participate regularly?(Check all that apply.)
____ a) Jogging
____ b) Swimming
____ c) Bicycling
____ d) Bowling
____ e) Other _____
_____ _____

45. To which of the following groups or clubs does your son or daughter belong? (Check all that apply.)
    ____ a) Church club   ____ d) Exercise class
    ____ b) YMCA or YWCA   ____ e) Adult education class
    ____ c) Scouts   ____ f) Other _____
                                          _____
                                          _____

46. Which of the following events does your son or daughter regularly attend?
    ____ a) Sporting event   ____ d) Fairs or festivals
    ____ b) Concerts or plays   ____ e) Other _____
    ____ c) Movies   _____
                                          _____

IV. Personal Life-Style/Quality of Life

47. Does your son or daughter spend most of his or her free time with
    ____ a) Family   ____ c) With general public (ex:
    ____ b) Friends   in a shopping mall or
                                         movie theater)
                                    ____ d) Alone

48. Does your son or daughter spend his or her free time outside of the family with:
    ____ a) Nonhandicapped   ____ c) Both handicapped and
          people   nonhandicapped people
    ____ b) Handicapped people   ____ d) Spends free time only
                                         with family

49. How often does your son or daughter spend his or her free time outside of the family with one person of the opposite sex?
    ____ a) Regularly   ____ b) Occasionally   ____ c) Seldom
    ____ d) Never

50. Did your son or daughter receive sex education:
    ____ a) At home   ____ b) In school   ____ c) Has not received sex education

51. Does son or daughter know about birth control methods such as the pill, condoms, and so forth?   ____ Yes   ____ No

52. Is your son or daughter registered to vote?   ____ Yes   ____ No

53. Does your son or daughter vote?
    ____ a) Yes, in all elections   ____ b) Yes, in some elections
                                    ____ c) No

54. Has your son or daughter ever been arrested?   ____ Yes ____ No

55. If yes, for what reason?
    ____ a) Traffic offense   ____ c) Assault
    ____ b) Shoplifting   ____ d) Drug-related issue
                                    ____ e) Other _____

56. How satisfied is your son or daughter with his or her life?
    ____ a) Very satisfied   ____ c) Somewhat dissatisfied
    ____ b) Satisfied   ____ d) Very dissatisfied

57. Which of the following items are a problem for your son or daughter? (Check all that apply.)

_____ a) Health

_____ b) Behavior outbursts/
   emotional control

_____ c) Transportation

_____ d) Making friends

_____ e) Loneliness

_____ f) Lack of money

_____ g) Lack of work skills

_____ h) Not enough leisure
   activities

_____ i) Other _____

_____

_____

Chapter 3   *Planning for Transition from School to Work*

TO THIS POINT THE AUTHORS HAVE PROVIDED A RATIONALE AND BASIS FOR local and individualized transition planning. However, the mechanics of evaluating local service options and of developing transition plans are difficult and time-consuming. Professional literature on transition planning for the most part has focused on the presentation of philosophical and untested models. These models have enabled professionals to describe what were felt to be the critical elements of transition planning (e.g., Halpern, 1985; McDonnell & Hardman, 1985; Wehman, Kregel, & Barcus, 1985; and Will, 1984a). As service providers began to implement these models, issues and concerns emerged concerning professional and parental roles and responsibilities, format of individualized transition plans, and methods of evaluating student outcomes as a result of transition planning. More recent literature has begun to identify several critical issues related to transition planning. These issues include the development of formal local interagency agreements, community-based vocational instruction, parental involvement, formal written transition plans, and secondary program follow-up to evaluate program effectiveness (e.g., Ballantyne, McGee, Patton, & Cohen, 1984; Benz & Halpern, 1986; McDonnell, Wilcox, Boles, & Bellamy, 1985; Rhodes, 1986). The concept evolved from relatively naive efforts to systematically effect the transition of youth with severe handicaps by indiscriminantly moving them from school programs into existing adult service programs. More recent opinion is that the transfer of youth from inadequate secondary programs into inappropriate adult service programs is inefficient and unacceptable. Furthermore, successful transition must be evaluated not only by the existence of written transition plans, reduced waiting lists, and increased placements in existing adult service programs, but also by the quality and timeliness of the placements and services ultimately provided.

Transition is defined here as an interagency planning and implementation process that takes place at the local level and that makes available new residential and employment opportunities for youth with disabilities. But effective transition planning and implementation is more than the development of individualized transition plans. It also involves evaluation of local programs and services and a coordinated and cooperative effort by all involved agencies to bring about systems change.

Recent literature assessing graduates of special education programs, as reviewed in Chapter 2, has carefully documented the scarcity or ineffectiveness of current transition planning in reducing unemployment rates, decreasing dependence on social service programs, and decreasing community isolation. It is essential that transition begins to be viewed not as a process that simply moves young adults with severe handicaps from one isolated and restrictive placement into another, but instead as a process that results in new and different outcomes. Effective transition planning involves coordinating existing services, changing service delivery systems, and developing new service options. *Transition planning that results in improved outcomes of employment, independence, and community integration must be a cooperatively planned and implemented process at a local community level.*

It is the purpose of this chapter to present a model for step-by-step interagency transition planning and implementation at the local level. Procedures are outlined for localities to use in five areas; developing local core teams, conducting needs assessments of local services, targeting changes in existing services, developing procedures for transition planning within a local education agency (LEA), and implementing and evaluating the outcomes of transition planning. This model, (see Figure 3.1), presupposes that in most states transition planning will take place on three levels: state, local, and individual. The state level provides fiscal and legislative guidance, but transition planning and implementation must take place at a local and individual level.

ELEMENTS OF THE TRANSITION PROCESS

Local Core Transition Teams

Developing Core Teams A local core transition team comprises a small number of persons (optimally between six and ten), in a local

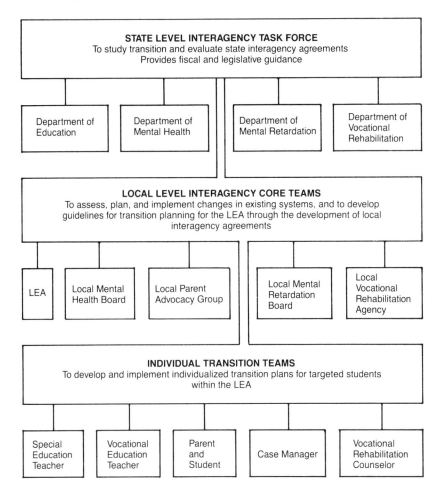

Figure 3.1.   Levels of transition planning: Local level core teams and individualized planning teams.

community who represent key agencies and adult service programs. A parent or consumer representative should also be present. A core team is a task force whose members agree to serve as catalysts for planning and implementing interagency procedures for the transition from school to work of youth with disabilities. The primary responsibility of the core team is the development of transition procedures as embodied in formal local interagency agreements. These agreements address transition planning issues and strategies for implementing the agreements. Team members must agree to work together for an indefinite period of time; therefore, each team member must support the concept of school to work transition, have the support of his or her own agency or organization, and occupy a key leadership position in that agency or organization. A core team may need to work together for as little as a year, or for as long as 5 years in order to plan and evaluate comprehensive transition planning and implementation guidelines for a locality.

A core team, or task force, may be initiated by one or more professionals within an agency, by a parent or consumer advocacy organization, or by several professionals across agencies. In some states, the development of local core teams has been supported by state level interagency task forces. In Tennessee (Bellephant, 1986), a state level interagency task force agreed to work together to train local core teams in selected localities throughout the state. Tennessee's state level task force recognized the need to provide guidance and leadership to localities who desired to assess and change local services. The state level task force also recognized a critical prerequisite to local change: the localities' willingness and readiness to change.

In many localities, the initial development of a core team will be assumed by the local education agency, since the agency is ultimately responsible for serving transition-age students (McCarthy et al., 1985). In the Philadelphia city school system, for example, a special education administrator was assigned responsibility for transition planning for all secondary students with severe and profound handicaps in his school district. He chose to assume responsibility for the initial development of a core team by contacting key agencies and organizations by telephone and letter to invite them to send a representative to a school-sponsored transition awareness meeting. The purpose of this meeting was to discuss the need for transition planning and to propose the formation of a core team to address local issues and needs. A secondary purpose of the meeting was for school representatives, adult service representatives, and parent and advocacy representatives to get to know each other in a nonthreatening situation. Because representatives from the local education agency, from vocational rehabilitation and mental retardation agencies, and from the Association for Retarded Citizens (ARC) were involved from the beginning, all members of the newly formed team were able to readily define their roles and responsibilities, and to build an environment of trust from the very first meeting.

Viable interagency teams have been formed in other locations as well. In Kanawha County, West Virginia (Cook, 1986), Johnson County, Kansas (J. Scarlett, personal communication, 1986), and Sonoma County, California (Rosenberg, 1986), interagency teams were formed using federal or state grants and the assistance of external consultants. In addition to financial incentives, teams in these localities were successful because of the team members' conviction that transition planning was a logical extension of interagency coordination activities already undertaken by the teams.

In those instances where local interagency teams have already been established, a reexamination of purpose and goals may be useful. An existing interagency team may form a core transition subgroup that is charged with the responsibility of developing a formal local interagency agreement for transition planning. This action is important because the decision to develop written local interagency agreements may be the first step toward coordinating existing services and developing new service options for youth with severe handicaps during the transition years.

Teams may be assisted during their initial development by an external consultant, but the ultimate success of a local core team depends upon each member's understanding and acceptance of the need for coordination of interagency services. Goal identification and involvement of all critical team members throughout the planning process is important if all team members are to take full responsibility for the final procedures and agreements.

Whether a core team is being newly developed or is already in operation, the participation of all key agencies and organizations is essential if successful transition planning and implementation is to occur. The key participants that must be included in a local core transition team are: 1) one or two school representatives, ideally representing both special education and vocational education; 2) a representative from the local vocational rehabilitation agency; and 3) one or more representative from the local mental retardation agency, mental health agency, or developmental disabilities planning council. The final key member is a parent advocate or client representative. These four or five team members together represent the agencies that are responsible for existing education, habilitation, and day support programs for young adults with developmental disabilities.

A locality may choose to add one or more additional members to the core team based on the individual needs of the community. For example, localities that have model demonstration programs in transition or supported employment would want to include representatives from these programs on the core team. Other local core teams, recognizing the importance of university preservice and inservice training for professionals, may include a representative from a community college or local university.

Although there are no definitive rules for choosing the number or positions of members who should serve on a core team, there are some general guidelines that local core teams have found to be important.

The team must be small enough for all participants to actively work toward a common goal, but large enough to include all relevant school personnel, adult service personnel, and parent or client representatives. In most localities, between six and ten members agreed to serve on the core team that is presented in Table 3.1. Representatives from all key agencies should occupy parallel positions of authority within the hierarchies of their agencies in order to minimize conflict, territoriality, and competition. Team members must also occupy positions that enable them to identify their agency's resources and limitations, and to make financial, staffing, service, and time commitments. Perhaps the most important requirement of core team members is that each member agrees to serve as a catalyst for bringing about local systems change. The identification of potential team members either by an external consultant or by local professionals requires knowledge of local politics and agency hierarchies.

Once a core transition team has been identified and has agreed to serve as a task force for developing and implementing local interagency transition procedures, the team members are ready to begin the step-by-step planning process. The overall goals of a local core transition team are threefold: 1) to assess and evaluate existing services, 2) to develop guidelines for interagency transition planning, and 3) to develop written local interagency agreements targeting transition planning and employment outcomes. Table 3.2 summarizes the activities core teams might engage during completion of each goal. A team may need to target one or both of the second and third goals depending upon the results of the local needs assessments. If local interagency agreements are developed, they must be outcome-oriented

Table 3.1. Potential members of a local core team

Critical team members	Special education administrator Vocational education administrator Vocational rehabilitation administrator Mental health/Mental retardation director Developmental disabilities planning council member Parent representative and/or client advocate

Other team members as identified in specific localities	University representative(s)
	Job Training Partnership Act (JTPA) program
	   representative
	Private Industry Council (PIC) representative
	Social security administration representatives
	Rehabilitation association representative
	United Way or other community services
	   representative

Table 3.2. Goals of a local core team

Goal 1: Conducting needs assessment or gathering existing needs assessment information
—Identify and assess school sponsored preemployment training programs.
—Identify and assess adult service employment, supported employment and postsecondary training programs.
—Identify and assess other adult services and environments that transition-age young adults might utilize.

Goal 2: Establishing guidelines for interagency transition planning
—Target a population to receive formal transition planning.
—Target an age to begin formal transition planning.
—Define procedures for developing individualized transition plans.
—Define roles and makeup of individualized transition teams.
—Plan inservice training programs related to transition for all personnel across agencies.
—Plan parent training program on transition.
—Plan community public awareness program.

Goal 3: Developing a local interagency agreement and action plan
—Identify mission and purpose of agreement.
—Identify measurable goals to be achieved by the agreement.
—Identify responsibilities and deadlines.
—Identify evaluation procedures.

and guided by the information gathered in local needs assessments. In addition, step-by-step implementation procedures should be included in the transition planning.

Conducting Needs Assessments

The initial task of the core team is to conduct a needs assessment of the local community or to gather existing needs assessments (McCarthy et al., 1985). These assessments should identify and evaluate services currently offered by school programs and adult service programs. For example, school programs should be assessed for: 1) the amount of time students spend in community-based vocational training sites and other vocational training sites, 2) the relationship between school curricula and local employment opportunities, 3) the number of students placed in employment settings prior to or immediately upon leaving school, 4) employment and community integration status of students who have previously left the school program, and 5) the number of former students currently on waiting lists for employment and residential services. Table 3.3 examines questions that core teams should address when assessing secondary school programs.

Table 3.3. Secondary education programs for students with moderate and severe disabilities: Sample needs assessment questions

1. What is the LEA's overall philosophy of secondary education for students with moderate and severe disabilities?
2. Does the LEA collect any follow-up data to determine what outcomes former students achieve and what services former students utilize? Are school personnel satisfied with former students' outcomes?
3. To what degree are students integrated into classes and activities with nondisabled peers?
4. How many students receive vocational education services? How are curricula adapted?
5. Do students receive community-based training (as opposed to intermittent field trips)? If yes, in what curricular domains? How frequently?
6. Does classroom training target functional age-appropriate activities?
7. Do vocational training programs support job placements prior to or immediately upon leaving school?
8. Do secondary vocational programs collect situational assessment data as well as formal assessment data?
9. Are students given the opportunity to participate in a variety of vocational training experiences? In sheltered settings? In simulated settings? In real work environments?
10. Do students receive formal transition planning? At what age?
11. What professionals and agencies are involved in transition planning?
12. Are parents and students actively involved in transition planning and implementation?
13. Are parents and students provided information on locally available adult services? Are school personnel knowledgeable about referral procedures and eligibility information?
14. Are release of information procedures in place to release student records to adult services providers?
15. Are parent and peer support groups available during the transition years?

Adult service programs should be assessed and evaluated for the types of postsecondary vocational assessment and training that they provide, the availability of job placement programs, and the availability of supported and sheltered employment options. Employment programs should be evaluated by: 1) the number of individuals placed into employment opportunities; 2) the retention rates of their placements; 3) the hourly, weekly, monthly, and or yearly wages earned by employees; 4) the use of Department of Labor subminimum wage certificates; 5) the average number of hours employees work daily, weekly, and the number of months worked yearly; 6) the availability and type of follow-along support services provided; and 7) the type and degree of integration employees have with nondisabled co-workers. Table 3.4 examines questions that core teams should address when assessing adult employment programs.

The core team should also identify and evaluate the availability

Table 3.4. Employment programs for adults with moderate and severe disabilities: Sample needs assessment questions

1. What is the program's overall philosophy toward employment for individuals with moderate and severe disabilities?
2. What is the program's eligibility requirements? Are there any prerequisite skills required? How many candidates are on the waiting list?
3. What population(s) does the program serve?
4. What specific service(s) does the program provide: postsecondary vocational training? vocational evaluation? job seeking skills? career counseling? job placement? supported employment?
5. How many candidates are placed in employment each year? How many are maintained in employment? What is the program's definition of "successful"?
6. What are the average graduate's earnings hourly, weekly, monthly, yearly?
7. What is the average number of hours worked by graduates daily and weekly? Is the work temporary or seasonal?
8. How much contact do graduates have with nondisabled peers? What is the ratio of workers with disabilities to nondisabled workers?
9. What is/are the agency's primary funding sources(s)?
10. What is the name of the program, and what image does the name invoke?
11. Is the program accessible by public transportation or does the program provide specialized transportation?
12. Are services facility-based or community-based?
13. What is the ratio of staff to candidates? (differentiate between direct and administrative)

and quality of other support services frequently requested and utilized by individuals with developmental disabilities. These services would include community living arrangements, transportation, recreation programs, peer support groups, counseling, and medical and therapeutic services. Special attention should be given to environments and services that nondisabled persons frequent and use, but that young adults with disabilities have not traditionally taken advantage of because of the unavailability of community-based training and support. For example, aerobics classes at local recreation centers are much more integrated than Special Olympics programs. Supported apartment programs are much less restrictive than 15-bed group homes.

Although the mandates of the 1983 Education of the Handicapped Act Amendments (PL 98-199) require state departments of education to conduct demographic studies on the number of students leaving public schools each year and the types of services they require, the applicability of the data to specific localities may be difficult to determine. McDonnell et al. (1986) posed the question, "Do we know enough to plan for transition?", as a result of their attempts to obtain accurate data from all 50 states and the District of Columbia on the numbers of former students requesting and obtaining employment and residential services after graduation. One of the needs these researchers identified was for the development of state-level data systems that would track students by disability, types of services requested, and types of services obtained. Until statewide needs assessments are available in all states to determine specific service needs for adults with developmental disabilities, each locality must rely on its own needs assessments to better serve its citizens. In some states, this is a role with which the Developmental Disabilities Planning Council, the Association for Retarded Citizens (ARC), or a University Affiliated Facility (UAF) may assist the core team. Elder and Magrab (1979) have suggested that an agency or organization external to the core team should conduct the needs assessments to avoid possible threats to participating agencies.

One of the primary reasons for the core team to conduct new needs assessments and to gather information from existing needs assessments is simply to draw attention to the fact that there may be a lack of accurate information on services requested and utilized by youth with severe disabilities. More importantly, examination of local needs assessments information will enable the core team to identify common referral procedures, eligibility criteria, and existing interagency linkages. Additional reasons for conducting needs assessments are to enable the core team to assess the type and quality of services currently offered by local programs, to target changes in existing programs, and to identify new programs for development. As individualized transition plans become operational, the discrepancy between the number of services required by youth with severe disabilities and their families, and the number of services available locally, will become increasingly clear. Procedures for the collection of ongoing needs assessment data from individualized transition plans are discussed in Chapter 4.

Establishing Guidelines for Interagency Transition Planning

Based on information obtained from statewide follow-up studies of youth with disabilities and from local needs assessments, the next step the core team should take is to make procedural decisions related to the transition planning process. The results of the needs assessments may indicate improvements are needed in all service areas, or instead, that there are critical needs in specific areas. The core team must analyze the strengths and needs of the locality, establish priorities, and develop guidelines for local service providers to follow. These guidelines should establish transition planning procedures for individual students and should suggest strategies for changing existing systems and developing new ones.

For example, the core team should target the age at which the student's formal transition planning shoud begin. The core team should also outline procedures for individual transition teams to use when developing written transition plans, and should specify what service personnel are required for individual transition teams. The core team will need to address a number of questions. For example, at what age should formal transition begin? At what age should adult service representatives be involved in the ITP process? Do all students in the LEA who receive special education services need formal transition planning? Will the transition plan be an addendum to the individualized education program (IEP) or will it be a separate document? Who will assume responsibility for organizing an individual student's transition team? What school and adult service providers are critical members of an individual transition team? How will confidentiality and release of information be coordinated? Although these and other questions are addressed in this chapter and in Chapter 4, the answers must ultimately be provided by each locality as they make decisions and set local guidelines for transition planning.

A core team working with students in Philadelphia's large urban school system (J. Murphy, personal communication, 1986) spent its first 2 years identifying a core team, conducting and gathering existing needs assessments, and developing six transition planning and implementation modules to be field-tested and revised. This would take place during the following school year with a small group of secondary students, parents, and professionals. Guidelines for expanding the procedures and disseminating the modules to the entire targeted population, to teachers, and to parents were also included. Because the core team was composed of interagency personnel, it recognized the need to provide guidance to individual transition teams. The Philadelphia core team also identified the need to establish new supported employment options in the Philadelphia area. This would be achieved through improved interagency collaboration and the development of local interagency agreements.

Developing Local Interagency Agreements and Action Plans

Planning Local Agreements　The culmination of the core team's activities is the development of a local interagency agreement for transition planning accompanied by an action plan with policy and implementation guidelines. This agreement will enable the team to formalize all of the informal agreements and procedures agreed upon thus far. Evaluation of state and local needs assessments should have enabled the core team to: 1) identify and verify participation of key agencies and organizations; 2) identify existing linkages between agencies and organizations; 3) identify flow patterns of youth with disabilities across local agencies and organizations; and 4) identify education, employment, residential, case management, and recreation needs of young adults in the local community. Procedural decisions based upon evaluation of the needs assessments should have enabled the core team to: 1) identify the overall mission and goals of local interagency transition planning, 2) target the population (including age, disability types, and geographical constraints) to be served, and 3) establish guidelines for interagency transition planning by individual transition teams. Figure 3.2 is a checklist that a

---

A small number of persons, usually six to ten, representing key agencies in the community, need to agree to serve as catalysts to generate an interagency agreement. These persons are the CORE team.

As a team, identify and then rank by priority the issues you would like to see addressed by a local interagency agreement.

Step 1: Is this a need?			Step 2: Is this a priority?
___ yes ___ no	1.	Purpose or mission statement of agreement	___
___ yes ___ no	2.	Process of eligibility determination for each agency's services	___
___ yes ___ no	3.	Referral procedures of each agency's services	___
___ yes ___ no	4.	Staff allocation for transition planning or supported employment services	___
___ yes ___ no	5.	Procedures for implementation of agreement	___
___ yes ___ no	6.	Plan for dissemination of local agreement	___
___ yes ___ no	7.	Plans for cross-agency inservice staff training	___
___ yes ___ no	8.	List of service options currently available	___
___ yes ___ no	9.	Identification of services targeted for development	___
___ yes ___ no	10.	Procedures for development of new services	___
___ yes ___ no	11.	Specification of target population for pilot services	___
___ yes ___ no	12.	Delineation of time-limited and ongoing services available from each agency	___

(continued)

Figure 3.2. *(continued)*

Step 1: Is this a need?			Step 2: Is this a priority?
____ yes ____ no	13.	Cost/sharing/funding coalitions planned or currently in place	____
____ yes ____ no	14.	Data sharing provisions	____
____ yes ____ no	15.	Release of information and confidentiality	____
____ yes ____ no	16.	Roles/attendance of personnel at IEP/ITP meetings	____
____ yes ____ no	17.	Schedules for implementation of agreement objectives	____
____ yes ____ no	18.	Schedule/procedures for re-negotiation or modification of agreement terms	____
____ yes ____ no	19.	Policies on specific service delivery related to transition planning/supported employment	____
____ yes ____ no	20.	Identification of agency liaisons in participating agencies	____
____ yes ____ no	21.	Other	____
____ yes ____ no	22.	Other	____

Figure 3.2. Needs assessment for local action plans and interagency agreements.

core team in Johnson County, Kansas found useful as they began to identify priority transition issues. This core team discussed all the listed issues, then used a modified Delphi process to determine the five issues they felt were most critical in their locality. These five issues, agreed upon by all the core team members, helped focus the team's goals for the upcoming year.

Nationally, there are few models for the development of local interagency agreements. Existing state level interagency agreements are often used as models even though they typically do not address coordination of specific client services or state desired outcomes in measurable terms. Viable local agreements must be more than simple cooperative agreements with broad goals if they are to achieve new and different outcomes for youth with disabilities. Formal interagency agreements enable localities to coordinate resources and services between agencies with similar objectives (Greenan, 1980). These agreements help maximize existing services and create a better understanding of what other agencies are doing (Schinder-Rainman & Lippitt, 1977). Table 3.5 describes the steps for developing local interagency agreements. These steps are discussed in more detail in Chapter 5.

Before beginning to write a local interagency agreement for tran-

Table 3.5. Developing local interagency agreements and action plans

Step 1: Planning local agreements
—Review state level interagency agreements and any available local interagency agreements.
—Identify components of successful and unsuccessful interagency agreements.
—Identify the team's purposes in developing an agreement.
—Ensure involvement of all key members and agencies.

Step 2: Writing local agreements
—Develop specific mission statement.
—Develop measurable goals to be achieved.
—Define specific agency responsibilities.
—Identify shared costs and resources.

Step 3: Implementing local agreements
—Develop an action plan with designated liaisons within each agency.
—Develop a dissemination plan to ensure understanding of agreement by all agencies.
—Determine program evaluation procedures.
—Design a schedule for evaluation of goals.
—Draw up a list of services being provided. Indicate renewal dates for service provision.

sition planning, the core team members should obtain and review copies of their state level interagency agreement and any local interagency agreements previously developed for other services needs. For example, some localities have already developed or are in the process of developing local interagency agreements for infant intervention services. Infant intervention programs were only recently federally mandated and thus do not fall under the auspices of just one agency. Core teams should also attempt to obtain copies of local interagency agreements from other localities in other states. Examination of existing local interagency agreements and discussions with the individuals who were instrumental in their development will enable the core team members to identify the components of successful and unsuccessful interagency agreements.

Writing Local Agreements

The first step in developing a local interagency agreement is for the core team to develop in writing the specific mission statement or purpose of the agreement. The mission statement should be expressed as broad social goals rather than specific quantitative objectives (Rhodes, 1986). Each team member must be encouraged to share with the team his or her reasons for wanting a local agreement and what his or her agency or organization hopes to achieve with the agreement. An example of a mission statement is:

> The purpose of this agreement is to provide for the cooperation and coordination of efforts in the delivery of services for youth receiving special education services between the ages of 13 and 23 years who reside in Johnson County in the transition from school to employment and adult life.

Rhodes (1986) has suggested that cooperative agreements that seek employment services for persons with severe disabilities should eliminate the emphasis on demonstration of one's ability or inability to work in favor of willingness to accept support services.

Unlike state level agreements, which generally seek to ensure the efficient delivery of services mandated by federal and state legislation, local level agreements may refer to the weaknesses or gaps in existing services as identified by the local needs assessments. The purpose or mission statement of a local agreement may be followed by a written rationale for the agreement. For example:

> Graduates in Monroe County experience more than a 50% unemployment rate and long waiting lists for existing services. The agencies participating in this agreement share a concern about these statistics and a willingness to cooperate in the delivery of services to the target population.

Local level agreements are often developed because team members see a need for *coordinated,* not just *cooperative,* services at the local level.

The next part of the local agreement may be a statement of measurable goals that the participating agencies hope to accomplish as a result of the agreement. An effective agreement reflects the constraints of each participating agency, but it also reflects a commitment to enhanced services for clients. For example, one goal might be the provision of a one-day inservice training workshop by the core team to provide training to other professionals in each agency concerning the goals of the agreement and the services each agency has agreed to provide. Another goal might be the development of an interagency transition implementation manual to be field tested and disseminated throughout the locality within, for example, a 2-year period. A third goal might be the achievement of cooperative efforts in the coordination of case management and referral services.

When designing these goals, core team members should bear in mind that the goals should reflect and enhance state and federal laws governing service delivery (Whitehead & Rhodes, 1985), but should not be used complacently to justify acceptance of the status quo.

The third and largest part of the local agreement is a delineation of specific responsibilities to be assumed and services to be provided by each of the participating agencies and organizations. This is the most difficult section of the local agreement to develop, because it requires each core team member to represent his or her own agency or organization in a give-and-take process. A reaffirmation by team members of their willingness to provide those services they are already mandated to provide is simply an agreement to maintain current services without modification or improvement. Instead, this list of responsibilities and services should reflect team members' commitment to sharing staff, costs, data, and other resources to produce better outcomes for individuals with disabilities.

This section of the agreement must state expected outcomes in measureable terms. Expected outcomes may be expressed in terms of numbers of individual transition meetings to be held annually, for example, or number of graduating students to be placed in supported competitive employment annually, or number of graduating students to be placed in group homes annually.

Interagency financing and cost sharing are considered the most difficult issues to address in cooperative agreements (Rogers & Farrow, 1983). Transition services and supported employment services face limitations resulting from new funding constraints and resistance to reallocation of existing funds. Effective models of transition planning with employment outcomes require cross-agency provisions for staffing and funding. An example of an effective local interagency agreement for transition planning and supported employment services is described in more detail in Chapter 5. The financing section of the agreement must also specify an agency responsible for case management (Rhodes, 1986), the staff to be shared for joint service provision (Elder & Magrab, 1979), and the sources and amount of funds and other resources (e.g., office space, materials,) that will be available to each participating agency (Whitehead & Rhodes, 1985).

Implementing Local Agreements

Once written, local interagency agreements must be disseminated and explained to all participating agencies as well as to parent and consumer groups that will be affected by the agreement. The action plan that is developed to accompany the agreement must specify: 1) designated liaisons within each participating agency; 2) schedules and objectives of cross-agency inservice training; 3) technical assistance to local transition teams, school programs, and adult service agencies; 4) procedures for documenting progress toward each goal;

5) mechanisms and deadlines for evaluation; and 6) provisions and dates for renewal.

Local interagency agreements formalize arrangements developed by the core team in earlier stages of transition planning. Effective documents ensure the coordination of existing services and enhance the development of new services, but they are not substitutes for open and ongoing communication between agencies. A relationship that has not been nurtured through the needs assessment and procedural decision-making stages of the transition planning process will not be cemented by formal agreements.

The purpose of a local interagency agreement is to coordinate services and to foster systems change. Each team member, if he or she has agreed to serve as a catalyst for local change, must be willing to assume two roles as services are delineated in the agreement. The first role to be assumed is that of spokesperson for his or her own agency or organization. The second role is that of risk-taker who is willing to effect change both in his or her own agency or organization and as a local core team member. Chapter 5 provides an example of a prototype of a local interagency agreement for transition planning that was developed and implemented by core teams in selected localities in Virginia and North Carolina.

Individualized Transition Planning Teams

An individualized transition planning team is an interagency group of professionals from various disciplines who currently provide direct educational services or who are targeted to provide adult services to a transition-age youth with a disability. The targeted youth and his or her parents or guardians are also considered to be part of the transition planning team. The team's primary responsibility is to develop, implement, and monitor the development of the individualized transition plan for a specific student. The individualized transition planning team should work within the guidelines established by the local core team to institute a plan that identifies adult outcomes in the areas of employment, community living, and recreation. The plan should also identify the services necessary to ensure the maintenance of these outcomes. An individualized transition plan (ITP) differs from an individualized education program (IEP) in that the ITP identifies outcomes and support services rather than skill deficits and remediation strategies. Optimally, a transition plan should identify a "vision" of what a young adult can become when appropriate outcomes are identified and services are provided. Such a plan is preferable to one that simply lists the services and programs that currently exist in the locality, because the services may or may not be beneficial for the young adult. Individualizing the transition process for a specific student requires an LEA to follow the steps outlined below in Table 3.6. The transition planning team works within the framework developed by the local core team to personalize transition planning for all targeted students in the LEA.

Organizing an Individualized Transition Planning Team

The lead agency, as designated by the local core team, is responsible for organizing an individualized transition planning team for each student targeted for transition during the year the student reaches the appropriate age for transition planning. In most localities, the lead agency will be the school, and the targeted age for formal transition planning will be age 16, or no later than 2 years before the student leaves the school program (McCarthy, Everson, Inge et al., 1985). Each locality must work within the procedural guidelines established by the local core team. At each school a professional will need to be designated to coordinate transition planning. This person might be the school guidance counselor, the school social worker, or the student's secondary teacher. Alternatively, transition planning for all targeted students may be coordinated by a full-time individual at the central office level.

The transition planning team should be made up of many of the same members of the student's IEP team, but it should also include representatives from local adult service agencies and programs that

Table 3.6.   Individualized transition planning team step-by-step process

Step 1:   Organize an individualized transition planning team.
  —Identify school personnel.
  —Identify adult service personnel.

Step 2:   Hold initial transition meeting as part of annual IEP meeting.
  —Develop an individualized transition plan.

Step 3:   Implement the transition goals through secondary program.
  —Use a transdisciplinary approach.

Step 4:   Update the ITP annually through annual meetings.
  —Phase-out involvement of school personnel while increasing involvement of adult service personnel.

Step 5:   Hold an "Exit" Meeting.
  —Ensure employment outcome.
  —Ensure recreation outcome.
  —Ensure community living outcome.
  —Ensure referrals to appropriate agency and appropriate support service.

provide services for the transition-age young adult. The team should include the special education teacher, the vocational education teacher, the vocational rehabilitation counselor, the parents or significant caregivers, the case manager, an employer, and/or a representative from a community residential program. In some cases, an occupational or physical therapist may also be included. The core team will have defined the roles of professionals, parents, and consumers for specific transition planning teams following the guidelines in Chapter 8.

The Initial Transition Planning Meeting As soon as a student is targeted for transition services, the transition planning team should develop the student's individualized transition plan as part of the IEP. The individualized transition plan should target transition goals such as vocational training in the student's community and a long-term strategy for employment or supported employment. The individualized transition plan should also address community living options such as remaining in the family home or making plans for residential services. Team members must also identify the skills needed to fulfill these goals, for example, using public transportation, using money to make personal purchases, caring for adaptive equipment such as wheelchairs and canes, and interacting appropriately with employers and coworkers. Team members must also designate the agency team member responsible for implementing the individualized transition plan goals. Chapter 4 describes an approach for identifying support services, approaches, activities, and strategies needed by individual students during the transition planning process.

Implement the Transition Plan Once a plan is developed and agreed upon by the individualized transition planning team members, the next step is to begin to implement the plan. If a student has been targeted to receive community-based vocational training at a local shopping mall as a janitor for example, the first step of the plan may call for the special education teacher to train the student along with several of his or her classmates in social skills 4 days a week for 4 hours a day. The vocational education teacher may be responsible for contacting the supervisor of the mall and setting up the training site. The vocational rehabilitation counselor may be responsible for visiting the student to make observations on a monthly basis. The counselor will also assign the student to his or her caseload once the student is in the final year of the secondary program and will assist the teacher with job placement services.

Update the Individualized Transition Plan Annually The transition planning team should meet annually or as needed to update and evaluate the transition plan. The original goals set by the team members should be evaluated for their appropriateness; the student's progress should also be evaluated. A student who was targeted for inclusion in a mobile work crew may be found 2 years later to be more appropriate for, and more interested in, supported competitive employment as a dishwasher. Parents who were uninterested in residential support may be interested in learning more about residential options 2 years later.

Hold a Final "Exit" Meeting During the Final Year of the Student's Secondary Program   If formal transition planning has begun by the targeted age, and if the transition planning team has been meeting regularly to develop, implement, and monitor transition goals, the student should be ready for an exit meeting by the final year in the secondary program. At this meeting, the team should make plans and assign responsibilities for implementing the final phase of the transition process: obtaining meaningful employment and community living options for the student. Procedures should be included to maintain communication between the school and adult service agencies before the student leaves school. Parental and family concerns about adult services and financial arrangements should have been addressed throughout the transition years, but care should be taken to ensure that families know what services are appropriate and available, and how to take advantage of these services as needed after the student's graduation.

SUMMARY

Effective transition planning at a local level accomplishes two goals: 1) the movement of youth with disabilities from school into employment and residential settings without a gap in service delivery, and 2) the coordination of existing local services and the development of new and different employment and other integrated community options for transition-age youth. In order for these goals to be met, transition planning must take place at two levels: by core teams at an interagency level and, on a more personal level, by the professionals who make up the transition planning teams.

Carefully planned and coordinated interagency services during the transition years are critical to the movement of young adults with disabilities into appropriate adult employment and residential settings.

Chapter 4   *Individualized Transition Planning*

CURRENTLY, THERE ARE NUMEROUS ARTICLES IN THE PROFESSIONAL literature calling for interagency cooperation and transition planning for young persons with disabilities who are graduating from school (Halpern, 1985; Hasazi, 1985; McCarthy, Everson, Inge, & Barcus, 1985; Wehman, Kregel, & Barcus, 1985). This abundance of professional literature is prompting initiatives by agencies at the federal level (Elder, 1984; Will, 1984a), as well as federal and state level legislation that addresses the development of formal procedures for transition planning (Federal Register, 1985, Vol. 50(759); Kansas House Bill 2300, 1986; Massachusetts House Bill 688, 1983). However, many states and communities still have no established procedures for coordinated needs assessment and transition planning between school and adult service agencies (McDonnell et al., 1986).

Without coordinated efforts in planning for individual students, there is a high likelihood of duplication or interruptions in service provision flow (Fenton & Keller, 1981). For example, some graduating students find themselves in endless cycles of adult services training programs repeating the same activities that they were doing in school programs. Even less fortunate are the many youth with more severe handicaps who will find services discontinued altogether because they and their advocates do not know what services are available, how to take advantage of local services, or how to meet eligibility criteria for available programs. Some students may end up at home requiring "babysitting" or some other form of less-than-optimal day care arrangements. In some cases, individuals will end up in institutions, in intermediate care facilities, or in nursing homes because parents and families find themselves unable to provide for their adult sons or daughters during the hours they used to be in school.

Chapter 3 of this text discussed the general issues of local transition planning, and highlighted the importance of cooperation between agencies serving youth and adults with disabilities. This chapter expands upon the planning process by discussing guidelines for individualizing transition planning for specific students. Five basic steps are included in procedures for formulating and implementing individualized transition planning (ITP):

Step 1: Organize ITP Teams for All Transition-Age Youth.
 — Identify all students who are transition age.
 — Identify school personnel.
 — Identify adult services/agency personnel.

Step 2. Hold Initial ITP meetings as Part of Annual IEP Meeting.
 — Schedule meetings.
 — Conduct meetings.
 — Develop the ITP.

Step 3. Implement the ITP through Secondary School and Adult Service Provision.
 — Operate according to guidelines defined in local interagency agreement.
 — Use a transdisciplinary and cross-agency approach.

Step 4. Update the ITP annually (during the IEP Meeting), and Implement Quarterly Follow-Up Procedure.
 — Phase out involvement of school personnel while increasing involvement of adult service personnel.
 — Contact persons responsible for completion of ITP goals to monitor progress of ITP.

Step 5: Hold an "Exit" Meeting.
 — Ensure most appropriate employment outcome.
 — Ensure most appropriate recreation outcome.
 — Ensure most appropriate community living outcome.
 — Ensure referrals to all appropriate adult agencies and support services.

Individualized transition plans cannot be implemented in isolation. Other important elements related to the implementation and success of ITP activities include the existence of an interagency agreement (as described in Chapters 3 and 5) and clear delineation of roles and responsibilities for individuals who participate in the transition planning process (as discussed in Chapter 8). In addition, long-range planning and local needs assessments are prerequisites to effective individualized transition planning.

IMPLEMENTING AN INDIVIDUALIZED TRANSITION PLANNING PROCEDURE

Initiating transition planning for students with disabilities is logically the responsibility of the local education authority because the school is the primary provider of services to youth during the transition planning years. The local interagency agreement (as described in Chapter 5) is one mechanism that enables school systems to initiate, implement and monitor an interagency ITP process. However, an LEA cannot be solely responsible for individualized transition planning without the cooperation of local adult service providers.

The steps below describe, in sequential order, the activities necessary for developing individual transition plans for youth with disabilities who are leaving the public school system. Suggestions are also offered regarding schedules and service personnel to be responsible for the completion of each step. There are many transition planning manuals available that have been developed for specific states and localities (e.g. Horton et al., 1983; Lambrou et al., 1986; McDonnell & Hardman, 1985; Stodden et al., 1986). These manuals, as well as this chapter, provide specific and tested guidelines for individual transition planning that may be adapted to the unique needs of a particular student in a certain community.

Step 1: Organize ITP Teams for All Transition-Age Students

Identify All Students Formal transition planning should begin for students when they have reached the age of 16. For students who are at a high risk of dropping out of school, age 14 might be the targeted age. A list of these students should be compiled in September or prior to the IEP meeting each year. Either a school teacher, social worker, guidance counselor, or other designated personnel may assume the role of transition planning coordinator or school transition liaison. This person will operate within the procedures that have been determined by the core team and documented in a local interagency agreement. The designated person should be responsible for compiling the list of transition students and overseeing the remaining steps in the transition process.

Identify Appropriate School Service Personnel School personnel, that is, teachers, therapists, and counselors who have been involved with individual students targeted for transition planning, should be identified for participation in the individualized transition planning (ITP) process. When enlisting school staff for involvement, the person organizing the transition participants should be careful to select staff from different disciplines who have had recent and meaningful contact with the student. The number of participants should be kept at a minimum so that teams will not be too large to be productive as a group. Also, the team must include all relevant disciplines.

Identify the Adult Service Agencies For students who are in their last 2 years of school, arrangements should be made for representatives from adult service agencies to participate in the ITP process. In some cases, it may be necessary to involve a representative of an adult service agency before the last 2 years of school. However, school officials should be aware of the very large caseloads of adult service workers and should refrain from requesting their involvement early except as required for individualized students. The idea is to involve adult agency representatives when their services can be best utilized and to avoid overloading them with involvement at a time when they cannot be active participants. Thus, during the early secondary years, adult service providers may best assist ITP team members in an informal consultative role rather than as active team members.

Adult service representatives will be able to provide valuable input on the services that will be available and most appropriate for a particular student as he or she leaves the school program. Community agencies from which representatives may be drawn include: mental health, mental retardation, vocational rehabilitation, social services, the local ARC, or the United Cerebral Palsy (UCP) group. The factor that determines which adult service agency becomes involved in transition planning for a particular student is the likelihood that the student will benefit from that agency's participation, or will be using their service in the future. The more knowledgeable the school liaison or transition planning coordinator is regarding the functions and service capabilities of adult service providers and agencies, the better able he or she will be to identify appropriate agency representatives for participation in ITP meetings.

Step 2:   Hold Initial ITP Meetings as Part of Annual IEP Meetings

Schedule the ITP Meeting Individualized transition planning meetings need to be scheduled for each student identified as being of transition age so that the student, parent(s) or guardian(s), relevant school personnel, and adult service representatives can attend. The student should always be included in the transition meeting so that he or she can have an active role in planning his or her future.

As decided by the core team and the local interagency agreement, the transition meeting may be conducted as part of the IEP meeting. This way, IEP goals and objectives can be written to reflect the ITP goals and objectives. Coordination of IEP skills and ITP services link the two agendas together.

Before the ITP meeting, the school liaison should make arrangements for cross-agency sharing of information on transition-age youth. (See the Interagency Release of Information Authorization form in Figure 4.1.) These arrangements are essential because the LEA is prohibited from releasing confidential information on students in special education programs without the signatures of a parent, a guardian, or the student.

Conduct the ITP Meeting   Transition meetings should progress through very definite stages to ensure that the goals and objectives are specific enough to achieve the desired outcomes. An individualized transition plan should identify adult residential and employment goals and the support services that the student will require to achieve and maintain these goals. In contrast, individualized education programs (IEPs) identify skill deficits and remediation strategies. An effective individualized transition plan matches the specific strategies and behavioral objectives from an IEP with the employment, residential, and community goals that a student must achieve in order to be an independent adult. The meeting format outlined and discussed below is based on a transition planning strategy that is used in several Virginia LEAs. These procedures should help professionals, parents, and students develop individualized transition plans that include: 1) clearly defined outcomes, 2) selection of appropriate services to achieve those outcomes, and 3) objectives that must be met to arrive at the outcomes.

Open the Transition Meeting   The person conducting the meeting should welcome and introduce all meeting participants. An informal atmosphere is recommended so that the student and his or her parents will feel as comfortable as possible. It is the responsibility of the professionals present to encourage honest and open participation by student and parents, as well as by the other persons in attendance.

After the introductions, the purpose of the individualized transition planning meeting should be explained. The purpose statement is very important to set the stage for what is expected in the meeting. (See example on the ITP cover sheet in Figure 4.2.)

Generate a Discussion of Desired Outcomes and Available Support Services   If appropriate, ask the student what he or she wants to do after graduation. Ask what type of employment and living arrangements he or she would like. Have the parent(s) verbalize what they want for their son's or daughter's postschool life. It is very important to encourage parents to express themselves openly so that any fears or uncertainties will be addressed in the discussion. Have a school representative discuss the postschool outcomes he or she feels the student can achieve given the appropriate support service. For example, the voca-

CHESTERFIELD COUNTY INTERAGENCY
RELEASE OF INFORMATION AUTHORIZATION

For the purpose of facilitating a smooth and uninter-
rupted transition from school to adult services this form
authorizes the agencies listed below to share confidential information on the student listed below during
the final 2 years he or she is enrolled in the Chesterfield
County Public School System. As a part of the interagency
transition planning process, the agencies listed below
will be working cooperatively during this period to arrange for postschool services and outcomes that are most
advantageous and desirable for the student and the student's family and/or primary caregiver. Care will be
taken by all agencies involved to release only that information which is required for effective and efficient implementation of services. Confidential information to be
included in this interagency information release agreement may include: educational, psychological, medical,
social and vocational information relevant to this student's needs as an adult in the community.

Student name: _____ D.O.B. _____
Social Security #: _____
Date of graduation: _____ Date information can be
released: _____

Agencies to share access to confidential information:

Chesterfield Public   VA Dept. of Rehabilitative
  Schools   Services
P.O. Box 10   11300 Iron Bridge Road,
Chesterfield, Virginia   Suite C
23832   Chester, Virginia 23831
Contact person: _____   Contact person: _____
Phone: _____   Phone: _____

Chesterfield Mental   OTHER: _____
  Retardation Services   _____
P.O. Box 92   _____
Chesterfield, Virginia   Contact person: _____
  23832   Phone: _____
Contact person: _____
Phone: _____

_____   _____
Student/client signature   Parent/guardian signature

_____   _____
Witness   Date

Figure 4.1. Release of information authorization. (Form developed by the Education to
Employment Project of the Rehabilitation Research and Training Center, Virginia Commonwealth University, Richmond, Virginia.)

This student has reached the age and point in his or her school services where the primary purpose of any training activities and/or instruction should be to facilitate normalized integration into the community as an adult citizen. Therefore this Individualized Educational Program (IEP) planning meeting should seek to develop goals and objectives which will bring about postschool living outcomes such as employment, community and domestic independence, and the ability to spend leisure time appropriately as an adult.

To assure continuity of service provision from school to adult services, the appropriate adult service agency(s) representative(s) should be in attendance and should participate fully in the ITP meeting process. The team should consist of: 1) school representatives; 2) adult agency representative(s); 3) parents; and 4) student. The purpose of the meeting should be to develop transitional goals and objectives designed to achieve employment and independent living outcomes for the student before he or she actually leaves the school service system and to delegate responsibilities to school and adult agency representatives for service provision.

Transition planning coordinator

Figure 4.2. ITP cover sheet. (Rehabilitation Research and Training Center, Virginia Commonwealth University, Richmond, Virginia.)

tional teacher may feel that the student can be successful in a full- or part-time job with supported competitive employment services or rehabilitation engineering. Such an assessment would of course be supported by evidence that the vocational training that has taken place throughout the school years has been appropriate and successful (see Chapter 6). Have the adult service representatives discuss the postschool support services that are, or will be, available to the student. It is helpful to provide ITP meeting participants with a written list of service options available. Figure 4.3 is a list of adult services that has been arranged according to levels of support required. The ITP meeting participants can refer to this list for a brief description of each service type and a ranking of the level of support each provides. Participants can then use this information to discuss and select the services deemed most beneficial for the student and most likely to achieve the desired outcomes.

Some programs or models described on the list may not be available in a given community. However, the possession of information on

Level of support	Employment	Residential/domestic	Recreation/leisure	Community access
A Minimal assistance to no support	Preemployment training and/or placement assistance 1. No assistance 2. Placement services 3. College/technical training services 4. Minimal job-site assistance	Independent living in privately owned or rented housing 1. No assistance 2. Intermittent case management or support 3. Independent living training	Participation in integrated recreation activities in the community 1. No assistance 2. Independent leisure skills	No support needed 1. Driver's license 2. Access to public transportation—no training or supervision required 3. Carpool arrangements made—no support needed
B Intensive training leading to ongoing or no support	Individual's employment models 1. Transitional Employment Services—Time-limited job coach services. Minimum wage or higher 2. Supported Competitive Employment—Ongoing job coach services. Minimum wage or higher 3. Supported Jobs—Ongoing job coach services; Contracted employment through support agency. Can be subminimum wage	Requires support and/or supervision part-time 1. Supported living—intensive training-phasing out-follow-along 2. Supervised living—constant supervision/training 3. Remain with family 4. Group home—part to full-time supervision 5. Adult foster care 6. Respite care 7. Case management	Integrated recreation activities in community with support 1. Time-limited support of peer/advocate or recreation coach 2. Ongoing support of peer/advocate or recreation coach 3. Time-limited training for independence during leisure times	Support required 1. Time limited training for utilization of public transportation 2. Carpool arrangements with co-worker or neighbor 3. Parent/sibling provided transportation 4. Special transportation

C — Intensive training with ongoing support

Group employment models—employment contracted through support agency; usually subminimum wages	Requires support/supervision full-time	Integrated or segregated recreation activities in community	Constant supervision required
1. Enclave—small work group; constant training and supervision; manufacturing, assembly, packaging	1. Supervised living—constant training/supervision	1. Ongoing support of peer advocate or recreation coach	1. Constant supervision needed for utilizing public transportation
2. Mobile Work Crew—small mobile work group; janitorial, grounds maintenance, etc.	2. Remain with family	2. Segregated special recreation programs	2. Carpool arrangements with co-worker advocate or neighbor advocate
3. Small Subcontract Shop—small entrepreneurial business with up to eight employees; benchwork. Segregated.	3. Group home—full-time intensive supervision	3. Careful training for independence during leisure time	3. Parent/sibling provided transportation
4. Sheltered Workshop—mid- to large publicly funded facility; benchwork tasks, sub-minimum wage Segregated	4. Adult foster care		4. Special transportation
5. Work Activity Center—publicly funded facility; 0 to minimal wages earned; segregated	5. ICF/MR		
	6. Nursing home		
	7. Respite care		
	8. Case management		

Figure 4.3. List of adult services, arranged by level of support. (Rehabilitation Research and Training Center, Virginia Commonwealth University, Richmond, Virginia.)

services that are desired but unavailable can be useful. For example, this information can be used to provide community leaders with valuable ongoing needs assessment information. One of the agency liaisons should be assigned the responsibility of compiling the information into report form at the conclusion of each year's ITP for submission to the administrators of the appropriate agency.

Identify Transition Goals   Having determined the long-term employment and residential objectives and the appropriate service delivery model, the short-term transition goals should then be determined and written down by the group. A goal should include the desired outcome (e.g., "full-time employment . . .") and the appropriate service delivery model to achieve the goal (e.g., ". . . utilizing a supported competitive employment approach"). Some examples follow:

Employment—Part-time employment in an enclave program.
Residential—Group home living.
Recreation—Participation in an integrated recreation program (beginners' swimming at the YMCA) using a peer-advocate program.
Community Access—Use of public bus system to get to job-site and recreation program. Training will be built into employment and recreation support services.

Include with each goal:

1. Projected date for achieving goal
2. Whether this goal should be completed before or after graduation (BEFORE/AFTER Graduation)
3. Names of the agencies that will work on this particular goal (Agency(s) involved: School VR MR/DD)
4. The person who has primary responsibility for seeing that the goal is achieved by the date set for completion (person responsible)

Determine Objectives/Steps to Accomplish Goals   The objectives or sequence of steps needed to accomplish transition goals need to be determined. This can be done in much the same way as writing a task analysis. For each of the sample ITPs in Figures 4.5, 4.6, and 4.7, a form such as the one in Figure 4.4 would be used to precede the document as a summary page of overall transition goals.

Figure 4.5 reflects a plan developed for a student with severe mental retardation. Ed is 18 years of age and is scheduled to graduate in 1½ years. His measured IQ is 32, he is nonverbal, and he makes only minimal vocalizations. His vocabulary is very limited and his speech is difficult to understand. He has been attending a segregated school program for students who are considered to be in the trainable, severe, and profound range of mental retardation. His previous vocational training consisted of learning benchwork skills such as collating and folding papers and participation in a community-based unpaid enclave with five other students.

Figure 4.6 shows an ITP that was written for a student whose primary disability is caused by cerebral palsy and whose mild retardation is a secondary handicap. Cathy is 19 years of age at the time of her meeting and is scheduled to graduate in 2 years. She has been attending a center-based education and treatment day program for youth with cerebral palsy. She can read very slowly on a third-grade level and can do simple addition and subtraction. Her previous vocational training included a community-based work microfilming documents.

Figure 4.7 represents an ITP that was written for a student with autism. Bill is 21 years of age and is scheduled to graduate at the end of the current school year. Although his measured IQ is 45, he can read at a sixth-grade level. He enjoys reading magazines, but is unable to answer questions about material he has read. His speech is echolalic, his verbalizations are abrupt, and the volume is inappropriately loud. He allows only momentary eye contact and becomes easily prompt dependent. He is in a self-contained classroom in a wing of an elementary school. He is currently involved in a paid vocational training job in the school's central office mail room and professional library.

Devise a Services Referral Checklist There may be actions necessary for effecting smooth transition that are not listed in the ITP objectives or in the "Steps to Accomplish Goals." To catch items that may have been left out, a Services Referral Checklist can be devised such as the one shown in Figure 4.8. Based on the goals and services identified by the ITP meeting participants, agency representatives should be designated as "persons responsible" to begin the formal referral and application processes that will initiate the appropriate adult services. Application and referral forms will need to be completed by each of the adult service representatives identified as having a role in the student's postschool life. This would include representatives from such agencies as the Department of Rehabilitative Services, Social Services, Community Mental Health and Mental Retardation Services, the Social Security Administration, or the local sheltered workshop.

Ending the Meeting At the end of the meeting, have all meeting participants sign the ITP document. The school liaison should have copies of the ITP sent to all participants as soon as possible after the meeting. Information describing adult community services should be given to the parents or to the student at this time. This may be a com-

INDIVIDUALIZED TRANSITION PLAN GOALS

Name: _____ Date: _____

SS#: _____

Date of Graduation: _____ Current Age: _____ D.O.B.: _____

Employment (see **List of adult services**): _____

Projected date of completion: _____   BEFORE   AFTER   Graduation

Agency(s) involved: _____ School   VR   MR/DD

Person Responsible: _____

Residential/Domestic (see **List of adult services**): _____

Projected date of completion: _____   BEFORE   AFTER   Graduation

Agency(s) involved: _____ School   VR   MR/DD

Person Responsible: _____

Recreation/Leisure (see **List of adult services**) : _____

Projected date of completion: _____
Agency(s) involved: School   VR   BEFORE   AFTER   Graduation
                                                                        MR/DD
Person Responsible: _____

Community Access (see **List of adult services**) : _____

Projected date of completion: _____
Agency(s) involved: School   VR   BEFORE   AFTER   Graduation
                                                                        MR/DD
Person Responsible: _____

Other notes:

Figure 4.4.   ITP goals sheet.

INDIVIDUALIZED TRANSITION PLAN GOALS

Name: _ED JONES_   Date: _1-12-87_

SS#:

Date of Graduation: _6-15-88_   Current Age: _18_   D.O.B.: _5-5-69_

Employment (see List of adult services): _To obtain full-time competitive employment through supported competitive employment services 2 months prior to graduation._

Projected date of completion: _4-15-88_ (BEFORE) (VR) AFTER   Graduation

Agency(s) involved: (School) (VR) MR/DD

Person Responsible: _Vocational Teacher_

Residential/Domestic (see List of adult services): _Group home with full-time supervision and residential services support_

Projected date of completion: _9-15-88_   BEFORE (AFTER)   Graduation

Agency(s) involved: School   VR   (MR/DD)

Person Responsible: _MR/DD Case Manager_

82

Recreation/Leisure (see List of adult services): *Special recreation program at the YMCA offered on Saturday mornings. Recreation coach for integrated program is unavailable.*

Projected date of completion: *4-30-88*

Agency(s) involved: School VR (BEFORE) (MR/DD) AFTER Graduation

Person Responsible: *MR/DD Case Manager*

Community Access (see List of adult services): *Ride city bus to and from work, training part of supported employment Service.*

Projected date of completion: *6-15-88*

Agency(s) involved: (School) VR (BEFORE) (MR/DD) AFTER Graduation

Person Responsible: *Vocational Teacher*

Other notes:

Figure 4.5. ITP written for a student with severe mental retardation. Sequence of steps to accomplish goals. (This ITP is provided as an example only. Each student and community is different, therefore, plans should be individualized.)

Figure 4.5.   (continued)

SEQUENCE OF STEPS TO ACCOMPLISH GOALS

Student: Ed Jones
Date: 1-12-87

EMPLOYMENT

Liaison: School	Comp. Date	Liaison: Rehabilitation	Comp. Date	Liaison: MR/DD	Comp. Date
1. Monitor students full time at community-based training site.	9-87	1. Attend regularly scheduled ITP meetings beginning on 1/12/87.	1-87 / 1-88 / 1-89	1. Introduce the range of available MR Adult Services in this community.	1-88
2. Provide an opportunity for the student to experience at least three different types of employment opportunities	12-88	2. Assist schools with selecting/identifying competitive employment placements.	1-89	2. Assist family with adjustments needed with SSI benefits, notification of employment, etc.	3-89
3. Look for a full-time employment opportunity 6 months prior to graduation.	1-89	3. Begin paying for transportation training.		3. Assign individual responsible for employment management.	5-89
4. Meet with student and family prior to accepting job position.	3-89				
5. Begin full-time job-site training 2 months prior to graduation. *Transportation training would also begin at this time.	3-89				
6. Phase out assistance and provide follow-along support.	5-89				
7. Transfer employment management to MR adult vocational services	6-89				

RESIDENTIAL	1. Review entrance criteria to local group home services. — 9–87 2. Assess student ability to meet residential services entrance criteria. — 9–87 3. Design program to assist student in meeting group home entrance criteria. — 10–87 4. Implement program to meet all necessary requirements for group home services. — 10–87		1. Assist family with residential services application. — 1–88
RECREATION			1. Contact YMCA and obtain application and schedule specialized programs. — 4–88 2. Select YMCA recreation events with student and family. — 4–88
COMMUNITY	1. Provide public transportation training to and from job. — 3–89	1. Pay for transportation training to and from work. — 3–89	1. Assist student and family in selecting feasible transportation option to recreation event. — 4–88 2. Arrange transportation to YMCA with family. — 4–88

INDIVIDUALIZED TRANSITION PLAN GOALS

Name: _Cathy Doe_

SS#:

Date: _10-10-85_

Date of Graduation: _6-18-87_   Current Age: _19_   D.O.B.: _9-5-66_

Employment (see List of adult services): _Full- or part-time_
competitive employment (probably micrographics area).
Service = _Transitional employment services._

Projected date of completion: _10-1-86_   (BEFORE)   AFTER   Graduation
Agency(s) involved: _____ School   (VR)   (MR/DD)
Person Responsible: _MR/DD Employment Specialist_

Residential/Domestic (see List of adult services): _Supervised_
apartment program with wheelchair accessibility.
Service = _Supervised apt., MH/MR Case Management Services._

Projected date of completion: _October, 1987_   BEFORE   (AFTER)   Graduation
Agency(s) involved: _____ School   VR   (MR/DD)
Person Responsible: _MH/MR Case Manager_

Recreation/Leisure (see **List of adult services**): _No assistance requested._

Projected date of completion: _____

| | School | VR | BEFORE | AFTER | Graduation |
| | | | MR/DD | | |

Agency(s) involved:
Person Responsible: _N/A_

Community Access (see **List of adult services**): _Will use Special TRAN for wheelchair transport. Service = Time-Limited training for SPECTRAN and wheelchair access city buses_

Projected date of completion: _6-1-87_

| | School | VR | (BEFORE) | AFTER | Graduation |
| | | | MR/DD | | |

Agency(s) involved: (School)
Person Responsible: _Special Education_

Other notes: _New supervised apartments are currently under construction in Rose Hill area. Construction should be completed by August, 1987._

Figure 4.6.   ITP written for a student with cerebral palsy and mild mental retardation. Sequence of steps to accomplish goals. (This ITP is provided as an example only. Each student and community is different, therefore, plans should be individualized.)

Figure 4.6. *(continued)*

SEQUENCE OF STEPS TO ACCOMPLISH GOALS

	Liaison: School	Comp. Date	Liaison: Rehabilitation	Comp. Date	Liaison: MR/DD	Comp. Date
EMPLOYMENT	1. Provide community-based work experiences in clerical situations.		1. Gather information to meet eligibility criteria for VR services.		1. Assign to employment specialist for transitional employment services.	2-86
	a) bank investigations: using automated microfilm reader-printer	9-85 thru 11-85	2. Apply for VR services.	5-86	*Employment Specialist will:*	
	b) microfilm clerk: document preparation and filming 4 days/week, 4/hours/day, 12 weeks	2-86 thru 5-86	3. Authorize and order construction of wheelchair ramp from family residence.	8-86	1. Complete candidate assessment.	5-86
			4. Authorize and procure transitional employment services.		2. Begin job development.	5-86
	2. Arrange for adult services employment specialist to visit work experience site (twice).	3-86 and 4-86			3. Place candidate into competitive employment and begin job-site training.	8-86
					4. Assist and train transportation skills if needed. (Talk with school liaison.)	8-86
					5. Fade from job-site intervention as indicated by training data.	11-86
	1. Examine adaptive living skills entrance criteria for supervised apartment program.	1-86			1. Make referral to supervised apartment program.	
	2. Complete candidate assessment to determine skill deficits if	1-86			2. Assist with move from family residence to apartment.	
					3. Write IPP to accom-	

RESIDENTIAL	3. Provide domestic/adaptive living skills training to meet entrance criteria.	1–86		agement needs for money management where candidate will continue to need assistance (e.g., tax forms, SSI).
	4. Assess money management skills.	1–86		
	5. Train money management skills to meet independent living criteria for apartment program.	6–87		
RECREATION				
COMMUNITY	1. Provide transportation training to and from community-based work sites.	9–85 thru 5–86		1. Provide assistance/training to use SPECTRAN to travel to grocery store, movie theatre, and to family home from supervised apartment.
	2. Student will arrange and use transportation (SPECTRAN) to go to and return from work sites independently on 5 consecutive days.	5–86		

INDIVIDUALIZED TRANSITION PLAN GOALS

Name: _Bill Johnson_

SS#:

Date: _9-18-86_

Date of Graduation: _June,1987_   Current Age: _21_   D.O.B.: _11-4-64_

Employment (see List of adult services): _Part-time employment_
(≥20 hrs/week). Entry-level clerical position.
Service = Supported competitive employment

Projected date of completion: _January,1987_   (BEFORE)   AFTER   Graduation
Agency(s) involved: (School)   (VR)   (MR/DD)
Person Responsible: _School Employment Specialist_

Residential/Domestic (see List of adult services): _Remain with_
family. Case management assistance as needed.

Projected date of completion: _N/A_   BEFORE   AFTER   Graduation
Agency(s) involved: School   VR   (MR/DD)
Person Responsible: _MH/MR Case Manager_

Recreation/Leisure (see List of adult services): _Participation in integrated youth bowling league (Saturday afternoons)._

Service = MH/MR Recreation Aide as recreation coach.

Projected date of completion: _3-1-87_   (BEFORE) (AFTER) Graduation

Agency(s) involved: (School) VR   (MR/DD)

Person Responsible: _MH/MR Recreation Aide + Special Ed. Teacher_

Community Access (see List of adult services): _Ride city bus to and from employment site and bowling alley._

Projected date of completion: _6-1-87_   (BEFORE) (AFTER) Graduation

Agency(s) involved: (School) VR   (MR/DD)

Person Responsible: _School Employment Specialist + MH/MR Recreation Aide_

Other notes: _Transportation training will be part of supported employment services and recreation coaching services (Special Ed. Teacher and Rec. Aide will work together for recreation activity)._

Figure 4.7. ITP written for a student with autism. Sequence of steps to accomplish goals. (This ITP is provided as an example only. Each student and community is different, therefore, plans should be individualized.)

Figure 4.7. (continued)

SEQUENCE OF STEPS TO ACCOMPLISH GOALS

Student: Bill Johnson
Date: _____

EMPLOYMENT

Liaison: School	Comp. Date	Liaison: Rehabilitation	Comp. Date	Liaison: MR/DD	Comp. Date
1. Observe student at one community-based training site.	10–86	1. Determine eligibility for VR services.	10–86	1. Assign Employment Specialist to provide follow-along support services.	2–87
2. Begin job development to discuss employment options.	10–86	2. Arrange with adult services to provide follow-along services after stabilization.	11–86	2. Meet with school employment specialist to gather employment information.	5–87
3. Make referral to vocational rehabilitation agency.	9–86			3. Visit employer with school employment specialist.	5–87
4. Place into competitive employment.	1–87			4. Meet with family.	5–87
5. Arrange school schedule with teacher.	1–87			5. Assist with job site training and transportation skills training if needed.	6–87
6. Provide job-site training.	1–87			6. Phase out intervention time as indicated by data.	6–87
7. Provide transportation skills training.	2–87			7. Develop a systematic follow-along schedule.	6–87
1. Observe student at home to assess independent living skills.	10–86			1. Complete referral process.	6–87
				2. Gather information	6–87

	Activity	Date		Activity	Date
RESIDENTIAL	2. Meet with student and family to develop independent living skills training program.	10–86		and identify case management needs.	
	3. Provide independent living skills training.	1–87		3. Provide case management services as needed.	6–87
	4. Make referral to MR/DD agency.	4–87			
RECREATION	1. Locate a Saturday youth bowling league.	2–87		1. Assign student to recreational peer trainer.	4–87
	2. Accompany student to bowling alley to register.	3–87		2. Provide bowling skills and social skills at the bowling alley.	4–87
	3. Make referral to MR/DD agency to provide peer training.	1–87		3. Provide transportation skills training.	4–87
	4. Assist with making transportation arrangements.	3–87		4. Fade intervention time as indicated by data.	6–87
	5. Provide transportation skills training.	3–87			
COMMUNITY	1. Determine city bus schedule.	12–86		1. Assist with transportation training to and from job and bowling alley, if needed.	6–87
	2. Provide transportation training to and from job and bowling alley.	1–87 and 3–87		2. Fade intervention time as indicated by data.	6–87

Service item	Date to be completed	Person responsible	Date completed
Referral to vocational rehabilitation			
Referral to MR/DD			
Referral to			
Referral to			
Social security card			
Medicaid application			
Medicare application			
SSI			
SSDI			
Guardianship			
Welfare			
Food stamps			
Medical exam			
Psychological exam			
Social history			
Educational summary			
Special transportation			
Residential services			
Group home			
Family support			
Foster care			
Respite services			
Counseling			
Waiver for minimum competency test			

Figure 4.8.   Services referral checklist.

munity services booklet prepared by the transition planning core team (as described in Chapters 3 and 5) or brochures or pamphlets from the various agencies listed above.

Step 3:   Implement the ITP

Operating under the terms of an interagency agreement, the persons designated as responsible for goals or specific steps in the ITP should implement the plans as prescribed. The achievement of most of the goals of the ITP will require cross-agency involvement. For example, some services may need to be utilized immediately, whereas other services may be utilized gradually over a period of several school years, and even into the years immediately following graduation.

Step 4:   Update the ITP Annually
and Implement Follow-Up Procedures

As the student nears graduation and as the individualized transition plan is implemented, adult service agencies should be increasing their involvement with the student. The schools should at this point be concentrating on transferring their information and service provision responsibilities to the agencies who will be providing services after graduation.

It is important that one of the agency liaisons be designated to follow-up on the progress of the ITP plan throughout its implementation. This may mean calling the "Person Responsible" as listed on the ITP form and checking on the status of their goal or item. Follow-up should occur at least quarterly to ensure completion of all steps and thus increase the likelihood of achieving desired goals. Follow-up may also involve organizing and scheduling another meeting of ITP participants if it is found that goals are not being achieved as planned. Annual or more frequent revisions of the original plan may be required.

Step 5:   Hold an Exit Meeting

Toward the end of a student's last year in school, the school liaison and adult service representatives should plan an exit meeting with graduating students (and/or their parents) to finalize plans for the transition from school to work. At this time, any final needs relevant to the transition process can be addressed. The group should examine which goals have been achieved, which have not been achieved by their scheduled completion date, and which are scheduled for completion shortly after graduation. Those goals that have not been achieved as scheduled should be reviewed by the group to see if they are still relevant, and if so, what steps should be taken to achieve those goals. Outcomes scheduled for completion after graduation should be reviewed in the same manner as those not achieved on schedule. Achieved outcomes should be discussed to see how the student and his or her family is doing with the new activities.

COMMUNICATION WITH PARENTS

Parental support is crucial to successful implementation of the individualized transition plan. The communication must begin in the first transition planning meeting and continue throughout all phases of implementation. Parents will be concerned about their son or daughter moving from the sheltered environment of the classroom to unprotected environments such as employment or community living settings. They may voice concerns about transportation to and from work, co-workers' attitudes toward their son or daughter, the pressures of the job, SSI and health care benefits, or supervision and safety in a group home. Parents particularly need to understand how employment will affect their son's or daughter's SSI and health care benefits. It should be stressed that care will be taken to maintain health care benefits for the individual either through the employment situation, or if possible, by maintaining SSI eligibility.

It is critical that the goals and objectives of the ITP reflect the desired priorities and life-style of the student and his or her parents or guardians. As a youth makes the transition from the mandatory and intensive involvement of the school service system to a nonmandatory adult service system, it will be left to the individual youth and the family to carry out the goals and objectives as decided by the ITP team. If the goals are more a reflection of what the professionals think are best and most appropriate for the student rather than what is desired by the youth and the family, then it is likely that achievement of the targeted outcomes will fail.

SUMMARY

Three factors are critical to the successful implementation of an individual transition plan. These factors are: 1) the involvement of ITP members who are knowledgeable about the availability of local services, 2) a process that ensures the identification of all desired outcomes within the least restrictive service options, and 3) the ability of community agencies to provide or procure the needed services.

Communities with well-written interagency agreements, a wide array of community service options, and a collaborative plan to address service needs will have the best chance for achieving desired outcomes for each student.

Chapter 5   *Interagency Cooperation*

EFFECTIVE TRANSITION PLANNING AND SERVICE PROVISION DEPEND ON functional linkages between school and adult service agencies (Ashby & Bensberg, 1981; Fenton & Keller, 1981; Hasazi, 1985). Although the agencies primarily responsible for serving individuals with handicaps are all seeking the same or similar outcomes for their clients, they have, in many instances, been operating in isolation or even in opposition to each other.

Recent statistics indicating the lack of successful employment outcomes for students leaving public school special education programs are revealing. The data point out transition-related problems such as the inability of different agencies to coordinate services and resources to accomplish meaningful postschool outcomes in the areas of employment and community living. The U.S. Commission on Civil Rights (1983) reports that 50%–75% of the individuals with disabilities are unemployed. Chapter 2 has indicated that many follow-up studies of special education graduates show similar data indicating low rates of employment for youth coming out of public education programs (Hasazi et al., 1985; Mithaug et al., 1985; Wehman et al., 1985b).

As a result of recent federal initiatives, interagency cooperation has been written into key pieces of legislation; the Carl Perkins Vocational Education Act (PL 98-524), the Rehabilitation Act Amendments of 1986 (PL 99-506), and the Education of the Handicapped Act Amendments of 1986 (PL 99-457) are examples of this. For example, in Section 412 of the Vocational Education Act, interagency and private industry cooperation is supported in the development of:

> projects that are examples of successful cooperation between the private and public agencies in vocational education and model projects providing improved access to quality vocational education programs for handi-

capped individuals . . . (that) can work together effeectively to assist vocational education students to attain the advanced level of skills needed
to make the transition from school to productive employment . . . *Federal Register* (1985), Vol. 50(759)

Further evidence of the federal government's interest in interagency cooperation is demonstrated by the interest in transition and
employment shared by the Office of Special Education and Rehabilitative Services (OSERS) of the U.S. Department of Education
and the Administration on Developmental Disabilities (ADD) of the
U.S. Department of Health and Human Services. These two agencies
provide leadership to agencies at the state and local levels. Madeleine
Will, the Assistant Secretary of the Office of Special Education and
Rehabilitation Services and Jean K. Elder, former Commissioner of
the Administration on Developmental Disabilities have demonstrated
that interagency cooperation works because there is a shared interest
in employment as an outcome for individuals with severe disabilities.

For interagency cooperation to take place, with tangible goals
being achieved for individuals with disabilities, state and local community leadership must follow the example of leadership at the
federal level. Terms for cooperation must be designed and written for
the local level agencies, and staff and participating agency resources
must be committed to accomplishing transition related outcomes.
Plans must be developed and implemented that provide for regular
and frequent face-to-face interaction of interagency teams at the service delivery level.

The purpose of this chapter is to discuss ways to develop cooperative interagency agreements so that transition planning activities are
implemented and targeted outcomes achieved. A checklist is
provided that will facilitate the implementation of a written interagency agreement. Interagency agreements at the state level are discussed along with several options for interaction at the local level. Finally, the chapter provides an example of a three-way community
level agreement as a model for implementing individualized transition planning and supported employment services.

INTERAGENCY COOPERATION AT THE STATE LEVEL

For state level interagency collaboration to bring about changes in local level activities, there must first be a strong and visible commitment by the leadership to a common mission (Fenton & Keller, 1981).
This sense of mission is necessary to focus the activities of an organization (Beer, 1980; Tichy, 1983). For most agencies serving individuals

with disabilities, the mission—that of service provision—is the same.

The purpose for providing educational programming to children and youth with disabilities is to maximize their independence as adults. Education is a preparatory activity in that children and youth are being prepared for adulthood. In contrast, adult service providers do not begin their service provision to individuals with disabilities until these clients are adults. The goals of service provision are the same, but the deadlines for accomplishing the goals are different. In order to use time more efficiently, adult service providers are looking for more immediate and diverse means to accomplish the same goals. But the goals are the same none the less.

Realizing that the mission is the same but that there are different approaches being utilized by the various agencies, it is useful for the different agencies to examine their methods and to coordinate their efforts. Gaining a better understanding of how and why the different agencies operate as they do will improve efficiency between the various organizations, and instances of duplicated services will be reduced. One example of the duplication that occurs is the repetition of expensive diagnostic evaluations because one state agency does not accept the records of another state agency, or because an agency is required to conduct its own evaluations as a part of eligibility determination. In some instances, an agency may complete diagnostic evaluations in advance, in anticipation of meeting the receiving agency's eligibility requirements. For example, individuals who have received services while in public school special education programs must have been determined eligible for those services because of a handicapping condition. Procedures for eligibility determination are carefully prescribed in the regulations as written in the Education for all Handicapped Children Act (PL 94-142). The existence of an individualized education program (IEP) as required by law for each handicapped student should therefore be sufficient documentation that there is a disability, and that the individual is eligible for the adult services provided for disabled individuals.

Other programs with similar service provision goals for persons with handicapping conditions include the Vocational Education, Joint Training Partnership Act (JTPA), and Developmental Disabilities programs. However, unlike educational services, these are all eligibility programs, not entitlement programs.

In order to highlight how these service providers are similar in mission, it is necessary to restate or reexamine each agency's mission and then to recognize goals held in common by other agencies. This might well serve as a preliminary activity for leaders at the state level to initiate interagency cooperation. Once a common mission is identified across agencies, the purpose for formalizing interagency collaboration—that of efficient provision of services—becomes clear and logical.

After recognizing that interagency cooperation is advantageous, the leadership at the state level needs to begin working with other agencies to commit staff and resources to initiating the transition process. For example, designating middle level management personnel to begin development of interagency activities is a logical starting point for realizing this commitment (Ashby & Bensberg, 1981). Management designees from the different agencies need to come together as a core team to examine the needs for interagency cooperation by conducting state and local level needs assessments to define what changes need to be made. The core team will also develop strategies and deadlines for planning and implementation (McCarthy, Everson, Inge, & Barcus, 1985). The information in Chapter Three provides more information on core team activities.

It is important for the agency designees to be of equivalent authority levels within the management structure of the participating agencies so that they will have similar power for planning and implementing interagency programs. Unequal appointment of leadership level staff would indicate an unequal commitment to the implementation of interagency transition planning activities. It is important that there be a balance of leadership across the participating agencies so that there is relatively equal power and ability to allocate and mobilize personnel to disseminate information regarding transition and interagency activities, and to utilize agency resources.

For most agencies at the state level, it is important that plans for interagency cooperation be built into the working document for the particular agency (Ashby & Bensberg, 1981). Most state agencies are required to write state agendas that reflect an agency's plan of operation for a period of 5 years. The state plan that includes procedures for transition planning is likely to show evidence of interagency service coordination. Without explicit procedures for interagency interaction written into the working document of the agency, interagency agreements may end up safely filed away in file cabinets or on shelves, with the result that there is little or no change in actual service provision.

For any new concept to be translated into activity, there needs to be evidence of active involvement. Management staff seeking to initiate interagency planning for transition will need to develop and implement schedules of interaction between agency representatives, to develop a list of activities and deadlines for their completion, and to identify expected outcomes. Needless to say, implementation of any new activity requires a commitment of funds. The information gathered by the core team at the state level will be useful for budget allocations that will ultimately affect local level programs and service delivery to consumers.

Agency representatives involved in interagency cooperation for transition planning activities must always keep candidate needs as the primary goal (Fenton & Keller, 1981). It is also useful for representatives to bear in mind that the service system also benefits by combining and coordinating resources to accomplish outcomes for consumers.

THE LOCAL LEVEL

Steps that have been outlined and discussed for the state level will be repeated by agency leadership at the local level. A local core team needs to be organized to write a local level interagency agreement that establishes the operating and interaction procedures between agencies for planning and implementing transition services. This plan for interaction should include an inter-organizational structure with responsiblities outlined for each participating agency.

One of the first tasks to be completed by members of the newly formed community level transition planning core team is to conduct a local community needs assessment. The needs assessment information will be valuable for the development and writing of the local interagency agreement as well as for implementation of the agreement from year to year. Therefore, the needs assessment activity is important for gathering initial planning information. This information will need to be updated at least annually if it is to be useful in the implementation of the interagency agreement.

Organization of a Local Community Core Team

The core team in a local community needs to include members from all of the key agencies providing services to individuals with disabilities. Agency representatives might include the special education director from the local school system, the director of vocational education services, the regional director or program supervisor from the local rehabilitation services office, the director of community services from the local mental health and mental retardation agency, a representative from a local client advocacy group, and parent representation. Other agencies serving individuals with disabilities in a given community should also participate in core team interagency planning activities. In Chapter 3 there is a discussion of who should initiate the development of a community level transition planning core team.

The initial activities of this local community core team will be: 1) to establish a reason for its existence, that is, to improve and coordinate the provision of services for youth making the transition from school to adult community living; 2) to delineate the goals of the transition planning core team, which would include completing a local level needs assessment and writing an interagency agreement; 3) to list and rank by priority the activities of the core team that will enable the group to accomplish its goals; 4) to divide the list of activities and assign persons or work groups to be responsible for completion of activities; and 5) to establish deadlines for completion of all activities.

Local Community Needs Assessment

A community level needs assessment should be conducted by the core team to provide the information needed to decide how to utilize community service options and agency resources for optimum service delivery. This information will also be useful in determining reallocation of resources for the development of new programs where and when they are needed. The community level needs assessment should be conducted to identify: 1) how many individuals will graduate from public school services in the next 5 years, 2) how many adults are currently being served in each existing program, 3) how many adults are waiting for services, 4) what the available services are in the community, 5) what the service capacities are of the programs currently available, and 6) what program or service options are still needed in the community.

Figure 5.1 is a chart that can be used to gather relevant information for a local community needs assessment. Once filled in, the information gives a quick summary of programs available in the community; provides quantitative data to indicate where, when, and how much of each different service option is needed; and which service types will have demands either over or under their existing service capacity.

Following are instructions for compiling information for a local community needs assessment.

Column 1: Projected number of individuals to initiate demands on the adult service system.

1. List the number of Special Education graduates to begin using adult service programs during the specified 12-month period.
2. List the number of students who will be using adult service programs during the specified 12-month period *prior* to graduation.
3. Estimate the number of adults who may be initiating demands on

adult service programs during the specified 12-month period. Include those individuals entering the catchment area from other localities, those reentering from institutional care, or those being identified as appropriate for services after a period of not being served.
4. Add the numbers from A, B, & C to get the total number of individuals estimated to initiate demands for adults services during the specified 12-month period (D), e.g., between 7–86 and 6–87.

$$A + B + C = D$$

Column 2:   Program Type and Service Capacity   The transition planning core team needs to identify the program types (Job Placement; Transitional Employment; Supported Competitive; Enclave; Mobile Crew; Sheltered Workshop; Adult Activity) that are available and the number of individuals that can be served in each program type. If a program type is not available in the community indicate this fact on the form.

Column 3:   Number of Individuals from Column 1 Targeting Specific Program Types   From the Individualized Transition Plan (ITP), Individual Program Plan (IPP) and Individual Written Rehabilitation Plan (IWRP) compile the number of individuals targeted for each program type. Requests or demands for program type(s) not currently available in the community should be noted and included in the needs assessment information.

Column 4:   Number of Individuals Currently on Waiting Lists   For each program type, identify and list the number of individuals currently on the providers waiting lists for services.

Column 5:   Projected Number of Program Slots to Open up Per Year   Based on the previous year's information, list the number of program slots projected to open in each program type, given the current funding and staffing level. Include the approximate number of individuals moving out of the catchment area, completing the program, discontinuing the program, or requiring a level of service that allows the program to accommodate new referrals.

Column 6:   Projected Percentage of Program Turnover   Compute by dividing the number in Column 5 by the Service Capacity (# in Column 2), then multiply by 100.

(Column 5/Column 2) × 100 = Projected Turnover %)

The Projected turnover percentage gives an indication of projected number of persons moving from each program type. (For example: 66% of the consumers will move out of the program or will require a level of service that allows the program to accommodate new referrals.)

Column 7:   Total Number to be Over Program's Service Capacity

1	2	3	4	5	6	7	8
Projected number of graduating students to initiate demands on adult service system.	Program type and service capacity (SC)	Number of candidates from Column 1 targeted for specific program types	Number of candidates currently on waiting lists	Projected number of program slots to open per year	Projected percentage of program slots to be open	Total number to be over Program's service capacity	Percentage of change (+ or −) in funding/resource allocation(s) indicated
A. Number of special education graduates to begin utilizing adult services between 7-86 and 6-87. $\frac{115}{8}$	Job placement SC = 50	44	8	35	70%	17	+34%
	Transitional employment SC = 40	28	15	21	52%	22	+55%
B. Number of special education students to utilize adult services prior to graduation between 7-86 and 6-87. $\frac{8}{\ }$	Supported competitive employment SC = 60	31	18	35	58%	14	+23%
	Enclave SC = 11	12	3	1	9%	14	+127%

104

1	2	3	4	5	6	7	8
Projected number of graduating students to initiate demands on adult service system.	Program type and service capacity (SC)	Number of candidates from Column 1 targeted for specific program types	Number of candidates currently on waiting lists	Projected number of program slots to open per year	Projected percentage of program slots to be open	Total number to be over Program's service capacity	Percentage of change (+ or −) in funding/resource allocations(s) indicated
C. Number of students expected to *begin* utilizing adult service programs between 7-86 and 6-87. $\frac{20}{\quad}$	Mobile crew SC = $\underline{NP}$	6	3			9	+100%
	Sheltered workshop SC = $\underline{65}$	16	15	9	13.8%	22	+34%
D. Total number of new individuals to potentially demand adult services between 7-86 and 6-87. $\frac{143}{\quad}$	Adult activity SC = $\underline{22}$	6	8	1.5	6.8%	12.5	+57%
	No services requested	36					

Figure 5.1. Local community needs assessment. (Instructions for completion of this form follow.)

1	2	3	4	5	6
Name of service provider, and program type	Targeted outcome(s) of service	Prescribed duration of service (and/or preservice referral period) to achieve targeted outcomes	Number of consumers achieving targeted outcome within prescribed service duration in last 12-month period	Total number of consumers served by program over last 12-month period	Percentage of program effectiveness
Vocational rehabilitation-job placement services	Candidates will be placed into competitive employment situations earning minimum wage or above and retain employment for at least 60 days.	3 mo.	25	45	55%
Carl County public schools vocational education job placement services	Candidates will be placed into competitive employment situations earning minimum wage or above and retain employment for at least 60 days.	3 mo.	15	30	50%
Supported employment of Carl County competitive employment	Candidates will be competitively employed earning minimum wage	8 mo.	18	24	75%

Program	Description				
	or above, require less than 10% job coach (employment specialist) intervention time by the end of a 5-month period and retain employment for a period of 6 months. Candidates will be accepted for ongoing follow-along services by the appropriate agency.	8 mo.	9	20	45%
Carl County ARC supported competitive employment	Candidates will be competitively employed earning minimum wage or above, require less than 10% job coach (employment specialist) intervention time by the end of a 5-month period and retain employment for a period of 6 months. Candidates will be accepted for ongoing follow-along services by the appropriate agency.				
Supported employment of Carl County enclave program	Candidates will be employed in an enclave employment program earning 50% of minimum wage by the end of a 4-month service delivery period.	8 mo.	8	12	66%

(continued)

Figure 5.2. *(continued)*

1	2	3	4	5	6
Carl County sheltered workshop program— Level I	Candidates will achieve earnings to equal 25% of minimum wage by the end of a 6-month service delivery period.	6 mo.	7	10	70%
Carl County sheltered workshop program— Level II	Candidates will achieve earnings to equal 50% of minimum wage by the end of a 6-month service delivery period.	6 mo.	14	20	70%
Carl County sheltered workshop program— Level III	Candidates will achieve earnings to equal 75% of minimum wage by the end of a 6-month service delivery period.	6 mo.	8	15	53%
Carl County sheltered workshop program— Level IV (competitive placement)	Candidates will be placed into competitive employment situations by the end of a 6-month service delivery period.	8 mo.	6	8	75%

Figure 5.2. Community services program effectiveness (percentage of candidates reaching targeted outcomes). (Instructions for completion of this form follow.)

mum wage by the end of a 6-month service delivery period.

Level III—Candidates will achieve earnings to equal 75% of minimum wage by the end of a 6-month service delivery period.

Level IV—Candidates will be placed into competitive employment situations by the end of a 6-month service delivery period.

3. **Supported employment by a local nonfacility company**
Competitive employment services—Candidates will be competitively employed earning minimum wage or above, requiring less than 20% job coach (employment specialist) intervention time by the end of a 5 month service delivery period, and will remain employed for a period of 6 months. Ongoing follow-along services will be arranged.
Enclave employment services—Candidates will be employed in an enclave employment program earning 50% of minimum wage by the end of a 4-month service delivery period.

4. **ARC adult activities center**
Independent living skills (Level I)—Candidates will be approved to enter Chesterfield County's supervised apartment program by the end of a 6-month service delivery period.
Independent living skills (Level II)—Candidates will be approved to enter Group Home A through Chesterfield County Residential Services by the end of a 6-month service delivery period.

The delineation, in measurable terms, of targeted outcomes offers both consumers and purchasers of services important information that will affect their decisions as to which services they want. In the past, candidates and service purchasers paid for a service such as work adjustment training for which expected results were never stated. The achievement of individual goals by a candidate is not to be confused with the targeted or desired outcome of the service at the completion of the service period.

The key activity in the cooperative effort of transition planning is the dissemination of information and to those individuals who will be best able to use it in a meaningful way. As competition for limited funds increases between service providers, service purchasers such as vocational rehabilitation agencies are likely to place greater demands on programs to demonstrate their effectiveness.

Developing and Writing Community Level Interagency Agreements

The most important goal to achieve from the development and writing of a community level interagency agreement is that service imple-

Table 5.1. Interagency agreement checklist

Does the agreement include or address the following:
1. Mission statement or purpose of agreement
2. Number and names of agencies involved in the agreement
3. Measurable goals to be accomplished by core team as preliminary activities to the writing of interagency agreement
4. Definition of terms
5. Descriptions of roles and responsibilities of each agency in implementation of the agreement
6. Description of eligibility determination processes for each agency
7. Delineation of referral procedures for each agency's services
8. Description of staffing allocations from each agency for transition and interagency operations
9. Implementation procedures
10. Plan for dissemination of agreement
11. Plan for interagency inservice
12. Time overlapping/service coordination
13. List of service options available (direct or purchase)
14. Procedure for development of new services
15. Provisions for individuals with severe handicaps
16. Time-limited and ongoing service provision
17. Cost sharing
18. Data sharing (formative and evaluative)
19. Procedures for release of information and confidentiality policy
20. Attendance at IEP/ITP meetings
21. Schedule for implementation
22. Schedule for renegotiation or modification of agreement terms
23. Policy on service delivery (duplication, repeating, initiation dates)
24. Identification of agency liaisons to participating agencies
25. Schedule of interaction between liaisons
26. Desired outcomes of agreement
27. Dissemination of services available to parents and candidates
28. Procedure and schedule for ongoing needs assessment

mentation is improved so that candidates succeed in achieving the outcomes stated in the agreement. All too many state and local level agreements have been written that do not achieve their goals, and thus never have any direct impact on service provision. Table 5.1 is a checklist of items that will facilitate the implementation of a written interagency agreement. A well-written document that only proclaims the rationale of interagency cooperation, the desired goals of the agreement, and only lists each agency's available services, will not bring about improvements in service provision or service outcomes. The written agreement must specifiy changes in the behaviors of staff persons of the participating agencies in order for implementation of services and achievement of outcomes to be effected. For example, a written agreement should designate a staff person such as a secondary special education teacher to coordinate individualized transition planning (ITP) meetings every year. Activities necessary for this coordination include: contacting all appropriate meeting participants, scheduling meetings, and getting release of information forms signed prior to meetings.

One example of how items contained in the Interagency Agreement Checklist can be incorporated into a written agreement is evident in a community level interagency agreement featured later in this chapter. This agreement, developed for Chesterfield County, Virginia, had a successful impact on services and outcomes for youth making the transition from school to adult community living. Staff and funds were redirected and new behaviors and activities initiated as a result of this written agreement. Most of the items in the Interagency Agreement Checklist are addressed in this example agreement.

MODELS OF INTERAGENCY INTERACTION

Interagency cooperation can be characterized by three basic models of interaction. These three models are used here to illustrate degrees or levels of interaction between agencies with regard to: 1) communication and information exchange, 2) service planning and implementation, and 3) cost sharing. Figure 5.3 illustrates these different levels of interaction.

In Model A of Figure 5.3, there is little or no planned procedure for communication between the different agencies. Information is transferred from one agency to another in the form of stacks of paper that usually consist of the educational, psychological, vocational, social, and medical histories of the individuals who have been served by one agency and who are being referred for the services of another. In many instances, services are repeated by a receiving agency that may have the egotistical viewpoint that services would have been successful if "our agency" had provided them. Similarly, the receiving agency may want to repeat their own evaluations to gather the same data because the information they received is out of date or they don't trust the sending agency as a reliable information source. In this model, services are unnecessarily duplicated and monies are utilized inefficiently because of poor communication and a lack of coordinated planning.

In Model B, there is careful coordination of the efforts of the different agencies to line up services so that as soon as one agency's involvement with a candidate ends, another agency's involvement begins. The services are preplanned in the interagency individualized transition planning (ITP) meetings so that there is smooth and unin-

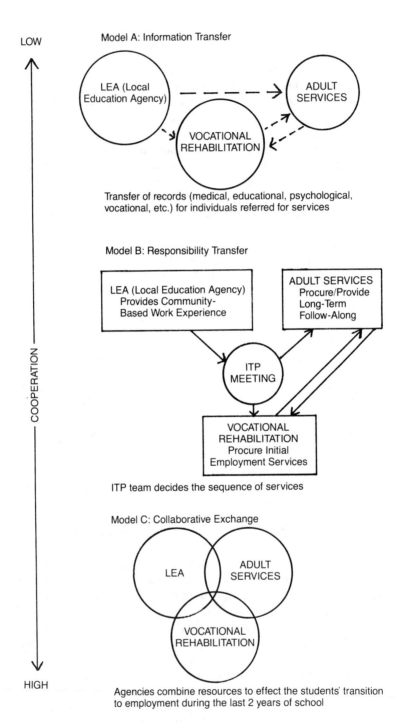

LOW

COOPERATION

HIGH

Model A: Information Transfer

LEA (Local Education Agency)

ADULT SERVICES

VOCATIONAL REHABILITATION

Transfer of records (medical, educational, psychological, vocational, etc.) for individuals referred for services

Model B: Responsibility Transfer

LEA (Local Education Agency) Provides Community-Based Work Experience

ADULT SERVICES Procure/Provide Long-Term Follow-Along

ITP MEETING

VOCATIONAL REHABILITATION Procure Initial Employment Services

ITP team decides the sequence of services

Model C: Collaborative Exchange

LEA

ADULT SERVICES

VOCATIONAL REHABILITATION

Agencies combine resources to effect the students' transition to employment during the last 2 years of school

Figure 5.3.   Models of agency interaction.

terrupted service delivery. Ongoing communication and comprehensive planning between agencies provides for procedural consistency, thus reducing the likelihood that services will be repeated from one agency to the next. Close communication enables the participating agency representatives to know what services have already been delivered by the preceding agency. This communication facilitates continuation of a logical and comprehensive service plan, and prevents inefficient backtracking and repetition of service activities.

In Model B, the interagency ITP team decides the sequence of service activities necessary to achieve the greatest success in effecting the transition of students from school to work. Each agency is responsible for providing or procuring the mutually agreed-upon services at the times set at the ITP meeting. For example, for student A to succeed in community employment, the team has decided that supported competitive employment is the most appropriate service delivery option. The activities outlined for each agency might be as follows:

Schools—The schools will provide work experience for Student A during his or her last 2 years of school in at least two different community-based work experience training sites. This will occur at least 4 days each week, 4 hours each day prior to his or her graduation from school. If a competitive employment position is identified prior to graduation, and conditions permit, the schools will confer with the agency liaisons. If it is deemed appropriate, the placement will be made. Training in the use of public transportation in the local community will be included as part of work experience training.

Rehabilitation—The rehabilitation counselor will procure supported employment services for Student A immediately following graduation. Or, if more appropriate, the counselor will arrange for services for Student A if he or she has already been placed by the school system and is still requiring 2 or more hours of job coach or employment specialist intervention time per week. The rehabilitation counselor needs to arrange for the provision of services far enough in advance that the school and the service provider can cooperate for a smooth transfer of services.

Mental Retardation Adult Services—The mental retardation agency representative will initiate long-term follow-along services for Student A once he or she has stabilized in the employment situation and once the rehabilitation counselor has terminated service involvement with the candidate. The MR services representative will allow time for transfer of information in the event of a change in service delivery personnel. In such a situation, the employment specialist who is providing job-site training intervention time, the student, the parent or guardian, and the employer will all need to be informed of the change and properly introduced to the new employment specialist.

In the service delivery arrangement described above, each agency has a definite point at which services will be turned over to the next agency. Adult service agencies, rehabilitation, and mental retardation community services do not provide services while students are still in school, but a comprehensive sequence and plan for service responsibility assures continuation of employment support for the consumer.

A third model, as illustrated by Model C in Figure 5.3, depicts interagency interaction that provides for coordinated overlap of service implementation without overlap of spending. The overlap occurs because agencies combine resources to serve a targeted population of students during the last 2 years of school. With this approach, all agencies are involved with the planning and implementation of services, but there is no duplication of spending on individual students.

Model C is an example of the interagency agreement developed for Chesterfield County, Virginia. Chesterfield is a rapidly growing suburban county outside of Richmond, Virginia. The three key agencies in the Chesterfield County community work together to develop individual transition plans and to implement supported competitive employment services. In this agreement, there is a planned procedure for communication and information sharing, there are arrangements for service implementation without duplication, and there is an equitable cost sharing arrangement.

Financial resources for each of the different public agencies serving individuals with disabilities are limited; therefore, efficient and effective use of funds is important. Duplication of services or misappropriation of funds due to lack of communication or coordinated planning is undesirable for agencies and candidates alike.

A THREE-WAY INTERAGENCY AGREEMENT FOR TRANSITION PLANNING AND SUPPORTED EMPLOYMENT SERVICE: MISSION STATEMENT

The following is a three-way interagency agreement for the implementation of transition planning and supported employment services. The agencies participating in this agreement are the Chesterfield County Public Schools, the Chesterfield County Mental Health and Mental Retardation Community Services Board, and the Virginia Department of Rehabilitative Services serving the Chesterfield County area.

MISSION STATEMENT

The purpose of this agreement is to provide for meaningful postschool employment outcomes for youth with severe disabilities who are leaving the public school system. It is understood that the students targeted for services in this cooperative agreement will be in their last 2 years of school. All students, at the point of graduation, will become the responsibility of the adult service systems. Formal transition planning for individual students will begin at age 16 or before, for the purpose of implementing meaningful functional and community-based instructional programs in integrated environments. Adult services involvement will be encouraged as needed during the years prior to the last 2 years in school, and required for two years after leaving school as part of this agreement.

By combining the coordinated efforts of these three key agencies during the 2 years prior to graduation, the transition process is initiated by each agency's participation in the provision of employment, independent living, recreation and leisure options, and community integration outcomes for graduating students. There are service provision and funding advantages to be gained by all three agencies involved in this agreement. Following are several reasons why it is advantageous to begin supported employment services prior to graduation:

1. The school's knowledge of individual students through past experience is channeled directly into the employment of the students making the transition from school to work.
2. The number of personnel assigned to employment outcomes is increased by involving the schools in the supported employment service provision, at no cost to the adult service system. Instead, a portion of the up front costs are born by the school system.
3. Teachers are trained to provide systematic instruction. This interagency agreement provides for this instruction to be provided at the job-site and at other community settings, rather than in the prevocational classroom.
4. Direct involvement by school personnel in actual employment situations provides important program evaluation and feedback to the schools facilitating school curriculum improvements regarding work in the "real world."

5. With the involvement of the schools, costs are shared in a three-way split rather than a two-way split between rehabilitation and (MR/DD) services. (See Figure 5.4.)

COOPERATING AGENCY LIAISONS

Each cooperating agency agrees to designate at least one individual to act as a transition liaison to facilitate communication between the three agencies. These liaisons will be primarily responsible for maintaining frequent and regular contact between the three agencies and for coordinating services for all students moving from school to adult services. The agency liaisons might be the school, MR services employment specialists, and the rehabilitation counselor assigned to serving the school population. Each agency liaison needs to be responsible for his or her agenecy at all ITP meetings. The agency liaisons may attend all or part of the meetings themselves or they may

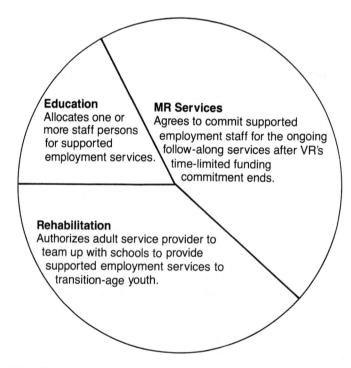

Figure 5.4. Three-way cost sharing pie for the implementation of supported employment services with transition-age youth.

assign a designee to attend. Each agency liaison is also responsible for providing ITP meeting designees with information regarding their agency's capacity to provide agency services and/or resources. Agency liaisons are responsible for training their agency's designees in areas of receiving referrals, eligibility for services, and schedules for authorizing or committing agency services or resources.

Schedule of Interaction of Cooperating Agency Liaisons

Participating agency liaisons will meet on the third Thursday of every month during the first year of implementing this interagency agreement. Relevant service delivery personnel or other involved participants should be invited to these meetings as necessary. The group's meeting agenda will include discussion of ITP meeting schedules, current services being provided to transition-age youth, new or planned services to be available in the community, examination of the outcomes of transition planning, and cooperative service delivery efforts.

INDIVIDUALIZED TRANSITION MEETINGS

The Chesterfield County Public Schools agree to initiate the planning and scheduling for individualized transitional planning meetings for a mutually agreed-upon target group of students age 16 or older. The required involvement of adult service agency representatives begins during the student's last 2 years of school. It is recommended that all students who are identified as "severely disabled" according to criteria established by the Virginia Department of Rehabilitative Services have ITP meetings during the last 2 years prior to their graduation.

The development of ITPs are to be completed as part of the IEP meeting, with transition planning issues being discussed first, so that IEP goals and objectives can be written to support the targeted post-school outcomes. The ITP goals and service provision plans will be developed as an addendum to the IEP document. The rehabilitation counselor and the MH/MR services representative should incorporate ITP goals into the Individual Written Rehabilitation Plan (IWRP) and the Individual Program Plan (IPP).

The school liaison will be responsible for ensuring that the release of information authorization forms are signed by the appropriate person(s) prior to scheduling ITP meetings. (See Figure 5.5.) Release of information forms must be signed for all students who are in their last 2 years of school; copies should be forwarded to the adult agency liaisons prior to scheduling ITP meetings.

For the purpose of facilitating a smooth and uninter-
rupted transition from school to adult services, this
form authorizes the agencies listed below to share confidential information on the student listed below during
the final 2 years he or she is enrolled in the Chesterfield
County Public School System. As part of the interagency
transition planning process, the agencies listed below
will be working cooperatively during this period to arrange for postschool services and outcomes that are most
advantageous and desirable for the student and the student's family and/or primary caregiver. Care will be
taken by all agencies involved to release only that information that is required for effective and efficient implementation of services. Confidential information to be
included in this interagency information release agreement may include: educational, psychological, medical,
social, and vocational information relevant to this student's needs as an adult in the community.

Student name: _____ D.O.B. _____

Social Security #: _____

Date of graduation: _____ Date information can
be released: _____

Agencies to share access to confidential information:

Chesterfield County	VA Dept. of Rehabilitative
Public Schools	Services
P.O. Box 10	11300 Iron Bridge Road,
Chesterfield, Virginia	Suite C
23832	Chester, Virginia 23831
Contact person: _____	Contact person: _____
Phone: 748-1892	Phone: 796-4124

Chesterfield Mental   OTHER:
  Retardation Services
P.O. Box 92   _____
Chesterfield, Virginia   _____
  23832   Contact person: _____
Contact person: _____   Phone: _____
Phone: 748-1421

_____   _____
Student/client   Parent/guardian
  signature   signature
_____   _____
Witness   Date

Figure 5.5. Chesterfield County interagency release of information authorization. (Form
developed by the Education to Employment Project of the Rehabilitation Research and Training Center, Virginia Commonwealth University.)

Notification of ITP meetings will be provided to the cooperating agency liaisons at least 5 days prior to each meeting by the school liaison. When advance notice is not possible due to extenuating circumstances, the schools will do whatever possible to communicate scheduling arrangements or other information to each of the other agency liaisons.

ITP meeting participants should include:

1. Student
2. Parent/guardian/primary caregiver
3. Rehabilitation counselor
4. Mental retardation case manager
5. School employment specialist
6. Mental retardation employment specialist
7. Special education teacher
8. Agency liaisons (if different from any of the above)
9. Special education administrator
10. Others who might be included: a current or previous employer, medical doctor, occupational, physical, or speech therapist

The ITP meeting is the appropriate forum for the different agency representatives to develop plans of long-term service provision for graduating students. Each agency representative should assume responsibility for referral to and delivery of the various services that will be required for an effective transition from school to work. Agency representatives must bring such materials as: referral/service application forms, program or agency brochures, and information on program eligibility to ITP meetings to share with parents and candidates. The coordination of the services at the ITP meeting should provide for smooth and continued delivery of services later on.

School Services

The Chesterfield County School system agrees to provide community-based work experience for students in actual work settings in the community. The settings can be paid or unpaid. Unpaid training programs must meet the criteria for non-paid training situations as described by the U.S. Department of Labor. Students should have work experience in at least two community-based work settings prior to graduation, with the last experience requiring 4 days per week, with at least 3 hours per day, for a period of at least 6 months. Other community-based training positions in integrated environments will also be provided for students prior to graduation from the public schools. These will include: public transportation training, grocery shopping, and integrated programs for recreation in the community.

Other services to be offered by the schools include: vocational evaluation, vocational education/training, guidance and counseling, job placement, time-limited job coach services, community access training, leisure and recreation training, and domestic skills training.

MH/MR Adult Services

The Chesterfield County MH/MR Services agrees to provide case management services to transition-age students. These services will entitle candidates to assistance in such areas as exploring residential option, providing for advocacy needs, adult day support, respite care, follow-along supported employment services, or other services necessary for maintaining integrated community living.

Rehabilitative Services

The Virginia Department of Rehabilitative Services agrees to provide or procure services for transition-age youth either before or immediately following graduation from the public school system. As outlined in the ITP or IWRP, services may include the following: vocational evaluation, job-seeking skills training, counseling, work adjustment training, time-limited job coach (employment specialist) services, independent living training, on-the-job training (OJT), time-limited sheltered employment, and rehabilitation engineering.

SUPPORTED EMPLOYMENT SERVICES

Intensive Training Role: Schools

The Chesterfield County Public Schools agree to provide one full-time certified teacher to act as an employment specialist to place *and train* specific students in competitive employment settings utilizing a supported competitive employment approach. The full-time teacher must be completely free from the day-to-day operation of the school building (e.g., bus or lunch duty or weekly staff meetings). The employment specialist's schedule must be flexible enough to allow planning around the work hours of any given student in any given employment situation.

Students identified for supported employment services must first be considered eligible for receipt of services by the Chesterfield County MH/MR Community Services Board agency representative. These criteria must be met before the agency will commit its resources for on-going follow-along services for supported employment candidates.

MH/MR Services

Chesterfield County MH/MR Commmunity Services Board agrees to designate at least one full-time employment specialist to team up with the one full-time school employment specialist for the purpose of placing and training designated school-age youth into competitive employment situations utilizing a supported competitive employment approach.

Rehabilitative Services

The rehabilitation counselor representing the Virginia Department of Rehabilitative Services agrees to authorize funds for supported competitive employment intervention hours to be provided by one in-kind match employment specialist employed by the Chesterfield County MH/MR Community Services Board. The Chesterfield MH/MR Community Services will provide supported competitive employment services as prescribed in the agreement with the Virginia Department of Rehabilitative Services (DRS). The MH/MR Services employment specialist will be directed to work with the school employment specialist for the purpose of placing school-age youth between the ages 20 and 22 into jobs 2 years prior to their graduation. Supported competitive employment services will be billed based on a prearranged fee, at a rate of $19.89 per hour. Records of intervention time will be maintained utilizing a Consumer-Specific Intervention Time Recording Sheet with billing to the Virginia Department of Rehabilitive Services on a monthly basis (see Figure 5.6).

Students served by the school employment specialist will be placed on Virginia Department of Rehabilitative Services caseloads, but the training and other intervention hours provided by the school employment specialist will not be billed to the Virginia DRS counselor. These clients will be Virginia DRS clients, whose full records are provided to the assigned rehabilitation counselor.

The rehabilitation counselor should make sure that all students targeted for supported competitive employment services have been accepted for services by the MH/MR Community Services Board so that on-going follow-along services will be provided. Those students who do not need follow-along services may benefit from transitional employment services, for example, job coach services, that are provided for a limited period only.

Responsibilities of MH/MR Community Services

Chesterfield County MH/MR Community Services agrees to assume responsibility for the on-going follow-along services for all employ-

Consumer name: _____

SSN: __ __ __ / __ __ / __ __ __ __

Recording period: ___ / ___
mo.   yr.

Staff member name: _____

ID Code: _____

Case managers: DRS: _____

MHMR: _____

Date (month/day)							
Intervention time directly related to job skills training (Hours:Minutes) 1. Active (candidate and job coordinator at job-site)							
2. Inactive (between periods of active intervention)							
Intervention time indirectly related to job skills training (Hours:Minutes) 1. Travel/transporting							
2. Candidate training							

3. Program development (task analysis and behavioral intervention programs)					
4. Direct employment advocacy (work-site related, includes candidate-specific job development)					
5. Indirect employment advocacy (non-worksite related)					
6. Screening and evaluation (screening consumer for service eligibility)					
Total (daily)					

Figure 5.6. Consumer-specific intervention time recording sheet. (Form developed by the Rehabilitation Research and Training Center, Virginia Commonwealth University, in cooperation with the Departments of Vocational Rehabilitation, Mental Health and Mental Retardation [revised 9/86].)

ment candidates who are placed in jobs by the supported competitive employment team prior to graduation. A firm commitment to this model is critical prior to placement of any individual in a job that utilizes the supported competitive employment approach. The employer, the client, and the client's parent or guardian will be depending on the continuation of follow-along services.

Data Collection

The Chesterfield County Public Schools, Rehabilitation, and MH/MR Community Services representatives agree to use the Virginia Commonwealth University/Rehabilitation and Research Training Center (VCU/RRTC) data management system by completing the prescribed forms according to the established schedules. The VCU/RRTC agrees to provide data analysis services and program evaluation feedback for the three cooperating agencies to begin March 1, 1986.

Interagency Inservice

Cooperating agency liaisons should coordinate at least one interagency inservice training program during each school calendar year that addresses issues surrounding transition, employment, residential options, secondary or postsecondary education, adult services, and so on. The agency liaisons are responsible for issuing invitations to cooperating agency staff to attend transition-related inservice sessions provided by any one agency. The interagency transition liaisons must work together as a team to plan or conduct at least one transition-related inservice training session.

EXCHANGE OF INFORMATION

List of Upcoming Graduates

The Chesterfield County Public Schools agree to provide the Chesterfield County MH/MR Community Services Board (the agency liaison) and the Chesterfield County DRS liaison with a list of names of upcoming graduates who are in their last 2 years of school. Release of information forms must be signed by students before names can be released. The school is responsible for getting the release forms signed.

Projected Graduates over a 5-Year Period

The schools agree to provide the number of students scheduled to graduate for the next 5 years. This information will assist the two adult service agencies in projecting the service needs of the future.

Adult Service Programs in the Chesterfield County Area

The Chesterfield County MH/MR Community Services Board and the Virginia DRS serving the Chesterfield area agree to provide a list of currently available adult services and programs accessible to youth who are making the transition from school to adult service system. The list will also include the service capacity (number of individuals that can be served) of each program, and the projected number of slots to open up by July 1 of each year.

Adult Services Selected for Graduating Youth from ITP Meetings

The school liaison having access to all completed ITP meeting forms must compile information from those forms for dissemination to the MH/MR Community Services Board and to the Virginia DRS liaisons. The report should indicate the number of students selected for each type of program or service. The categories include currently available services and services that are requested but are not currently available to Chesterfield County citizens with disabilities.

Post-graduation Follow-Up Data

MH/MR Community Services and DRS agree to provide the schools with follow-up data (employment or residential services data) of graduates from the program for at least 2 years following their graduation. This will ensure the ongoing commitment of the schools to the interagency agreement, and will provide educators with continual information about the graduate's employment and independent life.

EXPECTED OUTCOMES

Past data from supported employement programs indicate that one skilled employment specialist can place and train anywhere from four to ten individuals into competitive employment situations, depending on the skill level of the individual being placed and that person's compatibility with the requirements of the job. That is, the more complex the job, the higher the probability that the candidate will require extended training time. The job/candidate compatibility process should strive to match candidates to jobs that are complex enough to avoid boredom and apathy. Positions should require skills that are challenging yet obtainable when given intensive training with ongoing support, thus providing for improved employment retention.

Given a school and MR services supported employment team of two employment specialists (with the school person operating on a 10- or 11-month contract) the supported employment team should provide services to between 10 and 18 student candidates (depending on skill level of candidates placed) between the ages of 20 and 22 placed in competitive employment positions. Employment retention for these individuals should be 65% at the time of graduation from school.

ADMINISTRATIVE CONSIDERATIONS

Staff Competency

All staff from all three participating agencies will attend training internships on supported employment and transition planning. The employment specialists will also spend a 20-day period in intensive field work training. This training is to be done by highly trained experts in supported employment.

Liability

Employment specialists and other staff providing training in community-based settings will have liability insurance coverage provided by their employing agency. In case of an accident while training on employment sites or other community settings, the agency's insurance will provide coverage unless gross negligence is apparent on the community training site.

Office Space

The Chesterfield County MH/MR Services will provide office space, telephone, and office supplies for supported employment service delivery staff; this will include the school employment specialist.

Transportation

Each agency will provide mileage reimbursement for its staff for travel expenses incurred as a result of job-site training, community-based training, or other travel needs or services as related to the job.

Dissemination of Agreement

Written copies of this agreement will be disseminated to all core team members, designated agency liaisons, service delivery administrators, and other relevant agency personnel.

Review and Modification of Agreement

The transition planning core team members will plan to meet quarterly—January, March, July, and October—to reevaluate this interagency agreement. Written reports, program outcome reports, and yearly needs assessment information will be included in this evaluation.

Procedures for Development of New Services

At the quarterly meetings, the local core transition team will examine community services and needs assessment information to determine if there is need for expansion or development of new programs.

Dissemination of Adult and Transition-Related Services in the Community to Candidates and Parents

A booklet of Chesterfield County Community and Adult Services will be compiled for dissemination to parents, service delivery, and agency liaison personnel. This booklet will be completed 60 days from the signing of the three-way agreement. (See Figure 5.7.) The three-way agreement should be signed and dated by the appropriate administrator of each of the participating agencies.

SUMMARY

The previous pages have provided an in-depth look at how three different parties (the schools, vocational rehabilitation, and local com-

---

This agreement will be enacted immediately following the date of signing by all cooperating agencies.
_____ day of _____, 19____.

_____
Chesterfield County Public Schools
Director of Special Education

_____
Virginia Department of Rehabilitative Services
Regional Supervisor for the Richmond area

_____
Chesterfield County MH/MR Services
Director of Community Support Services

Figure 5.7. Schedule for implementation of interagency agreement.

munity services) can plan an *outcome-oriented* agreement for resources sharing.

Formal interagency agreements at both the state and local community level are necessary in order for comprehensive planning and service implementation to take place. Leadership at the state and federal level should provide impetus and guidance to leaders at the community level to work together. Community level leadership is charged with the responsibility of developing terms for interagency cooperation that provide for actual changes in service implementation and achievement of outcomes. Issues of territorialism and notions that one agency is superior to other agencies only serve to inhibit efficient and effective utilization of available resources.

All of the agencies need to be knowledgeable about the capabilities, strengths, and weaknesses of the other participating agencies. Staff persons at the level where actual services are provided to students need to be experts at coordinating and making available whatever resources are necessary to achieve the desired outcomes of transition planning for individual youth with disabilities.

Community leadership needs to be constantly aware of needs and demands for new services that may be the most successful in allowing individuals to achieve the desired outcomes. It is not the responsibility of the candidate to "fit" into what services are available; rather, it is the responsibility of the service agencies and providers to offer the services that "fit" the needs of the candidates.

To accomplish effective transition planning, participating agency leadership and service delivery personnel need to constantly bear in mind that the mission of the agencies is to provide successful outcomes to candidates. Service provision alone is not the goal; it is the means to an end. The goal, the desired result of the services, is to provide persons with disabilities with employment and the opportunity for independent living as adults in integrated communities.

Chapter 6   *School-Based Vocational Preparation*

THE FOUNDATION OF EFFECTIVE TRANSITION IS APPROPRIATE SCHOOL PRO-
gramming, for it is during a student's school years from ages 5 or 6 to
ages 18 to 22 that both employment and independent living skills
must be systematically taught. Effective school programming should
result in both placement into a paid job and movement into an age-
appropriate community living residence upon or just after school
graduation. It is also during this initial phase of the transition process
that school personnel such as special and vocational educators must
assume a leadership role in planning, implementing, and evaluating
the educational goals established by the core and transition planning
teams. The purpose of this chapter is to assist the transition team
members—particularly the teachers—in ensuring that students with
severe handicaps receive an education that will result in a decent job,
the best possible place to live, and skills that enable the students to be
independent and enjoy life. The practical emphasis of this chapter is
on "the how, where, and when" of teaching these skills.

SCHOOL VOCATIONAL PREPARATION:
A HISTORICAL PERSPECTIVE

A number of approaches have been used to teach students with disabilities the skills needed to function in jobs and in other community
settings. Historically, the first approaches were designed for persons
with mild and moderate handicaps, although these approaches were
also applied to individuals with more severe handicapping conditions. Later approaches were developed specifically to prepare students with severe disabilities to function as independently as possi-

ble in particular local situations, such as in the workplace or at home. This section briefly outlines a few of the most commonly used school vocational training strategies and lays the groundwork for a discussion of a school curriculum that enhances transition.

Career Education

Career education became a national education priority in the early 1970s; in 1974 the U.S. Office of Career Education was established. The Career Education Implementation Incentive Act of 1977 (PL 95-207) provided federal funds that enabled schools to build career education into their curricula, and in 1979 the Council for Exceptional Children (CEC) formed a Career Development Division (Brolin, 1982; Rusch, Mithaug, & Flexer, 1986). All of these events underscore the belief that developed in the 1970s that school-age individuals needed systematic and longitudinal training in developing work and community adjustment skills. The career education approach typically revolves around 4 levels of skill development that primarily occur at one of three points during the school years (Brolin, 1982). Skill instruction that takes place during these phases may be the most effective. Figure 6.1 indicates the points during the school years at which a student with severe handicaps is most responsive to training for skills. Table 6.1 provides examples of activities appropriate for students with severe handicaps that relate to these 4 phases.

Another important contribution of the career education movement has been the development of curriculum packages that underscore the importance of teaching both specific job skills and related social, daily living, and community access skills. An outline of the skills drawn from one career education curriculum guide (Brolin, 1982) is provided in Table 6.2. Although some skills need to be further analyzed for most students with severe handicaps, Brolin's outline provides a good base for general skill development, particularly in the earlier school years.

	Career awareness	Career exploration	Career preparation	Job placement
Elementary	▓	▓		
Junior high		▓	▓	
Senior high			▓	
At graduation				▓

Figure 6.1. Stages of career education.

Vocational Education

Vocational education is usually a means of career preparation for regular education students, but it should also be available for students in special education. This type of training usually reflects local labor market needs and thus provides specific skill training for particular occupations such as practical nurse, mechanic, beautician, or brick mason. Many vocational education programs provide laboratory classes in which a student spends part of his or her day learning job skills as well as related concepts (Rusch, Mithaug et al., 1986).

There are certain disadvantages inherent in the use of this approach with students who have severe handicaps. For example, Rusch, Mithaug et al. (1986) pointed out that some of the occupations stressed in a vocational education program that also serves regular education students may be inappropriate for students with disabilities. But it is often difficult for vocational educators to modify their course content or teaching techniques to meet the needs of the special education student. However, special and vocational educators can work together to serve all students through joint planning as described in Chapter Eight.

Work Experience and Workstudy

Work experience is a training approach that places students in community-based job-sites on an unpaid basis so that they can receive experience in several types of jobs prior to obtaining regular paying work. The original intent was for a work experience or workstudy coordinator to arrange a placement and then to evaluate a student's progress, with an additional person from the job-site responsible for the day-to-day training (Bellamy, Rose, Wilson, & Clarke, 1982). Although this approach has proven successful with mildly handicapped students (Brolin, 1982), it is difficult to implement with students with more severe handicaps because they typically require direct instruction on the job-site by specially trained personnel.

Job Training Stations In Industry

Job training stations or sites in industry are the terms used to describe community-based training in real job environments for students with severe handicaps (Pumpian, Shepard, & West, 1986). Community-based job training stations are specific to the local job market and include the presence of an instructor who is not a regular employee of the company such as a special education or vocational-special needs teacher or aide. Pumpian et al. (1986) provide a thorough description of the advantages of using job training stations, and they provide instructions for establishing these sites. The basic tenet of this approach

Table 6.1. Vocational preparation activities for students with severe handicaps

Guidelines for Vocational Training at the Elementary Level (Career Awareness):

—Become familiar with federal, state, and local regulations regarding vocational training and employment of citizens with handicaps. The earlier an educator becomes an advocate of mandated services in this area, the more likely the students are to receive proper training. Lobby for legislation that enhances employment opportunities.

—Make sure that vocational training is part of the IEP in the earliest school years.

—Visit upper-level school vocational programs and adult training programs to see if they match the variety of model programs that exist throughout the country. If local programs are good, determine what skills you need to teach to ensure a student's entry into programs.

—Make certain that the IEP addresses self-care and independent living skills, and functional academic and social skills that are needed in the work place. Such skills include eating, toileting, dressing, grooming, communication, independent mobility, money and time management, physical fitness, and the appropriate use of leisure time. If these skills are taught early, there will be more time for specific job training in later years.

—Emphasize the importance and rewards of work, and create opportunities for students to see and learn about different vocations. Get students into the community to see and be seen by nondisabled workers. Be certain to encourage realistic vocations such as office helper, receptionist, maid, orderly, janitor, auto mechanic helper, food service worker, farm laborer, and entry-level communications assistant.

—Let students sample at school and at home a wide array of work skills applicable to realistic jobs such as cleaning tables, washing dishes, taking messages to other people, emptying trash, and answering the phone. Enforcing a strict schedule of work duties teaches young students the importance of work quality and rate.

—Begin training skills in all curriculum areas outside the classroom. Integration into the community and training in natural settings at early stages of learning will promote generalization of learning and acceptance by other people.

Guidelines for Vocational Training at the Middle School Level (Career Exploration and Preparation):

—Continue to train communication, self-care, mobility, independent living, and recreation skills. Teach these skills within the context of job training whenever possible.

—Make sure the IEP addresses specific vocational training in a variety of potential jobs related to realistic employment in the local labor market.

—Provide job training in real job-sites such as hotels, restaurants, hospitals, and local businesses. At the very least, train in a variety of school sites such as the cafeteria, the office, the school building, and the school grounds.

—Begin working with high school personnel to identify possible permanent job placement. Make sure the transition from middle to high school programs is smooth and appropriate.

(continued)

Table 6.1. *(continued)*

—Identify a vocational track for each student so that more specific job training can occur at the high school level. Do this only after the student has shown job preferences and skill strengths and weaknesses from exposure to a variety of jobs in community-based settings.

—Continue training general work habits such as neatness, promptness, and responding to criticism within the context of specific job training. Use systematic data-based instructional methodology to monitor the mastering of general work habits and specific skills. Documentation of learning can be used later to ensure entry into the appropriate job.

—Continue to get students into the community for training in all curriculum areas.

—Contact rehabilitation and mental retardation adult service providers to identify who will be working with your students after graduation.

Guidelines for Vocational Training at the High School Level (Career Preparation and Job Placement):
—Develop a *transition team* composed of the student, parents or guardians, teacher, rehabilitation counselor, MR case manager, and other appropriate professionals to ensure movement from school to an appropriate job or postschool training program.

—The transition team must formulate a formal, written plan that specifies how a student will be trained and placed in a permanent job upon graduation. This *transition plan* specifies who is responsible for the timely completion of each goal of the plan.

—As part of the development of the transition plan, identify existing and potential job options. Work with adult service providers and businesses to create new jobs.

—Provide daily training in community job-sites that are realistic permanent job possibilities for the students. These potential job-sites should have been identified earlier with the assistance of middle school personnel.

—Once the student is placed in a job in the community, work with the student to improve work quality and production rate. Also, make sure the student has the endurance and stamina to work all day.

—Prepare job placement files with references, descriptions of acquired skills, work history, and community assessment information.

—Follow up on all graduates to make sure they are either employed or are receiving job placement services.

is that the number of training sites increases as the student progresses through school, enabling her or him to gain a variety of skills and to make choices about what kind of job he or she wants. As the student nears graduation, these experiences should help determine the paid job placement most appropriate for the student (McCarthy, Everson, Moon, & Barcus, 1985). Table 6.3 provides a sequence of steps that can be followed in establishing and running a job training station in industry.

Table 6.2. Career education curriculum competencies from The Life-Centered Career Education (LCCE) Program

DAILY LIVING SKILLS
1   Managing family finances:
1.1   Identify currency values and make correct change
1.2   Obtain and use bank and credit facilities

2   Selecting, managing, and maintaining a home:
2.1   Select adequate housing
2.2   Use basic appliances and tools

3   Caring for personal needs:
3.1   Dress appropriately
3.2   Exhibit proper grooming and hygiene

4   Buying and preparing food:
4.1   Demonstrate appropriate eating skills

5   Buying and caring for clothing

6   Engaging in civic activities

7   Utilizing recreation and leisure facilities:
7.1   Participate actively in group activities
7.2   Be familiar with community events and available community resources

8   Getting around the community (mobility):
8.1   Demonstrate knowledge of traffic rules and safety practices

PERSONAL-SOCIAL SKILLS
9   Achieving self-awareness of appearance and behavior:
9.1   Attain a sense of physical coordination

10   Acquiring self-confidence:
10.1 Express feeling of self-worth
10.2 Accept praise
10.3 Accept criticism

11   Achieving socially responsible behavior:
11.1 Know proper behavior in public places

12   Maintaining good interpersonal skills:
12.1 Know how to listen and respond
12.2 Know how to make and maintain friendships

13   Achieving independence

14   Achieving problem-solving skills

15   Communicating adequately with others:
15.1 Recognize emergency situations

OCCUPATIONAL SKILLS
16   Knowing and exploring occupational possibilities:
16.1 Identify the personal values met through work
16.2 Identify the remunerative aspects of work

17   Exhibiting appropriate work habits and behaviors:
17.1 Follow directions
17.2 Work with others
17.3 Work at a satisfactory rate
17.4 Accept supervision
17.5 Recognize the importance of regular attendance and punctuality
17.6 Meet demands of quality work
17.7 Demonstrate occupational safety

Adapted from Brolin (1982, p. 270).

Table 6.3.   Establishing and running community-based job training stations

A. Establishing job-training stations
1. Establish a philosophical commitment to implementing appropriate community-based training.
2. Outline the program's objectives for community-based training.
3. Identify target age and population.
4. Conduct a community job market screening of job types and available positions.
5. List potential training sites based on the community job market survey.
6. Initially contact potential training site employers by phone to set up a visit.
7. Visit potential sites and determine the job skills required.
8. Determine if the potential site reflects job skills required in other potential employment positions within the community. Does the site reflect the objectives of the program?
9. If yes, negotiate with the employer to use the site for training.
10. Draw up a written training agreement and have the employer sign the agreement.

B. Running job training stations
1. Establish program operation procedures that adhere to Department of Labor standards.
2. Analyze the job skills and related nonvocational skills for the training station.
3. Select students, usually one to three for each site.
4. Place and train students in the training station.
5. Utilize systematic instructional procedures.
6. Monitor student performance.
7. Collect evaluations and obtain frequent input from employers.
8. Provide student performance feedback to families and appropriate school and adult service personnel.
9. Reinforce employers and co-workers for their efforts.
10. Review the appropriateness of the training site on a monthly basis.
11. Maintain sites that are reflective of the community job market.
12. Expand the number and type of sites to reflect the local community job market.
13. Have each student move through several training stations during the year so that you can assess vocational preferences and skill differences.

Adapted from Hamre-Nietupski, Nietupski, Bates, and Maurer (1982) and Pumpian, Shepard, and West (1986).

Paid Job Placements

As a student nears graduation, he or she may be placed on a part- or full-time basis in a paid job as part of his or her school vocational training program. This has been done in some systems where educators and vocational rehabilitators work together closely. Paid job placement is a logical culmination of successful, long-term job-site training in community stations, but personnel must be careful not to place students too soon so that their options are limited by insufficient skill preparation (Bellamy et al., 1982).

UNDERLYING ASSUMPTIONS OF AN
INDIVIDUALIZED EDUCATION PROGRAM: WHAT TO TEACH

Whatever major strategies a program may use for vocational preparation, experts agree that there are certain characteristics fundamental to a successful individualized education program for a student with severe handicaps. Such characteristics apply to all curriculum areas including vocational, lesiure/recreation, domestic/residential, and community skills. Chapter 1 mentioned several of these characteristics, including a functional curriculum, integrated programming, and community-based instruction. This chapter elaborates on these and several other characteristics or assumptions. Adhering to the assumptions delineated in this section and using a combination of several of the strategies mentioned earlier should help the transition team move students into the best available adult work and living situations.

Developing a Functional Curriculum

A curriculum with goals and objectives based on the demands of adult life over a variety of settings is believed to be most effective for students with severe handicaps (Brown et al., 1979; Falvey, 1986; Wilcox & Bellamy, 1982). Such situations include the workplace, leisure and residential settings, and community facilities. The functional curriculum divides all activities into skill "domains" or categories that list the skills necessary to survive in both current and future environments within each of these domains. Chapter 4 presents a method for developing a list of activities within each domain that should be taught. Other sources have referred to the process of identifying activities for instruction as "cataloging local opportunities"

Table 6.4. Identifying functional activities for instruction across all curriculum domains

1. Select a broad curriculum domain category (i.e., recreation, community, vocational, and domestic) to be analyzed.
2. Identify a list of environments within home, school, and community settings where students may perform activities related to the identified domain category.
3. Identify additional environments by surveying other professionals, the parents, and the students.
4. Observe these identified environments and list those skills that are essential for competence in each environment.
5. Verify the list of skills with other professionals and with parents.
6. Repeat this process for all domain categories.
7. Review and revise as needed (with a minimum of one review annually).

(Wilcox & Bellamy, 1982) or "conducting an ecological analysis" (Wehman, Renzaglia, & Bates, 1985). Regardless of the method used for organizing activities, certain basic procedures such as those listed in Table 6.4 should be used.

After all possible activities needed to function in current and future environments have been identified, the teacher or transition team must rank by priority which activities should be taught initially. Table 6.5 provides guidelines for listing instructional activities.

A Longitudinal Functional Curriculum

Training in all skill domains must occur from the earliest school years. However, the emphasis during the elementary years will be on domestic, community, and recreation activities, as well as on communication skills. Vocational training is more general in focus, addressing not only career planning, but also job-site skills such as duty assignment, changing work stations, working at one task for a specific period of time, and taking breaks at appropriate times. As a student becomes older, more time needs to be spent on the vocational domain, and the training of specific job skills becomes critical. Table 6.6 provides examples of functional activities for three students at different school levels. Table 6.1 provides examples of specific vocational activities that should occur across the school years.

Rusch and Chadsey-Rusch (1985) point out that teaching social and vocational "survival" skills that have been identified by employers as crucial to job success is one way of developing a longitudi-

Table 6.5.   Establishing priority activities for instruction

1.   Identify with the student and her or his family the student's performance in each of the domain categories. Then identify desired relevant future environments in which it is projected the student will be functioning.
2.   Identify activities and skills relevant to the student's current environment; identify skills necessary to function in projected future environments.
3.   Review all relevant current and future activities and indicate those activities that occur in two or more domains and that are age-appropriate.
4.   List these activities from most- to least-frequent in occurrence.
5.   From this list, identify those activities that are crucial for the student's safety. Next identify those activities critical for functioning independently in the identified future environments.
6.   Select for immediate instruction:
    (a)   those activities essential to the student's safety within current environments.
    (b)   those activities that the student must perform frequently in order to function independently within her or his current and identified future environments.
7.   Select remaining objectives from the list of activities (Step 4).

Table 6.6. Curriculum activities across the school years

Student	Domestic	Community	Leisure	Vocational
Tim (Elementary school)	Picking up toys	Eating meals in a restaurant	Climbing on swing set	Picking up plate, silverware, and glass after a meal
	Washing dishes	Using restroom in a local restaurant	Playing board games	Returning toys to appropriate storage space
	Making bed	Putting trash into container	Playing tag with neighbors	
	Dressing	Choosing correct change to ride city bus	Tumbling activities	Cleaning the room at the end of the day
	Grooming			
	Eating skills			Working on a task for a designated period (15–30 minutes)
	Toileting skills	Giving the clerk money for an item he wants to purchase	Running	
	Sorting clothes		Playing kickball	
	Vacuuming		Croquet	Wiping tables after meals
		Recognizing and reading pedestrian safety signs	Riding bicycles	Following 2- to 4-step instructions
		Participating in local scout troop	Playing with dolls and other age-appropriate toys	Answering the telephone
		Going to neighbor's house for lunch		Emptying trash
				Taking messages to people

(continued)

nal, functional vocational curriculum. An elementary teacher can start with general applications of a skill such as independent mobility by teaching her students to move from the classroom to the cafeteria to the playground. A junior high teacher could extend this training by instructing the student to independently walk from home to the school bus and then from the bus stop at school to the classroom. At the secondary level, students would be trained to use a city bus to get to various places and to move about independently between various community-based job-sites. One way to ascertain vocational survival skills is to survey a variety of employers in the community. Another way is to observe workers. Rusch and his colleagues have provided guidelines for conducting both types of assessments (Rusch & Mithaug, 1980; Rusch, Schutz, & Agran, 1982). Career education

Table 6.6. *(continued)*

Student	Domestic	Community	Leisure	Vocational
Mary (Junior high)	Washing clothes	Crossing streets safely	Playing volley ball	Waxing floors
	Cooking a simple hot meal (soup, salad, and sandwich)	Purchasing an item from a department store	Taking aerobic classes	Cleaning windows
			Playing checkers with a friend	Filling lawn mower with gas
	Keeping bed-room clean	Purchasing a meal at a restaurant		Hanging and bagging clothes
	Making snacks	Using local transportation system to get to and from recreational facilities	Playing miniature golf	Bussing tables
	Mowing lawn		Cycling	Working for 1–2 hours
	Raking leaves		Attending high school or local col-lege bas-ketball games	Operating ma-chinery (such as dishwasher, buffer, etc.)
	Making a gro-cery list	Participating in local scout troop		
	Purchasing items from a list			Cleaning sinks, bath tubs, and fixtures
	Vacuuming and dusting living room	Going to neighbor's house for lunch on Saturday	Playing softball	Following a job sequence
			Swim-ming	
			Attending crafts class at city recre-ation center	

(continued)

guidelines such as those listed in Table 6.2 should also be helpful in determining skills for instruction.

Training in Integrated Community-Based Settings

One working premise of educational programs is that training occurs in integrated settings where the majority of participants in a particu-lar activity are not handicapped (Freagon et al., 1986; Rusch & Chadsey-Rusch, 1985; Wilcox & Bellamy, 1982). This implies that students with handicaps receive school-based programming in "regular" schools and that specific training in particular curriculum domains occurs in "regular" community-based sites. For example, the majority of school-

Table 6.6. *(continued)*

Student	Domestic	Community	Leisure	Vocational
Sandy (High School)	Cleaning all rooms in place of residence	Utilizing bus system to move about the community	Jogging	Performing required janitorial duties at J. C. Penney
	Developing a weekly budget	Depositing checks into bank account	Archery	Performing housekeeping duties at Days Inn
	Cooking meals	Using community department stores	Boating	Performing grounds keeping duties at VCU campus
	Operating thermostat to regulate heat or air conditioning	Using community restaurants	Watching college basketball	Performing food service at K St. Cafeteria
	Doing yard maintenance	Using community grocery stores	Video games	Performing laundry duties at Moon's Laundromat
	Maintaining personal needs	Using community health facilities (physician, pharmacist)	Card games (UNO)	Performing photography at Virginia National Bank Headquarters
	Caring for and maintaining clothing		Athletic club swimming class	Performing food stocking duties at Farm Fresh
			Gardening	Performing clerical duties at KATS Electrical, Inc.
			Going on a vacation trip	Performing job duties at company standards

age persons with severe handicaps need to receive employment training in community-based job-sites rather than in sheltered workshops, work activity centers, or adult day/developmental centers. Domestic activities such as cooking and clothing care should occur in group homes or in supervised apartments into which the students may move as adults.

Integrated school services are important not only because students with handicaps are exposed to the demands and expectations of their peers and supervisors in the "normal world" but also because the public at large gets an opportunity to observe and interact positively with the students who are handicapped (Wehman, Kregel, & Barcus, 1985). School administrators and teachers who are temporarily confined to segregated schools should refer to a number of excellent written resources now available on desegregated service delivery.

Community-Based Instruction

Regardless of whether a school program is based in an integrated or a segregated setting, most instruction should occur in the "natural" environment in which activities actually take place. As the student becomes older, more and more time must be spent in natural settings if the student is to become truly prepared for functioning in adult situations (Brown, Nietupski, & Hamre-Nietupski, 1976; Falvey, 1986; Wilcox & Bellamy, 1982).

To determine which environments are most appropriate as training sites, an ecological analysis of the four curriculum domains must occur. The process of conducting an ecological analysis involves the following basic steps (Wehman, Renzaglia, & Bates, 1985, p. 19):

1. Focusing on the primary home, community, recreational, and potential work environments where the student spends or will spend his/her time.
2. Visiting these environments and analyzing the skills that are essential for competence in each environment.
3. Determining which of those skills the student can already perform.
4. Prioritizing those skills that the student cannot perform in an order of the most important for instruction to less important.
5. Validating that these skills are appropriate by double-checking with parents and significant others in the student's living environments.

An analysis of community-based jobs that may be future employment settings for students with handicaps should provide training stations for students who are 12 or older (Hanley-Maxwell, 1986; Pumpian et al., 1986; Rusch & Chadsey-Rusch, 1985; Wehman, Renzaglia, & Bates, 1985). (The reader should refer to Table 6.4 for guidelines on establishing community-based vocational sites or job training stations.)

Problems and Solutions to Community-Based Training

It can be difficult to implement a community-based educational program, particularly in a school system where students have remained in a classroom for the entire day. Teachers may be concerned with the

Table 6.7. Solutions to community-based training problems

Staffing and Scheduling
—use of computer-assisted instruction
—use of computer-managed instruction
—team teaching
—use of volunteers
—use of paraprofessionals
—use of peer tutors
—use of university graduate students, student teachers, and practicum students
—teacher-student ratio of 1:4 or less
—heterogeneous grouping of students
—staggered student training schedules
—support personnel providing integrated therapy services

Transportation
—use of parents' car (reimburse for mileage)
—utilization of training stations within a short (walking) distance of the school
—utilization of volunteers (reimburse for mileage)
—coordination of regular bus schedules with community training
—use of public transit systems (i.e., bus, taxi, subway, train)
—teacher transport (reimburse for mileage)
—use of school district vehicles (i.e., vans, cars, drivers, school cars)
—bicycling

Liability and Safety
—board of education district-wide policy development
—specific school and/or student agreements
—district liability insurance policies cover teachers and students while in the community; insurance for students through school accident funds or employer's insurance coverage
—purchase of 24-hour coverage offered to families for a minimal fee at the beginning of school year
—worker's compensation insurance (for students being paid a wage)
—written training agreements between student, parent(s), teacher, and participating employer
—volunteers register with school system volunteer program for insurance coverage

Costs
—include money for community-based instruction in annual budgets
—use of individual classroom supplies budget
—use of career education monies
—use of vocational education monies
—use of funds allotted per class by the student government of the school
—establish open purchase order accounts with local merchants
—use of donation from local businesses for specific uses (i.e., bus passes for transportation training)
—structure purchasing training around regular family purchases using the family supply list and funds

staff-to-student ratio when there is only one teacher and an aide in a classroom of 8–12 students. Additional issues, such as transportation to job-sites, costs of changing an already established curriculum, and safety and liability may be of concern to administrators. Furthermore, parents may initially worry that supervision and structure could be weakened, or fear that the academic or therapeutic needs of their daughter or son may be neglected.

Several model training programs across the country have resolved these valid concerns, and solid suggestions for implementing community-based training are available. The suggestions from three sources (Baumgart & Van Walleghem, 1986; Hutchins & Talarico, 1985; Nietupski, Hamre-Nietupski, Welch, & Anderson, 1983) concerning the most often voiced concerns are summarized in Table 6.7.

Involvement of Parents and Other Professionals

There are two other major working premises of a successful educational program. First, parents or primary caregivers must be involved from the early school years in planning and monitoring their child's school training. Chapters 7 and 9 of this text provide guidelines for parents and for professionals in their efforts to jointly plan, implement, and monitor a student's progress through school and into the world of adult options. The final premise is that teachers and other school personnel will begin working together to plan the transition process long before the student prepares to graduate. The other chapters in this text, particularly Chapter 8, describe how professionals across all disciplines must be involved in the educational and transition process.

SYSTEMATIC, BEHAVIORAL INSTRUCTION IN NATURAL SETTINGS: HOW TO TEACH

Once community-based training sites and vocational instruction areas have been designated in the classroom, the teacher(s) must decide upon and write down lesson plans outlining how each student will be taught all essential activities. Many factors must be considered—including all the elements listed in Table 6.8. The remainder of this section briefly describes the elements listed in Table 6.8 that constitute a vocational (or other adult-life domain) instructional program.

Delineation of Appropriate Training Stations

As described earlier in this chapter, training in all skill domain areas should occur in the settings that will be available to the students

Table 6.8.   Elements of a vocational training program

1.   Delineation of appropriate community and school-based training sites
2.   Sequencing of training goals and related behavioral objectives
3.   Formulation of skill sequences and task analyses that break activities into teachable units
4.   Choosing appropriate instruction techniques for every student that will enhance acquisition and generalization of skill performance
5.   Deciding upon data collection procedures that will reflect the strengths and weaknesses of each student's performance
6.   Teaching related social and community survival skills
7.   Determining methods to phase out instruction from a training site so that supervision on that site can be transferred to "real" employers
8.   Designing staff and student schedules that permit the most students to receive the maximum amount of community-based training

when they become adults. The process of identifying training areas is described more fully in a later section.

In those situations where younger students are involved, where community access is difficult to arrange, or where the staff-to-student ratio is disproportionate, simulated training in a classroom may have to take place on a part-time basis. Whenever classroom instruction occurs, the teacher must make certain that performance of that skill is assessed regularly and frequently in the natural environment. Frequent assessment is important because research has shown that skills learned in simulated environments may not readily transfer into a natural work environment. Wilcox and Bellamy (1982) warn that simulation is appropriate on only a limited basis: 1) to provide intensive practice on difficult activity steps, 2) to train the use of prosthetics or alternative performance strategies, 3) to practice task variations or low probability events, and 4) to practice social skills that are related to skill performance in the community.

Sequencing of Training Goals and Related Behavioral Objectives

Whether they are part of the individualized education program (IEP) or the individualized transition plan (ITP) for a secondary student, yearly instructional goals in each domain must be established. Annual goals are based on the activities a student must perform in a particular environment; these are determined after an ecological analysis has been completed. By identifying activities across all domain areas within a community, an instructor should have no problem determining annual goals. If there is a difficult task ahead for the instructor, it will be in ranking by importance the activities for instruction (see Tables 6.4 and 6.5).

Developing specific instructional objectives that describe how a student will attain a goal requires more analysis than the annual goals, because this step sequence will become the basis of a written instructional program. Instructional objectives must contain the observable behaviors that will be taught, the conditions under which behaviors will occur, and the criteria that will be used to evaluate performance of a behavior (Snell & Grigg, 1986). Falvey (1986) also points out that vocational objectives must be coordinated with objectives from other domains. For example, if a student is learning to communicate with a picture book system, then that system must be incorporated into his or her vocational skills training program.

Table 6.9 illustrates some sample vocational goals and corresponding instructional objectives for those students whose functional curriculum activities were identified in Table 6.6.

Formulation of Skill Sequences and Task Analyses

Every functional activity that a student must learn has to be broken into teachable units. For example, in selecting job training stations for students, a teacher can identify the major duties involved in each job, and the sequence in which each job duty occurs. Noting the amount of time required for each duty to be completed is also helpful. Table 6.10 indicates the skill sequence for one training station: a janitorial position at a university student center.

Once an activity has been sequenced into component skills, each skill must be task-analyzed for instruction. The task analysis, once it is written on a data collection sheet, can be used for both assessment and instruction. Table 6.11 indicates a task analysis for the skill of "Getting the Supply Cart."

Choosing Appropriate Instructional
Techniques and Data Collection Methods

Once an appropriate instructional objective has been formulated, and skill sequences and task analyses have been written, a program must be developed for teaching each task to the student. This program should outline procedures for performance assessment. In addition, the program should include training methods for shaping or chaining, reinforcement procedures, prompting techniques, data recording, a schedule for training, and preliminary plans for ensuring maintenance and generalization. Such a program developed for one of the students working in the training station described earlier (see Table 6.10) is provided in Table 6.12.

Although it is beyond the scope of this chapter to describe in detail behavioral training methodology, there are a number of excellent sources that instructors should refer to in designing community-

Table 6.9. Sample vocational goals and objectives for students of various ages

Student	Vocational goal (See Table 6.6 for related curriculum activity)	Instructional objectives
Tim (Elementary)	Tim will clean up his work space independently by June, 1987.	Given his meal (breakfast or lunch) in the cafeteria and upon completion of eating his food, Tim will return his tray, plate, silverware, and glass to the dishroom window and independently sort the items (tray, plate, silverware, glass) into the appropriate dish bins with 100% accuracy. According to the task analysis, this will be performed over three consecutive data probes (probes taken once weekly).
		Given an opportunity to choose a toy for play time from the storage area, Tim will independently return the toy at the end of playtime to it's storage space on six consecutive trials over a 2-week period.
Mary (Junior High)	Mary will operate a lawn mower to mow the family yard by September, 1987.	Given a lawn mower and a gas can, Mary will independently fill the lawn mower gas tank accurately, performing 100% of the steps on the task analysis for three consecutive data probes (probe taken once each week).
		Given a lawn mower, Mary will independently mow the family yard accurately, completing 100% of the steps of the task analysis for lawn mowing for three consecutive data probes (probe taken once each week).
Sandy (High School)	Sandy will work for 4 hours a day in a competitive job training station.	Given a rake, Sandy will independently rake the leaves on the VCU Commons grounds, performing 100% of the steps on the job duty task analysis for three consecutive data probe trials (probe taken once each week).
		Given a checklist of the day's list of job duties, Sandy will independently perform all assigned job duties in sequence for three consecutive data probe trials (probe once each week).

Table 6.10. A skill sequence for a part-time janitorial position

Activities performed at training station	Times
1. Getting supply cart from janitor's store room	9:00
2. Blocking off men's room for cleaning	9:10
3. Emptying trash	9:15
4. Sweeping floor	9:20
5. Flushing toilets	9:30
6. Spraying toilets	9:35
7. Brushing toilets	9:40
8. Spraying counters/sinks	9:50
9. Wiping counters/sinks	9:55
10. Polishing sink faucets	10:00
11. Moving cart to women's room	10:05
12. Blocking off women's room	10:07
13. Opening men's room for use	10:12
14. Emptying trash	10:15
15. Sweeping floor	10:20
16. Flushing toilets	10:30
17. Spraying toilets	10:35
18. Brushing toilets	10:40
19. Spraying counters/sinks	10:50
20. Wiping counters/sinks	10:55
21. Polishing sink faucets	11:00
22. Opening women's room for use	11:05
23. Moving supply cart to hall window	11:05
Break time	11:10–11:20
24. Wiping window ledges	11:20
25. Spraying entry doors	11:40
26. Wiping entry doors	11:45
27. Returning supply cart to janitor's store room	11:55

Note: The authors wish to thank Carole Jesiolowski who developed this skill sequence for a janitorial training site used by the VCU-RRTC and Amelia Street School in Richmond, Virginia.

based training programs for students who are severely handicapped. A few of the very good commercial sources available are listed in the Appendix at the end of this chapter, and can be purchased by the school or program responsible for curriculum and individualized student program design.

Data Collection Procedures The instructor must have a method of documenting a student's progress during community-based training. This is particularly true of job skill training, as proof of performance can lead to either paid job placement or placement on a state vocational rehabilitation agency caseload. Several of the primary methods of data collection that should be conducted for job training are described here.

Table 6.11.   Task analyses for janitorial position (training station)

GETTING SUPPLY CART	EMPTYING TRASH
1. Get out of car.	1. Pick up stopper from cart.
2. Acknowledge "Hello" (shake hands say "Hello").	2. Open door.
3. Close door.	3. Put stopper under door.
4. Walk to building entrance door.	4. Pull door over stopper.
5. Go in.	5. Kick in stopper.
6. Walk to service elevator.	6. Push cart into room.
7. Push "down" button.	7. Stop at trash can.
8. Wait.	8. Put hands on container.
9. Go into elevator.	9. Lift.
10. Push "1."	10. Move away from wall.
11. Get out of elevator.	11. Place can on floor.
12. Turn left.	12. Pull out bag.
13. Walk to B4.	13. Empty into cart bag.
14. Enter room.	14. Put bag back in container.
15. Take off hat.	15. Pick up container.
16. Take off coat.	16. Put on ledge.
17. Place hat and coat on shelf.	17. Lift up flap.
18. Find cart.	18. Push container to wall.
19. Push cart into hallway.	19. Drop flap.
20. Turn left.	20. Return to cart.
21. Walk to elevator.	
22. Push button.	
23. Wait.	
24. Enter.	
25. Push "2."	
26. Get out of elevator.	
27. Push cart down ramp.	
28. Turn right.	
29. Stop at desk.	
30. Ask for key.	
31. Place key on cart.	
32. Push cart to restrooms.	
33. Stop cart next to restroom doors.	

Recording Performance Level During Initial Training   Job trainers need to record the performance of a student while he or she is learning to perform job tasks. Regular data collection is the only objective way of determining whether or not new skills are being acquired sufficiently enough that the trainer can begin phasing out his or her assistance. Two types of data can be recorded during this phase of training. Both types are based on the task analysis of each job skill and both indicate whether the student is beginning to work independently. The same data sheet can be used for recording the two types of data.

Table 6.12.   Instructional program

A. TERMINAL OBJECTIVES:
When given the cue, "Spray the counters and sinks" the student will pick up the can of Lysol, remove the top, walk to the counter/sink area and spray each section. The student will do this independently for 4 consecutive training days with 100% accuracy.

Environment: Training will take place in the restrooms on the first floor of the Student Commons at Virginia Commonwealth University on Monday, Wednesday, and Thursday from 11:00 A.M. to 12:30 P.M. for 6 weeks.

Rationale: Student is participating in a community-based training program for a duration of 6 weeks to assess vocational skills, to receive exposure to nonhandicapped peers, and to experience a community work environment with its inherent expectations and responsibilities.

B. MATERIALS:
—cleaning cart with supplies
—can of Lysol disinfectant

C. TASK ANALYSIS (TA): See attachment.

D. TEACHING PROCEDURES:
1. *Assessment:*   Baseline data will be collected during the student's first week at the training site. Both probe and prompt data will be collected for 3 days to assess student's performance (see TA for codes). This data will be graphed.

2. *Positioning of materials:*   Lysol can will be positioned on top of the cleaning cart along with the other supplies. This supply position is customarily used by the regular custodial workers.

3. *Position of trainer:*   Trainer is positioned next to cart for instructional cues, moving along with student as necessary (see prompt sheet). Trainer will increase distance from student but will remain present in restroom.

4. *Sequence of steps:*   A forward-chaining system will be utilized as the initiation of each new step is dependent upon completion of the previous one. If a step is done incorrectly, trainer will complete and position student for the next step.

5. *Reinforcers:*   Two reinforcers will be used—verbal praise and physical gesture (pat on the back).

Verbal praise will be given each time student correctly completes a step of the TA. When the same prompt is given for 3 consecutive training days and the student completes the step, the reinforcer will stop. Praise will then be given when the step is completed using the next lower level of prompting. The rationale for this procedure is to move the student through the prompting hierarchy toward independent completion of the step. When student completes all 23 steps of the TA, trainer will pat student on the back and say: "Nice job. You sprayed the counters and sinks quickly and completely."

(continued)

Table 6.12.   *(continued)*

6. *Teaching the skill* (behavior change procedures):   The instructional method of least intrusive prompts will be utilized.

E. METHODS OF EVALUATION:
Probe data will be collected on Thursday, using a multiple-opportunity assessment. If step is done incorrectly, trainer will complete the step and position student for the next step.

Prompt data will be collected on Monday and Wednesday using a prompt hierarchy as outlined.

Criterion for acquisition is the completion of all steps of the TA with 100% accuracy independently for 4 consecutive work days.

Opportunities for generalization will occur across settings when the student cleans the women's restroom, which contains additional counter space and sinks. (Cleaning this restroom also provides opportunities for repeated practice of the skill.)

Generalization across people will occur during the 5th and 6th weeks of training when a different trainer will provide the instructional cues.

Note: The authors wish to thank Carole Jesiolowski for developing this program.

The first type of data is referred to as "probe" or "continuing assessment" data and indicates how well a student performs a job duty without any prompting or nonnaturally occurring reinforcement. It should be collected at least once a week and preferably at the beginning of a training period. Probe data, recorded simply with a (+) for a step done correctly and (−) for a step done incorrectly, lets the job trainer know when the student is performing a specific task correctly and independently. We typically consider a job task to have been learned by a student when the student performs all of a task analysis correctly on three consecutive probe trials.

The task analysis recording sheet in Figure 6.2 shows how a student, Tom, performed on pot scrubbing on five probe trials that were conducted over a 5-week period. (His performance was assessed each Monday as the dates indicate). On the third, fourth, and fifth trials he performed all steps of the pot scrubbing task analysis correctly, so from that point on the trainer would expect Tom to perform this task without assistance. Of course, if he began to make an error in this task, instruction would begin again.

One way to ensure correct performance is to continue to collect probe data at least once a week. This type of assessment can be done on visits to the job-site long after the job trainer is no longer present on a daily basis. Note the directions for conducting a probe in Table 6.13.

The second type of data that can be collected between probes indicates the kinds of prompts that are being provided to the student

Trainer: _J. Trainer_
Trainee: _Tom_
Environment: _Henrico Hospital_
Instructional cue: _"Scrub the pots."_

Program	probe 8/28	train 8/29	train 8/30	probe 9/2	train 9/3	probe 9/4	train 9/5	probe 9/8	train 9/15	probe 9/11	follow-up 10/2
4.1 Place 10 pots in sink #1.	+	+V	+	+	+	+	+	+	+	+	+
4.2 Remove one pot from sink #1, empty water and place on counter, right of sink.	–	P	P	+	+	+	++	+	+	+	+
4.3 Grasp pot in upright position with nondominant hand, pick up green scouring pad with dominant hand.	–	PM	PM	PM	+	+	+	+	+	+	+
4.4 Scour the bottom inside surface of the pot until all visible food particles are loosened.	–	V	M	–V	V	+	+	+	+V	+	+
4.5 Position pot on its side and scrub inside wall of pot until all visible food particles are loosened.	–	V	+	+	+	+	+	+	+	+	+
4.6 Continue to rotate pot in a clockwise fashion until all inside wall surfaces are scoured.	–	V	+	+	+	+	+	+	+	+	+
4.7 Dip pot in sink #1, empty water out of pot.	+	+	+	+	+	+	+	+	+	+	+
4.8 Visually inspect pot for remaining food particles, rescrubbing any necessary spots.	–	M	V	–V	V	+	+	+	+	+	+

Figure 6.2. Task analysis recording sheet. (Code: + = independent/correct; – = incorrect; V = verbal prompt; M = modeling prompt; P = physical prompt.)

(continued)

Figure 6.2. *(continued)*

4.9 Dip pot again in sink #1, visually inspect for remaining food, and spot scour as needed.	−	M	∨	+	+	+	+	+		+
4.10 Turn pot over, bottom facing up.	+	∨	+	+	+	+	+	+		÷
4.11 Scrub bottom of pot.	÷	+	+	+	+	+	÷	÷		+
4.12 Position pot on its side and scour outside wall of pot until all visible food particles are loosened.	−	M	M	−	∨	+	+	÷		+
4.13 Continue to rotate pot in a clockwise fashion until all outside wall surfaces are scoured.	−	∨	∨	+	+	+	+	+		÷
4.14 Dip pot in sink #1, pour out water. Visually inspect for remaining food particles, rescouring as needed.	(	∨	÷	+	+	÷	+	+		÷
4.15 Drop pot in sink #2.	÷	÷	÷	÷	÷	+	+	+		÷
4.16 Repeat steps 2 through 13 until all pots in sink #1 have been scoured.	−	∨	+	+	+	+	+	+		+
4.17 Dip pot in sink #2 (verbal cue "dip and throw").	+	+	+	+	+	+	+	+		+
4.18 Place in sink #3.	+	+	÷	+	÷	+	+	+		+
4.19 Continue until the original 10 pots and pans are in sink #3.	−	÷	+	+	+	+	+	+		+
4.20 Take pots out of sink #3 and place on counter to drain.	−	÷	÷	+	÷	÷	+	÷		÷
4.21 Repeat steps 4.1 through 4.18	−	÷	+	+	+	+	+	+		+
Total correct steps										
Percent correct steps										

154

Table 6.13. Directions for collecting probe data

1. Have the student move to the appropriate work area unless movement is part of the task analysis.
2. Stand beside or behind the worker so that you do not interrupt work flow.
3. Say to the worker, "Scrub the pots."
4. Do not provide any prompts or reinforcement.
5. Record beside each step of the task analysis a (+) for correct performance or a (−) for incorrect performance.
6. After the student has finished the task, stop the worker and begin training the task.

during the completion of tasks. The same task analysis recording sheet used for probe data collection is used for recording this prompt data. In this case, the job trainer records a symbol representing either independent performance of a step or the provision of a verbal, gestural, or physical prompt. Directions for recording prompt data when using "a system of least prompts" is provided in Table 6.14.

Keeping track of the number and type of prompts that are provided to a student on a specific task over a period of time allows the trainer to determine whether or not to start gradually moving further away from the student during training to reduce dependency on

Table 6.14. Directions for collecting prompt data

1. Have student move to appropriate work area unless movement is part of the task analysis.
2. Stand behind or beside workers so that you can quickly provide prompts when necessary.
3. Say to worker, "Scrub the pots."
4. Wait 3–5 seconds for self-initiation of Step 1.[a]
5. If correct, record (+) and proceed to Step 2.
6. If no response is given, provide verbal prompts specific to step.
7. If correct, record (V) by step, and proceed to Step 2.
8. If no response is given after verbal prompt, provide model or gestural prompt specified in Step 1, with same verbal prompts.
9. If correct response is given, record (M) by step and proceed to Step 2.
10. If no response is given after a model prompt, provide a physical prompt to complete the step.
11. Record a (P) by the step and proceed to Step 2.
12. Repeat this procedure for each step until the student completes the entire task.

[a]After a few seconds, go ahead and provide the prompt so that the student does not make an error.

the trainer's physical proximity. For example, if the student is receiving mostly verbal prompts, or is performing most steps of the task independently, the trainer can move back from the student 3 feet or so on the first day. The trainer continues to increase the distance from the student as appropriate, until the trainer is observing the student alone in a work area during the first several days of employment without notifying a floor supervisor.

The data in Figure 6.2 show that Tom is learning to scrub pots quickly. In fact, he rarely needs anything more than a verbal prompt on a few of the steps in this task. Since he is performing so well, the trainer can begin to move further away from the student as he works. Eventually, after three consecutive 100% correct probe trials, the trainer can begin leaving the pot scrubbing area totally.

Even a small amount of data collection on the job-site can be time-consuming. It is recommended that the job trainer concentrate on recording *prompt* data on only one or two tasks per day. *Probe* data can be collected on several job tasks since only one trial, that is, one completed task analysis has to be recorded on any given day.

Improving Work Rate   Once a student has learned to perform a few job tasks correctly and independently, the job trainer helps the student to increase his or her rate of work production up to company standards. The first step in increasing work rate is to establish a standard rate based on the performance of nonhandicapped co-workers. This information can be gathered during job-site observations before placement and during the initial phase of job-site training. It is advisable to observe several workers performing a particular task over a period of several days. An average rate of production can then be determined from these observations.

Several methods can be used for improving work rate. These methods include: using a changing criterion reinforcement program in which a student has to work progressively faster in order to receive a particular reinforcement, using a timer to encourage speed (the student strives to complete a job before a buzzer sounds), having the student chart his or her work performance, and having the student talk about ways to improve performance before and after a work period with the job trainer. Whatever method is chosen, the job trainer must eventually remove all intrusive prompts such as timers and artificial reinforcers from the job-site.

Work rate should be assessed throughout job-site training and during follow-up visits once the trainer has phased out his or her presence from the job-site. Regular rate checks help to ensure successful job performance and can alert the job trainer if a problem is occurring.

Name: **Tom**   Month: **OCT/NOV 1986**
Task: **Scrubbing Pots**   *Standard: **30 units in 10 min.***

Date	Time started task	Time ended task	Total time worked	Units completed	% of standard
10-30	8:40	8:50	10 min.	10	33 %
11-2	8:20	8:30	10 min.	13	43 %
11-3	1:43	1:53	10 min.	18	60 %
11-3	11:20	11:30	10 min.	22	73 %
11-3	2:15	2:25	10 min.	24	80 %
11-4	11:30	11:40	10 min.	25	83 %
11-4	1:18	1:28	10 min.	26	87 %
11-5	10:15	10:25	10 min.	28	93 %
11-5	2:11	2:21	10 min.	29	97 %
11-6	10:00	10:10	10 min.	30	100 %
11-6	2:40	2:50	10 min.	30	100 %
11-9	9:40	9:50	10 min.	30	100 %
11-9	3:15	3:25	10 min.	30	100 %
11-10	9:40	9:50	10 min.	27	90 %
11-10	11:35	11:45	10 min.	30	100 %
11-10	3:10	3:20	10 min.	30	100 %

Figure 6.3. Production rate recording form. (*Standard is the average number of units completed by nonhandicapped co-workers performing the same task within a specified period of time. Rate equals number of units completed within specified time frame divided by standard number of units completed within same time frame.)

A form such as the one in Figure 6.3 can be used to collect rate data at any point during or after the job training phase.

Attention to Task During job-site training it is important to monitor a student's on-task behavior. Knowing that a student is attending to task allows the trainer to decide when it is appropriate to phase out his or her presence from the job-site. When a student is having problems staying on-task this affects work rate as well as the relationship with the supervisor and co-workers.

An interval recording method can be used for assessing on-task behaviors during brief observation periods, and a data sheet such as that in Figure 6.4 can be used for recording on-task data. In this method, the job trainer sets aside a short time period, such as 5 minutes, during which the student is observed performing a particular job task. During this 5-minute period the job trainer does not prompt or reinforce the student in any way. Every 10 seconds the job trainer records whether the student is on-task by writing down a plus (+) or a minus (−) if he or she is off-task. At the end of the 5-minute observation period, the trainer determines the percentage of time the student

Trainee: _Tom_____ Job site: _Henrico Hospital_____

Trainer: _J. Trainer_____ Job title: _Pot Scrubber_____

Date	Observation period	Time started task	Time ended task	10-second intervals (+ = on-task; − = off-task)	Percent time on-task	Job duty
9/1	1. 5 min.	8:05	8:10	++−+++−+++−−−++ ++−+++−+++++++	80 %	Scrub pots
9/1	2. 5 min.	9:20	9:25	+++−+++++++++− +++++++++++++++	94 %	empty trash
9/3	3. 5 min.	3:30	3:35	++++++++++++++ +++++++++++++++	100 %	CLEAN STA-TION
9/4	4. 5 min.	2:45	2:50	++++−+++++++++ +++++++−++++++	94 %	scrub pots
9/5	5. 5 min.	1:50	1:55	++++++++++++++ +++++++++++++++	100 %	scrub pots
	6.					
	7.					
	8.					
	9.					
	10.					
	11.					
	12.					
	13.					
	14.					
	15.					
	16.					
	17.					
	18.					
	19.					
	20.					

20 session totals: 20 session average:

Figure 6.4.   Sample of work regularity/percent time on-task.

(continued)

Figure 6.4. *(continued)*

Definitions

On-task: _____

Off-task: _____

is on-task by dividing the number of (+)s recorded by the total number of observations:

$$\frac{(+)s}{(+)s + (-)s} = \text{\% time on-task}$$

Teaching Related "Survival" Skills

While students are learning specific vocational activities in job training stations in the community, they also must learn particular social,
community, domestic, and survival skills that are necessary to hold
a job (Moon, Goodall, Barcus, & Brooke, 1986; Rusch, Chadsey-
Rusch, & Lagomarcino, 1986). Some of the more commonly identified
survival skills include: riding a bus or some other form of public transportation, using vending machines, depositing a paycheck in the
bank, communicating basic needs such as the need to use the bath-
room, following one-step commands, dressing appropriately and staying groomed during the day, and displaying no disruptive behaviors.

One of the best ways to identify important survival skills is to ask
employers both in paid jobs that students are aiming for and in job
training sites what skills they consider essential. Rusch, Schutz, and
Agran (1982) identified specific vocational and related survival skills
that employers in Illinois considered requisite to job placement. Results of this extensive survey plus data obtained by a survey of local
employers can be used to identify the functional activities that constitute a vocational curriculum.

Determining Methods for
Fading Instruction During Job Training

During the later stages of a student's work in a particular job training
station, he or she should be given the opportunity to work directly
with the job supervisor and co-workers without direct instruction
from the teacher. This allows the employer to see competence,
provides the student with the confidence that he or she can function
independently, and gives the teacher extra proof that the student is
capable of surviving in a real work environment. However, getting to
this point is a process that requires weeks or months of systematic
fading of instruction.

The criteria a trainer uses to begin fading consists of results from

Table 6.15.   Fading instruction from the job-site

1. Programming naturally occurring cues such as:
    placement or location of materials
    presence of co-workers, student, or supervisor, or verbal, gestural, or pictorial instruction

2. Programming naturally occurring contingencies such as:
    corrections from co-workers or supervisors
    consequences of performing an action (leaving water on the floor in pot scrubbing area brings complaints)
    consequences of performing a job duty (job duties performed well brings increased co-worker praise)

3. Programming naturally occurring reinforcers:
    break times   vacation
    paychecks   social interaction with co-workers
    bonuses   pay raises

4. Expanding performance across:
    job duties (the entire job duty task analysis)
    job situations (situations such as fire alarms that occur infrequently)

5. Utilizing co-worker facilitators:
    to identify break time
    to increase on-task behavior
    to assist in emergency situations and in following emergency procedures
    (i.e., fire, bomb scare)

6. Training self-management:
    self-instruction   pictorial job duty booklet
    labeling   pretaped instructions
    picture cues   tactile cues
    checklists

7. Increasing production rate to company standards:
    self-recording
    model appropriate production rate
    use of a timer
    use of reinforcement
    use of systematic instruction procedures (i.e., changing criterion design)

probe data, and the student's work rate and ability to stay on task without prompting. As the data reflect increasing independence and improvements in work rate and quality, the trainer can be absent from the immediate work area for longer periods of time. Of course, this schedule of fading must be approved ahead of time by the employer, and the trainer's whereabouts should always be known to the employer and to co-workers.

Some of the methods for fading instruction on a job training site are provided in Table 6.15.

Developing Staff and Student Schedules

One of the most complex jobs for a teacher is the development of a classroom instruction schedule that reflects the daily and weekly routine for all students and instructors. Although it may be difficult to design, this schedule is critically important for several reasons. First, a written schedule is necessary to ensure instruction on all priority IEP or ITP objectives for each student (Wilcox & Bellamy, 1982). Second, a schedule provides an organized flow of activities that will serve to decrease "down time" or instances of miscommunication about what activities each staff person is responsible for performing (Snell, 1986). Finally, a schedule provides an additional form of documentation of the services being provided to students.

The references listed in the appendix contain guidelines for developing instructional schedules, and most of the sources even contain several sample schedules for one or several age groups. Following are several of the guidelines most frequently mentioned in those sources.

First, a schedule must contain a list of the specific tasks for which each student and staff member is responsible during every instructional period of the day. This may require more than one master schedule and, in fact, many instructors prefer a schedule for themselves, one for the class as a whole, and then a separate student daily schedule for each member of the class. Instructional periods are typically broken down into 6 to 15 smaller periods, each running from 15 minutes to an hour in length.

Second, the schedule needs to reflect, by priority, the IEP/ITP goals for each student. If the schedule of activities does not match these objectives, then training will be ineffective. As Wilcox and Bellamy (1982) stated, a good schedule will maximize the amount of instruction provided on priority goals for each student. It will also ensure that the staff who are teaching the skills considered most important for each individual student are the most skilled. Similarly, a good schedule will ensure that it is the most skilled instructors who are spending the most time with students who have the hardest time learning.

Another guideline is to make sure that community-based programs get scheduled first, since these are most difficult to implement. After scheduling community-based programs, inflexible activities over which the classroom teacher has no control, such as music or art class, must be scheduled. Time for staff monitoring and routine administrative duties must be built into the schedule. As much as possible, activities should be scheduled to occur at their natural time. In order to enhance generalization of learning, activities must be scheduled after there has been initial instruction by various instructors in a variety of settings. The schedule should also include as reinforcement some maintenance of instruction even after learning criteria have been met, in order to ensure that critical skills are not forgotten.

Students should be taught to independently follow an individualized daily schedule, as this survival skill is crucial to functioning successfully in almost all adult domains, particularly work. The type of schedule and the assistance provided in following a routine will depend on the student's age and his or her skill level in areas such as reading, telling time, and picture or symbol identification. Freagon et al. (1983) provided examples of different types of student schedules from those with words to those with pictures. Some of these schedules were designed in a book format with one activity per page, while some schedules contained activities for an entire week on a single page.

A Job Training Schedule   Ideally, the identification of specific job training areas for each student should take place at the beginning of

	Michael	Bob	Andrea	Jill	Joe	Sam
Sept 1– Oct. 15	Janitor-VCU (RRTC Staff)					
Oct. 15– Dec. 1	VCU B&G Area (Aide)			VCU B&G area (Aide)		VCU B&G crew (Aide)
Jan. 1– Feb. 15	Stock clerk at Bradleys (Aide)		Janitor-VCU (RRTC staff)		Stock clerk at Bradleys (Aide)	
Feb. 15– April 1				Janitor-VCU (RRTC staff)	Janitor-VCU (RRTC staff)	
April 1– June 15	Part-time paid janitorial position (MH/MR Job coach)	VCU maintenance grounds crew (Student teacher)	VCU maintenance grounds crew (Student teacher)		VCU maintenance grounds crew (Student teacher)	Janitor-VCU (RRTC staff)

Figure 6.5.   Class job training schedule for 1986-1987. The teacher utilizes a classroom aide, student teacher, a university grant program, and an adult service agency to enhance training. The aide, student teacher, and RRTC program can work with two or three students during any 6-week period. One student is placed in a paid job during the last 6 weeks of the school year.

each year, but the schedule should be flexible enough to allow for modification during the year. When there are limited job training stations in a community or limited staff to provide the training, an initial schedule that includes at least one or two training opportunities for each student will at least ensure some work exposure for every pupil. The classroom training schedule provided in Figure 6.5 indicates an initial plan for one high school class.

SUMMARY

The provision of appropriate school programming that results in quality student outcomes upon graduation is an extremely challenging and often overwhelming responsibility for educators. However, the issues that may arise are not insurmountable, and the benefits to students are numerous. This chapter has briefly outlined strategies and techniques that have been effectively used in organizing instruction and systematically effecting the process of transition for students into adult community life. Utilization of these strategies requires professionals to philosophically depart from traditional school-based educational practices and to implement innovative instructional procedures in natural community-based sites.

APPENDIX

Sources on Curriculum Design and Instructional Programming for Community-Based Programs

Brolin, D. E. (1982). *Vocational preparation of persons with handicaps*. Columbus, OH: Charles E. Merrill.

Falvey, M. A. (1986). *Community-based curriculum: Instructional strategies for students with severe handicaps*. Baltimore: Paul H. Brookes Publishing Co.

Gaylord-Ross, R. J., & Holvoet, J. E. (1986). *Strategies for educating students with severe handicaps*. Boston: Little, Brown.

Horner, R. H., Meyer, L. H., & Fredericks, H. D. (1986). *Education of learners with severe handicaps: Exemplary service strategies*. Baltimore: Paul H. Brookes Publishing Co.

Kokaska, C. J., & Brolin, D. E. (1985). *Career education for handicapped individuals*. Columbus, OH: Charles E. Merrill.

Rusch, F. R. (Ed.), (1986). *Competitive employment: Issues and strategies*. Baltimore: Paul H. Brookes Publishing Co.

Snell, M. E. (1986). *Systematic instruction of persons with severe handicaps*. Columbus, OH: Charles E. Merrill.

Wehman, P. (1981). *Competitive employment: New horizons for severely disabled individuals*. Baltimore: Paul H. Brookes Publishing Co.

Wilcox, B., & Bellamy, G. T. (1982). *Design of high school programs for severely handicapped students*. Baltimore: Paul H. Brookes Publishing Co.

Chapter 7

Adult Service Alternatives

Day Care or Employment?

UP TO THIS POINT DISCUSSION HAS CENTERED PRIMARILY ON TRANSITION program development and planning. The preceding chapters have thus set the stage for reviewing and discussing the major adult service options available to disabled youth after they leave school. As the model in Chapter 1 indicates, adult service and employment outcomes should be a primary goal of secondary special education and transition planning.

In the United States today there is a civil rights movement advocating improved employment opportunities for adults with disabilities. Historically, adults with disabilities have been either grossly underemployed or without work altogether. There are millions of people with mental, physical, and sensory disabilities who would like the opportunity to work but who are being denied this opportunity. The many reasons for this situation include: limited expectations and attitudes of professionals in the field, the unwillingness of businesses to make reasonable accommodations for people with disabilities, lack of sufficient funds for training and placement, and government disincentives to work.

It is the authors' belief that the problems suggested above are currently being resolved and will, in the near future, be overcome. A recent Harris Poll (February, 1986) indicated two out of three persons with disabilities are not working. The authors feel this situation is unacceptable. Furthermore, such a high unemployment rate for persons with disabilities is unnecessary. Research programs and innovative

---

This chapter was partially developed in conjunction with Dr. John Kregel, and we are indebted to him for his assistance.

practices currently taking place at centers in various parts of the country have shown that many more persons with disabilities are capable of full-time employment than are currently being placed.

The authors believe that society as a whole is not opposed to the employment of persons who are disabled. To the contrary, research suggests that business persons can and will be highly accommodative to the idea, especially in businesses needing to strengthen their labor force (Shafer, Hill, Seyfarth, Wehman, & Banks, 1987). However, it is the authors' belief that professionals in the field, special educators, rehabilitation counselors, adult basic skills educators, and vocational evaluators do not have high vocational expectations for the people they serve. These lowered expectations are shaped by outdated or inadequate training experiences or by lack of exposure to a program that is functioning successfully. Essentially, this civil rights movement is a plea to professionals in the field to seriously evaluate their potentially outdated methods of delivering vocational services and of creating real work opportunities for persons with disabilities.

This chapter discusses services that are currently available and how those services can be improved as totally new job opportunities are developed for persons with disabilities. The chapter considers two themes: 1) appropriate values of normalization, that is, real work for real pay, and 2) existing research that provides an empirical base for different types of adult/vocational service options. Normalization is a philosophy that suggests that people typically devalued by society, such as mentally retarded or mentally ill persons, should be treated in a normal fashion. The tens of thousands of handicapped youngsters that leave school each year will require one or more of the alternatives that are described below. The challenge to professionals will be to create as many viable options as possible within a given community.

EMPLOYMENT FOR INDIVIDUALS WITH DISABILITIES: A RATIONALE

Employment is a major element in the life-style of all people with or without handicaps. Type of employment, amount of money earned, and advancement opportunities directly affect how we look at ourselves, how society evaluates us, and the amount of freedom we have financially and socially. Meaningful work that pays a fair wage is everyone's goal.

Let us consider more closely some of the points noted above. For example, how much does type of employment affect our behavior and the behavior of others toward us? Often entry-level manual labor is seen as less desirable than office work, even though the laborer's wages may be equivalent to, or higher than, that of the office worker. In contrast, consider the situation of a person who is restricted to a developmental adult day program that serves only individuals with mental and physical handicaps, and that offers no opportunity for employment. A person in that position might find the prospect of even our entry-level manual labor position much more attractive. Employment offers that person not only financial gain but also the social rewards of family and community acceptance. The opportunity to make nonhandicapped friends would be a major advantage to non-sheltered employment. Hence, the type of employment we have can be an important determinant in how we evaluate ourselves.

The amount of money one earns is another major determinant in the material and emotional quality of one's life. If a person volunteers his or her services all the time without earning an income, society perceives that person differently than if he or she earns a wage comparable to that earned by nonhandicapped workers performing the same job. Generally, the more money one earns, the more freedom one has to make purchases and to establish personal independence as a consumer in the community. A person who earns $5.00 per week in a day program or sheltered workshop will probably have a lower perception of herself or himself than a person who earns $190.00 per week working in a community bank or bakery. Unfortunately, many disabled people earn very little money and this can be a major problem. Wolfe (1980) reports that disabled persons, on average, earn $2.55 per hour compared with over $4.50 per hour for nondisabled people. This type of signficant wage discrepancy denies a higher quality of life to individuals with disabilities.

The flexibility to switch jobs and to move to a more favorable work setting with better working conditions, higher salary, and increased job stability is an important employment option both for non-disabled persons and for persons with handicaps. Similarly, career advancement and mobility should also be available to people with disabilities. Also, jobs in real work settings that yield a decent wage often lead the way to better jobs with more pay.

The astute reader will observe that the word *opportunity* has been used several times already. No one has a right to a job. Jobs are not available for everyone, and one must demonstrate a certain degree of skill and aptitude to obtain a job. However, all nonhandicapped people have an opportunity to work if they so choose, and every effort should be made to provide job opportunities to the thousands of individuals with handicaps who would like to work and who *can* work if given the opportunity. That this potential labor force has remained untapped is especially unfortunate when one considers that this is not a "new" problem. The abundant literature spans the past 20 years; the articles consistently point out the vocational potential of handicapped people as workers. This literature indicates the progressively greater vocational potential of individuals with both mild and severe disabilities. What is unfortunate, however, is that there is an enormous schism between what we know can be done to improve opportunities, and what is actually happening in practice. What follows is a discussion of several of the most pressing issues concerning the employment of handicapped individuals.

THE COSTS OF UNEMPLOYMENT FOR PERSONS WITH DISABILITIES

In considering the seriousness of the unemployment problem for persons with disabilities, it will be helpful to review the costs of unemployment to society, to business, and to individuals with all types of disabilities. It is not difficult to see how the impact of this pervasive high level of unemployment can affect thousands of people, disabled and nondisabled. The points that follow address some of the adverse effects of denying meaningful employment opportunities to capable handicapped persons.

Human Dignity

Human dignity and self-worth of individuals with disabilities are not enhanced. The opportunity and ability to work in a real job that pays a fair wage is an important option for everyone, not just for persons with disabilities. It is apparent to the authors that, after talking with persons with disabilities and friends of individuals with handicaps, sustained employment is a critical avenue to other successful aspects of life such as health, friendship, self-esteem, and a feeling of purpose. Employment is often the key to improving an individual's self-image to reducing feelings of loneliness, and to progression toward a richer quality of life (Brolin, 1985).

Family Concerns

The concerns and doubts of families and friends of persons with disabilities must also be considered. The concerns of parents often center around the question of: "What will happen to my son or daughter after I'm gone?" or "Will my son or daughter be able to get a job after he or she completes school?" Sustained employment can help answer these legitimate and serious questions. While a job may not solve all problems, it will be a major step in the right direction, and families need professional service support and assistance in helping disabled individuals enter the labor force (Seyfarth et al., in press; Venn et al., 1977).

Earning Power

As noted earlier, wages for individuals with disabilities are poor. However, earning competitive unsubsidized wages provides the person an opportunity to have more independence within his or her lifestyle. Even at minimum wage levels of $3.35/hour the wage accumulation over time is considerable enough to allow workers with disabilities to spend money on housing, meals, and other discretionary items. Often fringe benefits are made available as well. Wages and benefits provide greater independence and improvement in the quality of life for citizens with disabilities. Hill, Wehman, Banks, and Metzler (1987) note that over 2 million dollars was earned by slightly over 200 people with IQs in the 30–55 range over an 8-year period. The wage accumulation and earnings associated with competitive employment is powerful indeed.

Economic Benefits to Society

Wages earned by citizens with disabilities typically flow back into the local and state economy. The impact of these wages on the local economy should not be minimized. When combined with the taxes that are paid, it is apparent that signficant reductions in the disabled employment rate would quickly add up to a considerable benefit for state and federal budgets and the economy as a whole. Again turning to the Hill, Wehman, et al. (1987) study, it is clear that the savings from adult service day program participation by clients who are competitively employed was incredible. In this study almost 2 million dollars was saved in alternative program costs alone for 225 clients with moderate mental retardation (IQ mean 44) placed in competitive employment over an 8-year period. Total public savings exceeded 3 million dollars when social security savings were included. These clients accumulated 2½ million dollars in wages. The grand total in Table 7.1 refers to all clients served by the Virginia Commonwealth University program.

There are other economic benefits of employment as well. For example, there are signficant costs to taxpayers in subsidizing restrictive "prevocational" or nonfunctional work adjustment programs that often do not lead to employment of persons with disabilities who have the potential to work. In addition to these program costs, the supplemental security income savings to the government can be tremendous for those who are able to work. While it is important not to take away

Table 7.1. Financial ramifications of competitive employment; cross section of clients with moderate and severe retardation

Code name	SSI	Estimated alternative program cost	Estimated total taxes paid	Public savings	Targeted Job Tax Credit	Project expenditures	Consequence to taxpayer	Cumulative wages
Ted	23,266.62	51,560.44	15,571.78	90,398.84	0.00	30,542.78	59,856.06	67,703.38
Bill	17,391.81	31,150.88	17,473.53	66,016.22	0.00	40,633.09	25,383.13	75,971.88
Len	11,095.71	24,508.29	11,615.21	47,219.20	0.00	28,404.58	18,814.62	50,500.90
Clyde	1,530.37	8,974.34	1,970.34	12,475.05	0.00	2,014.81	10,460.25	8,566.71
Donald	3,193.94	13,941.30	3,086.09	20,221.33	3,420.79	13,488.18	6,733.14	13,417.77
Jason	810.18	6,416.40	1,398.77	8,625.35	2,466.17	3,786.38	4,838.97	6,081.59
Charlotte	0.00	3,971.74	628.04	4,599.78	1,347.80	1,838.37	2,761.41	2,730.60
Ralph	0.00	3,994.04	918.30	4,912.34	1,978.72	4,341.26	571.08	3,992.61
Dottie	0.00	585.71	98.04	683.75	0.00	380.52	303.23	426.25
Arnold	0.00	2,062.48	199.80	2,262.28	0.00	2,313.06	−50.78	868.70
Horace	0.00	183.90	37.26	221.16	0.00	772.92	−551.77	161.99
Andy	0.00	4,570.46	652.00	5,222.46	121.45	5,916.54	−694.09	2,834.76
Cheryl	0.00	2,142.54	969.14	3,101.68	2,106.83	4,869.52	−1,767.84	4,213.65
Sara	0.00	795.92	217.26	1,013.18	0.00	3,197.51	−2,184.33	944.63
Harry	0.00	1,922.97	591.44	2,514.41	804.47	5,045.82	−2,531.41	2,571.50
Rudy	6,853.43	21,145.76	6,646.53	34,645.72	4,918.16	37,556.30	−2,910.58	28,897.95
Frank	168.00	7,802.60	636.97	8,608.45	1,384.71	12,033.27	−3,424.82	2,769.42
Wanda	1,242.51	7,760.81	2,702.10	11,705.41	3,472.74	18,557.39	−6,851.98	11,748.26
M + S total	306,756.83	1,055,194.83	351,689.76	1,627,618.20	192,730.44	1,212,117.88	525,071.88	1,503,779.72
Grand total	452,554.50	1,803,604.16	587,545.48	2,843,704.14	296,299.82	1,787,712.58	1,056,991.56	2,554,545.58

Social Security benefits from those in need, it is also fiscally and morally necessary to help those who can work to find employment. Service agencies, however, need to continue moving in a direction that fosters joint development of training efforts with industry. These training efforts need to culminate in employment that is not government subsidized.

Impact on Business and Industry

Business and industry lose an excellent source of good labor when competitive employment opportunities are not made available to citizens with disabilities. For example, one industry in which many workers with mental handicaps are employed is the hotel and restaurant industry. In a study conducted by the National Hotel and Restaurant Association (P. Nelson, personal communication, May, 1983), it was found that the average length of employment time for over 2,000 nondisabled workers was only 5 months; yet, data from supported competitive employment efforts in Virginia (Wehman, Hill et al., 1985) indicate that for 150 workers with mental handicaps in similar jobs, almost 19 months was the average tenure on the job. This is a reasonable figure, particularly when compared to the 175% turnover rate reported by the well-known fast food chain of McDonalds Inc. in a single 12-month (1981) period. This type of turnover is terribly expensive to business and industry, it can be partially offset by a pool of well-trained workers with disabilities.

Expectations of Family and Friends

Finally, the attitudes and expectations of family, friends, service professionals, and above all, the citizens with disabilities, are greatly influenced negatively when persons with handicaps are continually shut out from opportunities to earn decent wages and have a meaningful job. One is often viewed by others in the context of whether one has a job, how much money one makes, how long one has held his or her job, and what type of work one does. The gratuitous and chronic unemployment of persons with disabilities casts an unfair light on the capabilities of these persons.

MAJOR VOCATIONAL ALTERNATIVES FOR ADULTS WITH DISABILITIES

Listed in Table 7.2 are the numerous types of adult service activities and vocational alternatives for people with substantial disability. Very few local communities have more than two or three of these options, yet an ideal city or region would offer most of the employment

Table 7.2.   Adult services and employment alternatives

Adult developmental centers (activity centers, day centers)
Sheltered workshops
Job placement to competitive employment
Transitional employment
Supported competitive employment
Enclaves in industry
Mobile work crews
Small (specialized) businesses

alternatives. What follows through most of the balance of this chapter is a description of these adult service and vocational alternatives.

Adult Development Centers

In most cities and towns, young adults with mental and physical handicaps go to special centers after they finish school. Many go to places that are variously called adult activity centers, developmental achievement centers, stimulation centers, and the like. These day programs have grown enormously in number, with approximately 2,000 in the country. Many other young adults are accepted in work activity or sheltered workshop programs. Sheltered workshops number well over 5,000. But the majority of young adults with disabilities are at home because services are not available.

On the one hand, participants in day programs have the opportunity to learn daily living activities, to learn academics, and to be involved in recreation and in some work skill activity. Sheltered workshops, on the other hand, provide participants with contract bench work under sheltered conditions, and only with other persons with mental or physical disabilities. Sheltered workshop employees typically earn an average of $1 to $4 per day. Most young people with severe handicaps, as well as parents and professionals, have come to expect this form of service. With increasing numbers of students leaving school and needing adult services, there have been efforts to increase the number of segregated adult day programs. In most states, adult activity centers annually cost anywhere from $5,950 per client (Virginia) to $7,500 per client (Maryland or Ohio). Sheltered workshops usually cost approximately $2,500–$3,500 annually per client.

The special day program that takes place in a segregated center must come to an end. This arrangement focuses too many fiscal resources into buildings, not staff. Such a situation does not yield movement of persons with disabilities into employment: it minimizes their employment potential. Even more regrettable, the special day program segregates people with severe handicaps away from the community. The goal of these programs is not on finding clients community employment with decent pay—even though research has shown that programs with these goals are successful. The underlying assumption has been that clients are not "ready" for "real" jobs and need much more training before they can work in the community. The stigmatizing nature of these programs must stop, and funds channeled in this direction must be diverted to higher quality outcomes.

In the period between 1955 and 1975 there were very limited data or published research suggesting that individuals with significant mental and physical handicaps could benefit from real jobs paying unsubsidized salaries. During this time, it went without question that enrollment at a special day care center where individuals were offered continued special education and developmental activities was the best option for persons with disabilities. Often, in fact, it was the only option. Unfortunately, this kind of program is still very much in evidence, since the center-based approach is still popular across the country.

What needs to be considered is how to best convert these existing centers from day-care activity to supported employment activity. The emerging initiative toward enclaves, workcrews, and supported employment, that is, supported *competitive* employment, provides a basis for alternative day activity that is much more productive. Adult service administrators must evaluate and review the following issues as they consider converting center-based day program activity to industry-based supported employment:

1. What training is necessary to develop new skills and philosophies in service staff?
2. Conduct an analysis of funding sources and determine the best ways to utilize resources from different agencies.
3. Mobilize staff opinion, parent attitudes and the business community to accept the employability of clients with no previous work histories.

Sheltered Workshops

Sheltered workshops have for a very long time been considered the foundation of our nation's adult vocational service system for persons with disabilities. Over the past 2 decades the number of sheltered workshops in the country has grown tremendously. More recent data (National Association of Rehabilitation Facilities, 1984) indicate that the number of sheltered workshops has risen to over 5,000 nationally.

At the same time that the number of sheltered workshops in the country has risen substantially, these programs have come under attack from a number of different government agencies, and have been challenged by professionals and advocates as well (Buckley & Bellamy, 1985; U.S. Department of Labor, 1977; Whitehead, 1979). This public outcry over the limited results achieved by sheltered workshop clients has left the facility operators in a state of confusion. Many sheltered workshops are facing increasingly greater financial constraints, at the same time, they were struggling to redefine their position in relation to the newly emerging community-based employment programs.

Operational Problems in Sheltered Workshops   The major criticisms of the existing sheltered workshop system have been described earlier. Clients in these programs often earn insignificant wages. In addition, client earnings have not risen at a rate comparable to overall wages for workers in our country. Sheltered workshops by their very nature are segregated facilities, with no mission to provide clients regular contact with nondisabled individuals. These programs have come to be viewed as "dead end" facilities with little client movement into competitive employment (Buckley & Bellamy, 1985). The U.S. Department of Labor (1977) study cited previously found that only 12% of regular program clients were placed into competitive employment annually. Furthermore, for clients who had remained in workshops for over 2 years, the placement rate dropped to 3% annually. Similar findings were recently uncovered by Bellamy and his colleagues (1986). In addition to the previously cited concerns, sheltered workshops have traditionally been plagued by operational and organizational problems. Following are several examples of these problems.

1. *Sheltered workshops have generally been underfunded.* Funding levels provided to sheltered workshops have often been inadequate to meet the actual costs of these programs. Workshops have too frequently been forced to rely on United Way contributions, fund-raising activities, or other charitable contributions to support wages, staff salaries, and overhead costs. This situation has led to many workshops focusing their efforts on "keeping their doors open," that is, to keep the workshop operating, rather than on efforts to move clients into competitive employment.

2. *Sheltered workshops have failed to incorporate the most efficient business and industrial technologies.* Sheltered workshops are generally labor intensive, nonautomated industries. Many times workshops fail to incorporate state of the art practices in market-

ing, production, and management. This situation is frequently caused by a lack of available jobs. In order to provide work for the greatest number of individuals for the greatest amount of time, workshops frequently divide jobs into small units that provide activity for the largest number of clients. Workshops may fail to procure equipment or machinery that would make production more efficient, or they may fail to diversify, relying too heavily on the manufacture of crafts or other low profit merchandise.

3. *Sheltered workshop staff are frequently not prepared to perform the marketing and production management activities necessary to maximize profits and client wages.* In many instances, workshop and work activity center staff are human service professionals who do not possess the industrial management skills required in contract procurement and production activities. These staff members are frequently hired because they possess the skills and motivation to work in settings that serve persons with disabilities. While these individuals are highly dedicated and skilled in working with individuals with disabilities, the lack of business knowledge among workshop staff members, coupled with the low salaries they generally receive, serve to limit the ultimate financial and employment outcomes for workshop clients.

The Future of Sheltered Workshops The preponderance of problems associated with the sheltered workshop programs in this country have led some professionals to suggest that these programs should be phased out or eliminated entirely (O'Neill, 1983). It is the authors' belief, however, that this suggestion should be viewed with caution. A more effective course, in the authors' opinion, would be to assist these facilities in making the transition into programs that provide an array of supported employment options described later in this chapter (Wehman, Kregel, Banks, Hill, & Moon, 1987). Additional financial resources should be made available only when programs provide paid integrated employment opportunities for clients. This approach would allow these programs to transfer their resources into employment options that hold the promise of greater client job success at equivalent or reduced public costs. Start up monies will need to be provided to assist workshops in making this transition. Parent and consumer education programs should be initiated to assist clients and caregivers in accepting the risks and challenges associated with such a change. Finally, staff development programs must be designed to prepare existing workshop staff for the new roles and job responsibilities associated with the supported employment movement. Table 7.3 provides a summary of major characteristics associated with the

Table 7.3. Sheltered work

Feature	Description
Economic benefit to society	Limited
Economic cost to society	$2,500–$3,500/year per client
Fringe benefits	None
Integration	None
Job-site training	Minimal to none
Service provision	Ongoing
Service provision location	Facility-based
Staff to client ratio	1 Staff for every 10–15 clients
Type of work	Subcontracted bench work
Wages of clients	$1–$5/day

sheltered workshop option for youth who are leaving special education programs.

Placement into Competitive Employment The majority of students with special needs who leave public school special education programs will be able to enter competitive employment with the assistance of a vocational rehabilitation counselor. This traditional approach to competitive employment placement involves providing individuals a variety of *time-limited* services, that is, services that may be of an intensive nature, but are only provided for a specified period of time (See Chapter 1, OSERS transition model). Traditional placement services have the greatest applicability for individuals with mild disabilities (Vandergroot, 1987).

Vocational rehabilitation services can be divided into four categories. *Evaluation* services are intended to identify client strengths and weaknesses and to identify potential job placement alternatives and the services required to secure these alternatives. *Preplacement* services are designed to allow individuals to maximize their employment potential through traditional vocational training and work adjustment services. *Placement* services assist individuals in securing a job that allows them to realize their vocational potential. Finally, *postemployment* services are provided for the purpose of enabling the client to maintain employment and for assisting the client in future career advancement. Vandergoot and Worrall (1979) describe this process as: 1) preparation for a job, 2) finding a job, and 3) keeping a job.

Time-limited placement services are most frequently initiated through a comprehensive vocational evaluation. While a tremendous amount of professional and financial resources continue to be expended in the evaluation process, in recent years this activity has seriously been called into question. Critics have charged that the outcomes derived from this activity do not justify the large expenditures for vocational evaluation, and that financial resources should be channeled to other areas of the placement process. Wehman and McLaughlin (1980) have identified four types of vocational evaluation data. These include: 1) clinical assessment, that utilizes formal testing procedures to evaluate medical conditions, educational skills, adaptive behavior, vocational interests and aptitudes, and other factors; 2) work samples that are simulated activities intended to assess an individual's interest in and capacity for tasks associated with various job clusters; 3) situational assessment, in which clients are placed in employment settings to assess their general work behaviors, skills, and attitudes; and 4) job tryout, that focuses on an individual's ability to adjust to a natural job setting. The latter two types of assessment are increasingly being viewed as optimal for persons with severe disabilities. Individuals with significant disabilities often do not perform very well on formal tasks, and do better in real life learning situations.

Placement services lie at the heart of the time-limited services approach. Generally, placement strategies fall into two categories: client-centered or selective placement. The client-centered approach focuses on teaching the client general job-seeking skills. Rather than trying to obtain a job for the client, the rehabilitation professional tries to develop the client's skills to the point where the client can locate and obtain his or her own job. In the selective placement approach, the rehabilitation professional takes a much more directive role. In selective placement the counselor attempts to match the skills and needs of a particular client with the requirements and rewards of a specific job in the local community.

Postemployment services have traditionally been underemphasized in the vocational rehabilitation process (Dunn, 1979). Postemployment services refer to follow-up activities that may be provided after an individual has successfully secured a job. These activities may include assessing client and employer satisfaction with job performance, initiating needed work adjustments, and preparing the client for future career enhancement and job mobility.

The key feature of all these services is their time-limited nature. After an individual has successfully adjusted to the initial job, services are terminated shortly thereafter. While this action may exclude many individuals with severe disabilities from success within this model, for others time-limited services are entirely adequate. Some individuals may require assistance in determining the job for which they are best suited, need additional training to prepare themselves for the job, require specific help in obtaining their first job, and need support to adjust to the performance and social demands of the job. For these individuals, the traditional time-limited approach to competitive placement continues to meet their needs.

However, this time-limited approach has several shortcomings when applied to persons with truly severe disabilities. The typical vocational rehabilitation counselor may have an active caseload of well over 100 clients, which makes it impossible for the counselor to be actively involved in all facets of the placement process for all individuals. This forces the counselor to purchase services from a variety of different providers for a given individual, a situation that too often results in disjointed and uncoordinated service programs. Another major shortcoming is the lack of postemployment follow-up services provided in the model. Services to many individuals are terminated after the client has completed just 2 months of successful employment. The authors' research on the placement of persons with mental retardation using a more intensive placement approach, known as supported competitive employment, indicates that individuals with mild mental retardation are no more likely than persons with moderate or severe mental retardation to be successfully retained in competitive employment when a 6-month employment criterion is utilized (Hill, Banks, Wehman, & Hill, in press). While the time-limited approach may be appropriate for many individuals with mild handicaps, it seems clear that other mildly handicapped individuals require more intensive services to adjust to and maintain employment for extended periods of time.

Transitional Employment

An extension of time-limited job placement that has gained popularity in recent years is transitional employment. This model involves placement followed immediately by weeks or even months of relatively intensive job-site training. Work adjustment and social skills training activity is delivered while the person is already employed. However, this is a time-limited option; that is, once the student is stable on the job and needs no further assistance from the staff person, he or she will be left alone. There is no follow-along support. This model can be very helpful for the first time workers or for individuals who need some initial assistance. Transitional employment is an effective extension of time-limited job placement, since it allows for a more intensive approach to correcting any problems that the clients may have. Table 7.4 provides an overview of transitional employment. This approach is frequently more efficient and effective than trying to remedy problems arising before placement.

Table 7.4. Transitional employment

Feature	Description
Economic benefit to society..........	High
Economic cost to society	$2,500–$3,500/year per client
Evaluation........................	Clinical assessment, work samples, job tryout, and situated assessment
Integration........................	Moderate to high
Job-site training...................	Intensive work adjustment and social skills training delivered while client is employed
Placement.........................	Selective placement
Postemployment service	None
Service provision...................	Time-limited
Service provision location	Community-based
Staff to client ratio	1 to 1
Types of work......................	Service industry related positions
Wages of clients	Sub-minimum wage and minimum wage or above

SUPPORTED EMPLOYMENT

The preceding discussion of adult developmental programs, sheltered workshops, and job placement suggests that many persons with substantial handicaps will never gain entrance to employment in industry under the current service delivery system. Also, many significantly impaired persons will never earn money at a real job in the community without professional support. In response to this, the concept of supported employment has evolved within recent years as an alternative for persons with severe disabilities who cannot get a job or cannot hold a job without permanent follow-along support placement. Supported employment provides opportunities to work for the first time for many people who were previously unable to gain and maintain employment. Supported employment may take the form of different arrangements within industry or outside of industry, and may involve differing staffing patterns in different occupations. The major characteristics of supported employment can be found in Table 7.5 and are described below.

Supported employment was included in Title VII(c), of the Rehabilitation Act Amendments of 1986 for the first time as a major rehabilitation objective. The amendments define supported employment as:

Table 7.5.   Supported employment characteristics

Emphasis on people with severe disability who cannot hold employment without
  ongoing support
Integration with and around nonhandicapped co-workers
Permanent ongoing or intermittent support through the duration of employment
Real pay for real work—not work experience or volunteer work
Tangible outcome—not a process service activity

> . . . competitive work in integrated settings—(a) for individuals for
> whom competitive employment has not traditionally occurred . . .
> services available (but not limited to) provision of skilled job trainers,
> on-the-job training, systematic training, job development, follow-up ser-
> vices . . . (p. 8911, October 2, 1986).

This law provides for the allocation of funds for supported employment activity and development planning. The law also calls for
funds to be made available for major state level discretionary projects
to change day program systems for adult activity centers to industry-
based employment programs. In 1985, 10 states were funded for this
activity, and in 1986 another 17 states were funded, all by the Rehabilitation Services Administration, OSERS at the U.S. Department of Education. If the efforts for systematic change are successful within
these states, transition-age youth will have better employment opportunities after they leave school.

Paid Employment

*Supported employment is paid employment that cannot exist with-
out a regular opportunity to work.* The federal government has suggested that an individual should be considered to have met the paid
employment criteria of supported employment if he or she engages in
paid work for at least 4 hours each day, 5 days per week, or if he or she
works at least 20 hours per week. This standard is insufficient: it neither establishes a minimum wage nor determines a productivity level
for supported employment.

The amount of hours worked should not be viewed as the only
criterion for supported employment, because some people (such as
adolescents with severe handicaps) may choose to work only 15 hours
a week. The stipulation that there should be a minimum number of
work hours, however, does convey the seriousness that paid employment should have for the young person with disabilities.

Community Integration

*Work is considered integrated when it provides frequent daily social
interactions with people without disabilities who are not paid care-*

givers. The federal government has defined integrated supported employment programs as those programs where: 1) no more than 8 people with disabilities work together in a program not immediately adjacent to another program serving persons with disabilities, and 2) where persons without disabilities who are not paid caregivers are present in the work setting or immediate vicinity.

For example, an individual with severe cerebral palsy who works in a local bank producing microfilm records of transactions clearly meets the integration criteria for supported employment. Also meeting the criteria would be: four individuals with severe emotional disorders who work together in an enclave within a manufacturing plant, a mobile janitorial crew that employs 5 persons with moderate mental retardation in community worksites, and the staff of a small bakery that employs persons with and without disabilities.

Ongoing Support

Supported employment exists only when ongoing support is provided. In contrast to time-limited support, such as transitional employment, that may only be provided for a few months, ongoing support continues as long as the client is employed. Ongoing support takes place when public funds are made available on a continuous basis to an individual or service provider who is responsible for providing employment support and who uses these funds for specialized assistance directly related to sustaining employment. It is this aspect of supported employment that distinguishes the model significantly from other models. The ongoing nature of this support is reassuring to parents and employers.

Severe Disability

Supported employment exists when the persons served require ongoing support; it is inappropriate for persons who would be better served in time-limited preparation programs leading to independent employment. The most meaningful way to determine who should receive supported employment is to assess how likely an individual is to gain and retain employment. Youths who are highly likely to lose jobs shortly after placement because of their disability may be prime candidates for supported employment. This means that individuals labeled autistic; moderately, severely, or profoundly mentally retarded; or multiply handicapped are the most appropriate target groups for this approach. Without permanent, long-term, follow-along services at the job-site, these individuals would not be able to hold jobs.

Since supported employment has become such a widespread mode of employment in recent years, it is essential that service providers understand the above four characteristics clearly and without ambiguity. As this is written initial regulations in the May 27, 1987 Federal Register have not been published. Approximately 60–90 days after comments and further revision, the final regulations will be issued.

What follows are descriptions of several emerging supported employment models. These models are among the principle models currently receiving attention in the field, and they are among the most likely placement alternatives for youth with severe disabilities.

THE SUPPORTED COMPETITIVE EMPLOYMENT MODEL

Competitive employment is defined in this book as a real job providing the federal minimum wage in a work area with predominantly nonhandicapped workers.

The supported competitive employment model requires special assistance in locating an appropriate job, intensive job-site training for clients who are usually not considered "job-ready," and permanent ongoing follow-along services. A qualified staff person establishes a 1:1 relationship with a client in need of individual employment services and places and trains the client right at the job-site. *The person is employed immediately with wages paid by the employer.* Follow-along is differentiated from follow-up in that follow-along entails daily and weekly on-site evaluation of how the client is performing, while follow-up suggests only periodic checking at established intervals of time.

Supported competitive employment contrasts with traditional placement into competitive employment in that the latter is time-limited. That is, once the client has been placed and trained to the employer's satisfaction at the job-site, the service is terminated. With supported employment, there is a permanent commitment for follow-along services provided by professional staff. An approach that has worked well in Virginia has been for Virginia Department of Rehabilitative Services to fund the initial job placement and intensive job-site training costs through case service funds. The permanent follow-along component is paid for through local and state health/mental retardation funds. This interagency responsibility sharing is now taking place in at least four locations in Virginia (Hill, Hill et al., 1987).

Why Establish Supported Competitive Employment Services?

One question concerning supported employment that vocational rehabilitation experts who have been in the field for a long time are asking is: "Why do we need another service when we barely have enough case service dollars now to meet the increasing demand for services?" There are several answers to this question. First, most persons with truly severe disabilities will not be able to obtain a real job without ongoing professional assistance. In these cases, substantial planning and direct assistance is required to overcome such problems as transportation difficulties, parental concerns, employer skepticism, and the search for an appropriate job. Additionally, a specialized and individualized approach is required to ensure job retention.

A second justification for this approach is that many persons with severe disabilities will be unable to maintain employment without professional support. The amount and nature of support will vary from person to person and will, of course, be influenced by the nature of the disability. For example, one would expect that the amount of intervention required by an individual with severe cerebral palsy would decline over time, eventually reaching a point of very little follow-along. In contrast, the individual with a history of long-term institutionalization and a dual diagnosis of mental retardation and emotional disturbance would require greater periods of long-term support (Anthony & Jansen, 1984).

The inability of many persons with severe disability to transfer those skills learned in special centers to real jobs is a third reason for using a supported employment approach. Although "readiness" is a long and time-honored concept of vocational preparation in day programs, in reality, it has not helped us. Clients do not "flow" from work activity to workshop to competitive employment (Whitehead, 1979). Furthermore studies by Kiernan, Smith, and Ostrowsky (1986); Sowers, Thompson, and Connis (1979); and Wehman, Hill, Hill et al. (1985) clearly show that many persons who are considered unready for competitive employment do quite well with a supported competitive employment.

A fourth rationale for considering supported competitive employment is that it is the most effective use of limited case service dollars. Setting aside one's professional biases toward one adult service or vocational rehabilitation service versus another, the successes of supported competitive employment (see Rusch, 1986, for description of many of these programs, the March, 1985, *Psychology Today* (McLeod, 1985a), or the October 21, 1986 *Wall Street Journal* [Ricklefs, 1986]), suggest that the outcomes and costs associated with day center nonvocational skill programming, vocational evaluation, or work adjustment contrast strongly with the more successful outcomes and costs of supported competitive employment. Stated another way, why spend $2,000–$3,000 on "preemployment" preparation activity for a given client if roughly the same amount can be spent immediately on job coaching services (Wehman & Melia, 1985) in supported competitive employment? These are the types of questions and decisions that rehabilitation administrators and counselors will increasingly need to face.

A final rationale for use of this specialized placement approach is to meet the labor demands and needs of certain businesses and industries. The hotel and restaurant industry and the cleaning industry are two high growth areas in entry-level service occupations. Similarly, micrographics and basic computer operation are also growth industries in which persons with severe physical disabilities might be able to enter with support. Previous experiences in Virginia (Wehman & Hill, 1985) suggest that business personnel welcome this placement approach because it includes training and follow-along services.

Staffing Issues Related to Supported Competitive Employment

Traditionally, neither rehabilitation counselors nor special education teachers—two professionals that might meet staffing needs in this area—have been completely trained in the skills necessary for successful supported competitive employment. Thus, university field-based training programs will need to be developed in business settings. This is because close relationships must be established with business and industry, and because professionals working in supported competitive employment must understand personnel practices in business. The success of the entire supported employment initiative, in fact, is highly dependent on: 1) the willingness of business to hire disabled persons, and 2) the likelihood that business will allow professional staff to work at job-sites. The authors' research in Virginia as well as around the country (Rusch, 1986) demonstrate a high level of business support.

It is probable that two types of job coaches are necessary; a senior person with either a Bachelors or Masters degree, and a junior person. The senior person would provide job development, job placement, and initial intensive training and employer relations work. Once the client became "stabilized" at the job-site with greatly reduced staff assistance, a less skilled job coach could then be employed for follow-along (Harold Russell Associates, 1985). At this point, much more emphasis must be placed on job development, placement skills and behavior training, and on working with parents, social security representatives, and other key agencies. In short, rehabilitation, special education, business, and social work skills are essential for effectiveness in this role.

There are, of course, a number of ways to provide this service. For example, there is the intact unit approach that many rehabilitation facilities and other special center-based programs might find attractive. With this approach, approximately $20,000 (including fringe benefits) would be allotted for the senior staff person, $10,000 would be allotted for the junior person, and $5,000 would go for travel and supplies. The total cost would be $35,000. This group could expect to place approximately 12 persons with severe mental disabilities annually. Data from the Virginia group show 66%–75% 6-month job retention at the end of such a program (Wehman, 1981).

A second approach might be to deploy a small team of senior job coaches who, upon placement and training of clients, turn over their cases to follow-along and retention specialists. These specialists would have large caseloads of businesses, all geographically close to each other. There undoubtedly is no shortage of ways to determine the best deployment of staff. As noted earlier in Chapter 5, interagency agreements can be utilized to maximize the sharing of resources.

What Are the Best Settings in Which to Establish Supported Competitive Employment Programs?

Supported competitive employment programs are labor intensive, not capital intensive. Therefore, there is no need for a large physical space to house persons with disabilities during the day, since work with clients will take place directly in business and industry. The reasonable cost is an attractive feature of this vocational option. Many supported employment programs (e.g., Kiernan & Stark, 1986; Rusch, 1986) are established on this basis. However, there is no reason why effective placement and training programs cannot also result from community-based adult day programs, rehabilitation facilities, schools, and vocational technical centers. If there is already an aggregate of professional personnel existing in a given setting, then it may be possible to direct some of these persons into supported competitive employment activities.

In Virginia there are local rehabilitation facilities that receive rehabilitative case service funds to provide supported competitive employment for at-risk clients (Hill, Hill et al., 1987). As noted earlier in this chapter, facilities may become licensed to provide transitional and supported employment services until clients bcome stabilized in their new jobs. This may last from 6 to 12 weeks or longer, depending on the client's progress. At this point, the participating staff and business decide the level of involvement necessary by the supported employment specialist. Follow-along employment support services are then funded by the local mental retardation/mental health services. These costs are typically much less expensive (Wehman & Hill, 1985). It appears that this approach to implementing the program is successful, but is may be too early to evaluate these efforts. Finally, schools can also be logical settings from which supported competitive employment efforts can occur. With such a major push toward transition from school to work nationally, many schools are feeling greater amounts of pressure to provide placement for students with severe handicaps before graudation.

In short, we do not yet know which settings are ideal for supported competitive employment. In all likelihood, all of the settings described above may be appropriate given the right staff attitudes, funding base, and local economy. Table 7.6 is a summary of the principle characteristics of the supported competitive employment model.

Supported Competitive Employment and Severe Disabilities: Needs and Concerns

It would not be appropriate to close this section without emphasizing that a supported work approach to competitive employment has the ability to meet the needs of individuals with several types of severe disabilities. While the majority of the supported competitive employment programs nationally have focused on persons with mild, moderate, or severe retardation, it should be noted that individuals with autism, severe physical disabilities, head injuries, and significant psychiatric impairments can also benefit. Each of these populations exhibits behavior in travel and social situations that have typically

Table 7.6.   Supported competitive employment

Feature	Description
Economic benefit to society:	High
Economic cost to society:	Limited, especially over long-term period
Fringe benefits:	Equivalent to co-workers
Integration:	Moderate to high
Job-site training:	Intensive
Placement:	Selective placement
Postemployment services:	Ongoing follow-along
Service provision:	Ongoing
Service provision locations:	Community-based
Staff to client ratio:	1 staff to 1 client
Type of work:	Service industry related positions
Wages of clients:	Minimum wage or above

reduced their likelihood for competitive employment. What is not fully understood yet is how much staff intervention is necessary to begin to overcome the behavior problems associated with each of these disabilities. Also unknown is how much of this staff intervention would be distributed over the life of an individual's employment. Furthermore, specific job coach competencies may vary according to type of disability.

The overriding issue is not what type of disability is involved, but rather: Is this person likely to have difficulty gaining and maintaining employment? If so, then a supported competitive employment arrangement may be planned and undertaken by an appropriate service provider.

MOBILE WORK CREWS AND ENCLAVES

Mobile work crews and enclaves for adults with disabilities are employment options that have existed for many years (McGee, 1975), but that have recently received renewed attention within the supported employment initiative (Mank, Rhodes, & Bellamy, 1986). Both enclaves and work crews allow individuals previously served in sheltered employment alternatives an opportunity for meaningful employment in more integrated community-based settings. In both options, individuals with severe disabilities are provided continuous support by a human services professional in order to better succeed in more challenging employment settings. Workers are paid based on performance, and wages are equal to those paid nonhandicapped workers performing the same duties. While similarities exist between enclave and work crew programs, the focus of the following discussion will be on the contrasting array of approaches currently used to implement these two models.

Mobile Work Crews

Mobile work crews or work force teams generally comprise four to six individuals with severe disabilities who spend their day performing service jobs in community settings, away from a center-based rehabilitation facility or adult vocational program. Mobile work crews may operate independently as private, not-for-profit corporations, or they may be one of a large number of employment options administered by a rehabilitation or adult service agency. Whatever the organizational structure, the sponsoring agency contracts with community businesses or individuals to perform grounds or home maintenance, janitorial, or similar tasks. Workers are generally paid by the sponsoring agency based upon productivity. A training supervisor or manager accompanies the crew on a full-time basis and is responsible for training work crew members, for providing ongoing supervision to maintain productivity and quality control, and for guaranteeing that the contracted work is completed to required standards.

The work crew is staffed by a single supervisor or manager. The supervisor is responsible for all facets of the operation, including securing and negotiating contracts, training and supervising crew members, and maintaining program records. While the small size of the crew permits close supervision, the inclusion of individuals with significant learning and production problems and the reliance on a single staff member for supervision makes the operation of the crew challenging. Since the crew functions away from the service agency or rehabilitation facility, the manager's task is made even more difficult because the manager is often isolated from other professionals. Also, the need to provide continuous supervision to crew members often prevents the supervisor from performing the required contract procurement and administrative activities. In larger communities, establishing a number of crews may be one way in which direct and management functions may be shared to maximize total program effectiveness.

The flexibility of the work crew, both in terms of the type of work performed and in the composition of the crew, allows the model to accommodate the needs of individuals with a wide array of disabilities. The majority of work performed by work crews is in the area of building and grounds maintenance, although housecleaning in suburban areas, farm work in rural areas, and motel room cleaning in areas with large tourist industries have also been identified as successful alternatives. A crew may have contracts with a number of different agencies and may perform work in a large number of settings in the course of a week. While work crews have been successful in areas with high unemployment rates, securing enough contracts to provide work during all standard work hours is frequently a problem (Mank et al., 1986). Table 7.7 provides an overview of the features of work crews.

Mobile work crews are an option that may have particular applicability in small communities and rural areas. Service agencies in rural areas attempting to provide supported employment alternatives to persons with severe disabilities face a unique set of challenges. Many rural areas have a relatively high unemployment rate. With little or no industrial base, service agencies encounter serious problems providing access to an adequate amount of work for their clients. In addition, the small number of individuals requiring services within a large geographical area creates severe logistical problems for the

Table 7.7. Mobile work crew

Feature	Description
Economic benefit to society:	Moderately high
Economic cost to society:	Moderately high
Fringe benefits:	Usually very limited
Integration:	Moderate
Job-site training:	Moderate to intensive
Placement:	Selective placement
Postemployment services:	Ongoing follow-along
Service provision:	Ongoing
Service provision location:	Community-based: Multiple contracts with businesses in the local community
Staff to client ratio	1 staff to 3–6 clients
Type of work:	Home or grounds maintenance, janitorial, etc.
Wages of clients:	Paid by sponsoring agency; based on consumer productivity

agency. Furthermore, it is often difficult for centers to identify and recruit highly trained staff with the skills necessary to implement supported employment alternatives. A major strength of the mobile work crew model is its ability to provide stable employment for a small number of workers with severe disabilities in the types of work found in a rural area.

Enclaves

Enclaves are employment options in which small groups of workers with disabilities (generally six to eight) are employed and supervised among nonhandicapped workers in a business or industry. Continuous long-term supervision is provided on-site by a trained human services professional or host company employee. Workers may be employed directly by the business or industry, or they may remain employees of the not-for-profit organization that placed them (Rhodes & Valenta, 1985). Enclave members work alongside nonhandicapped workers performing the same work, although in some situations workers with disabilities may be grouped together to facilitate training and supervision.

Enclaves have excellent potential for inclusion in either supported competitive employment or traditional sheltered employment programs. The model provides intensive on-site supervision designed to maximize worker productivity and prevent job termination. Enclaves allow access to community-based employment settings for workers with substantial handicaps who might otherwise have trouble remaining employed when daily training and supervision is phased out. At the same time, enclaves provide extended employment in an integrated community setting for individuals who were previously served exclusively in segregated workshops or work activity centers.

The model may also be contrasted with the mobile work crew approach. Within mobile work crews, workers will generally move to different work settings on a daily basis, or may work at several different sites in the course of a single day. Enclave employees, however, are able to work in a single setting for a prolonged period of time. Additionally, enclave employees in some instances will be paid wages and will receive benefits directly from the company, whereas work crew members will remain employees of the sponsoring service agency for an indefinite period of time. In one demonstration (Rhodes & Valenta, 1985), workers who had reached 65% of standard productivity were hired as employees of the host company at a competitive rate and with full fringe benefits.

The critical features of the enclave model are the extended training and supervision provided to remedy low worker productivity and the difficulties inherent in adapting to changing work demands. Systematic intervention is necessary to allow workers to acquire all needed skills and to work at an acceptable rate. This extra support may in some cases be provided by the host company, but in most instances it is the responsibility of the sponsoring service agency. The enclave supervisor is the person most responsible for seeing that this support is provided. It is a major commitment for the company to hire a group of workers with severe disabilities, and to allow the involvement of an outside service organization. The enclave supervisor must be highly skilled in effective instruction and supervision techniques while also being sensitive to the production demands and concerns of the host company. Table 7.8 indicates a summary of enclave characteristics.

Major Outcomes Associated with Mobile Work Crews and Enclaves

The major goals achieved by mobile work crews and sheltered enclaves have been the physical and social integration of individuals with severe disabilities in natural work settings, and the generation of opportunities for workers with disabilities to earn significant wages. Wages paid to work crew and enclave members are based upon productivity, with members earning a percentage of the standard hourly wage for nondisabled individuals performing similar work. Since the workers in most instances are clients of a not-for-profit service agency,

Table 7.8. Enclave

Feature	Description
Economic benefit to society:	Moderately high
Economic cost to society:	Moderately high
Fringe benefits:	Limited
Integration:	Moderate to high, depending on type of enclave
Job-site training:	Moderate to intensive
Placement:	Selective placement
Postemployment services:	Ongoing follow-along
Service provision:	Ongoing
Service provision location:	Community-based: in a host company
Staff to client ratio:	1 staff to 6–8 clients
Type of work:	Assembly work for a host company
Wages of clients:	Workers are paid based on productivity. Wages are often comparable to those paid to nonhandicapped workers.

fringe benefits are generally not provided. Mank et al. (1986) report data from two mobile work crew agencies in which individuals earned from $130 to $185 per month. Rhodes and Valenta (1985) report total wages of $295 for six individuals in an enclave after 8 months of employment. Public costs are required to make up the excess costs incurred in both models due to low worker productivity and the expense of intense, continuous supervision. While these figures may not seem particularly high, they are significant when compared to earnings of clients in sheltered employment alternatives (Noble, 1985). For example, in the enclave described above (Rhodes & Valenta, 1985), the individuals involved had averaged less than $40 per month prior to placement in the enclave.

The outcomes associated with the work crew and enclave options must be evaluated in the context of the individuals served by these models. In most cases, workers are not making minimum wage, or they are making only a percentage of the prevailing competitive wage, and the public cost for the programs is not significantly less than the cost of traditional workshop programs. In spite of this, the models are justifiable on the grounds that they provide employment in integrated settings for individuals who traditionally would have no opportunity for such work. Individuals who have medical conditions such as seizure disorders or severe diabetes, or individuals who exhibit significant maladaptive behaviors such as stereotypic or inappropriate behavior may at long last have an opportunity to secure and maintain employment in a natural work setting.

THE SMALL BUSINESS OPTION

Another type of possible employment option has been the small business alternative. This option usually reflects a manufacturing, production, or assembly operation that occurs in a building located in the community. Two major characteristics of this option are: 1) its small size, that is, a maximum number of 8–10 disabled persons with an equally small number of nonhandicapped employees; and 2) homogeneity of the business—all employees are involved in the same trade. Potential businesses for this option would be: printing, electronics, or micrographics. Bellamy, Horner, and Inman (1979), who have been leaders in this type of vocational alternative, have successfully used this model with persons who are the most severely handicapped. Generally, persons who work in these settings are in continual need of behavior training and production training. For example, such workers frequently exhibit inappropriate social behaviors, move slowly, lack verbal and communication skills, and have limited self-care skills. Table 7.9 briefly summarizes this model.

DECIDING WHICH OPTION TO CHOOSE

Deciding which vocational alternative is the most appropriate for a particular situation can be difficult. Obviously every job situation in a specific industry is different. And as is evident from the models listed above, vocational alternatives vary. The mobile work crew program

Table 7.9. Small business

Feature	Description
Economic benefit to society:	Usually limited
Economic cost to society:	High
Fringe benefits:	Very limited
Integration:	Low
Job-site training:	Moderate to intensive
Placement:	Selective placement
Postemployment services:	Ongoing follow-along
Service provision:	Ongoing
Service provision location:	Center-based—usually within industrial park
Staff to client ratio:	1 staff to 8 clients
Type of work:	Printing, electronics, baking, micrographics
Wages of clients:	Sub-minimum based on client productivity

may be an excellent option because of special government contracts; the actual amount of work available during a 40-hour week may be limited by seasonal constraints. Movement out of restricted enclaves into a more dispersed arrangement may be an excellent or a poor choice, depending on the management philosophy toward integration.

What is most important for persons with disabilities and their families is to push hard for having multiple employment choices available in their community. The more employment options an individual has, the greater the likelihood that that individual will find job satisfaction and achieve long-term employment. It is a testament to the progress made in adult services that there are an increasing number of diverse vocational opportunities available to persons with disabilities in more and more communities. Ultimately, it will be best if vocational arrangements are offered in a variety of industries—not only in food service or benchwork assembly. This type of job development will depend directly on the economic conditions of the local community and on the creativity and ingenuity of the participating vocational professionals.

Chapter 8   *Defining Professional and Parent Roles and Responsibilities*

MR. WALKER[1], A SECONDARY SCHOOL CLASSROOM TEACHER OF STUDENTS with moderate levels of mental retardation, was conducting an individualized transition planning meeting for Mary, one of his students. Mary, age 15, had been targeted to receive formal transition planning for the upcoming school year. Because this was the first formal transition planning meeting conducted in Greenlake school, Mr. Walker had carefully selected a transition planning team that included all school personnel who were actively involved in Mary's daily schedule. He had been careful to invite the vocational rehabilitation counselor who was assigned to the students in Greenlake school. In addition, Mr. Walker invited the director of Community Living Alternatives, a private residential services provider in the Greenlake area. Mr. Walker had also explained the purpose and importance of the meeting to Mary and her parents and had persuaded them to attend.

At the scheduled time, Mr. Walker opened the meeting with Mary, her parents, four representatives from the school (the usual

---

[1] Although the examples in this chapter represent compilations of actual experiences, the names and localities have been changed.

This chapter is an expansion of an earlier article by Everson, J. and Moon, M. S. (in press). *Transition services for young adults with severe disabilities: Defining professional and parental roles and responsibilities.* Journal of The Association for Persons with Severe Handicaps.

members of Mary's IEP team), and two representatives from adult service agencies in attendance. Based on the workshops he had attended on transition planning, Mr. Walker began by announcing that the team's purpose in meeting was to develop an individualized transition plan (ITP) that reflected employment, community living, and recreation goals for Mary once she left the school system. Additionally, the team would outline the training and support services Mary would need in order to achieve these outcomes. Mr. Walker suggested supported competitive employment as an employment objective for Mary during her final year of school. He also suggested community-based vocational training for Mary as a kitchen assistant at a local restaurant during the next school year. The vocational training would be provided by Mr. Walker and the vocational special needs teacher.

Ms. Jackson, the vocational rehabilitation counselor, protested, "There are no supported work providers in the Greenlake area! I don't understand why I am even here; Mary won't be assigned to my caseload for another 6 or 7 years!" Mary's parents spoke up, "You always told us that the best placement for Mary when she finished school would be the sheltered workshop. What in the world is supported work? And why is this person from Community Living Alternatives here? We've already decided that Mary will continue to live at home with us as long as we can take care of her." Mary's occupational therapist protested, "Mary can't be placed in a training program next year. She has to have her therapy twice a week." The vocational special needs teacher pointed out, "I work with 15 students at the vocational technical center already. I can't possibly work with Mary at another site."

What happened to cause so much confusion and territorialism at Mary's meeting? Could this situation have been avoided?

A local core team had been meeting for the past 9 months as a task force charged with addressing local transition needs in Greenlake County. After nine meetings, the team was unable to reach agreement on what changes were needed in the secondary special education programs, what new employment and residential opportunities were needed for graduates of Greenlake school, or whose responsibility it was to provide these new vocational and residential services. Each meeting ended with the agreement that no decisions could be finalized until each team member had cleared the decision with his or her supervisor. Several team members were ready to disband the core team because of their own frustration and the team's lack of progress.

What happened to cause so much confusion and territorialism with this local core team? Could this impasse have been avoided?

DEFINING ROLES AND RESPONSIBILITIES

In both of the examples described above, the difficulties experienced by the team members were caused, at least in part, by unclear definitions of the roles and responsibilities each person was expected to play as a member of the transition team. In transition planning and implementation, each team member plays a vital role as a representative of his or her agency or discipline. Additionally, each team member must also be willing to explore and assume new and creative roles as the transition process unfolds. Because no single agency or discipline currently has the technical skills or the fiscal resources to plan and implement the transition process on its own, all participating agencies, disciplines, and parents must agree to work together to combine their skills and resources. Thus, clear definitions of roles and responsibilities of all participating professionals and parents are crucial prerequisites to the development of coordinated interagency and transdisciplinary transition services. (See Chapters 3 through 5.)

The purpose of this chapter is to define the participants' "optimal" roles, and to outline both the administrative and direct service responsibilities that should be assumed by professionals and parents participating in the transition process. Additionally, the chapter presents strategies for developing parental and professional roles in interagency and transdisciplinary transition planning teams. These roles are defined as "optimal" because they are not roles that professionals and parents are currently playing as they struggle with planning and with implementing the process of transition from school to adult life. The roles and responsibilities that are described in this chapter are based upon two assumptions: 1) that transition planning is by definition an interagency process that requires the coordination of skills and resources by core team members and ITP team members, and 2) that transition planning requires the exploration and assumption of new roles and responsibilities by participants in order to maximize the coordination of existing skills and resources.

Roles and responsibilities for all participants are defined on an administrative level and a direct service level, because commitment to change and coordination of resources are essential at both levels. Administrators must extend financial and policy support to service providers and youth; service providers must implement transition procedures, collect necessary outcome data, and provide feedback on their needs and their client's needs to administrators. Change at one level without equal commitment to change from the other level will result in a system that is misaligned and that frustrates the efforts of administrators and service providers. Comprehensive transition management therefore requires alignment of services and resources at both the administrative and direct service levels.

Special Education

A special education director or other educational administrator is a critical member of a local core team because he or she is charged with the responsibility of planning interagency transition procedures. In a recent survey of secondary special education administrators in Oregon, 62% of the administrators surveyed felt that it was important for their district to assume responsibility for transition (Benz & Halpern, 1986). These same administrators also expressed concern about the quality of transition services being offered by their districts. At a direct service level, the special education teacher and the voca-

Table 8.1.   Secondary education preparation responsibilities assumed by special educators

Administrative responsibilities

Establish redirection of curricula funds for community-based vocational training.

Establish flexibility in teachers' and aides' classroom roles and responsibilities to enable teachers and aides to teach in the community.

Ensure liability coverage for community-based training and modify written policies and procedures to reflect service delivery changes.

Establish local follow-up studies of graduates of secondary programs to provide feedback to secondary programs.

Establish cross-agency inservice training and parent training and support efforts.

Establish a business advisory committee in cooperation with the vocational education administrator to obtain feedback and support from local employers on vocational curricula and community-based job-sites.

Direct service responsibilities

Identify and evaluate vocational training sites in the student's local community.

With the assistance of the vocational education teachers and other ITP planning team members, provide students access to two or more community-based vocational training experiences during the secondary years.

Identify and evaluate domestic, leisure, recreation, and community functioning sites in the student's local community.

Provide students access to a variety of activities in integrated community sites during the secondary years.

With the assistance of the vocational rehabilitation counselor and vocational educator, collect and analyze evaluation data.

Assure "optimal" parent, family, and student involvement in the educational preparation process.

tional rehabilitation counselor are the pivotal people in the implementation of the transition from school to work process for students (Everson & Moon, 1987). In the Benz and Halpern study, 36% of teachers and 32% of administrators felt that transition coordination was the responsibility of the secondary special education teacher.

Because special educators are mandated by law to provide educational services for youth with disabilities through early adulthood, they are the professionals most likely to be asked to assume two key roles in the transition process: 1) preparing students for transition, and 2) initiating the transition process. Preparation of students with disabilities for transition assumes that the goal of secondary special education is to identify the future environments that graduates are likely to utilize, and to train students in the skills needed in these environments (Wilcox & Bellamy, 1982). The implied objectives of this preparation are employment—either supported or non-supported—increased community integration, and decreased dependence on social service systems.

If special educators accept the preparation of students for adult life as the goal of secondary special education, then they must also be willing to accept responsibility for graduates' achieving or not achieving these outcomes. Recent literature focusing on secondary special education curricular and graduate follow-up studies (e.g., Falvey, 1986; Freagon et al., 1986; Hasazi et al., 1985; McDonnell & Hardman, 1985; Mithaug et al., 1985; Wehman, Renzaglia, & Bates, 1985; Wilcox & Bellamy, 1982) has isolated the following responsibilities that special educators should assume in order to better prepare students for adult employment and community living outcomes. These responsibilities are described in Table 8.1.

Special educators who agree to accept and implement the responsibilities outlined in Table 8.1 will increase the likelihood that secondary students with moderate and severe disabilities will receive an education that will serve as a strong foundation for the transition process (Wehman, Kregel, & Barcus, 1985; Will, 1984b). But these responsibilities require significant changes in the way secondary special education services are currently provided to youth with moderate and severe disabilities. A change in the typical secondary special education delivery system from predominately classroom-based to predominately community-based requires administrators, classroom teachers, and paraprofessionals to both define the goals they expect students with disabilities to achieve, and to accept responsibility for students who are not prepared to achieve these outcomes. This change in educational philosophy and service delivery procedures requires teachers to accept new and creative roles in their local community. In several locations across the country, special educators have expanded their role of vocational preparation to include job placement for students in their final years of school (Wehman, Hill, Wood, & Parent, 1987). Although this is a controversial role among many teachers and administrators, it is an example of creative partnership between educators and vocational rehabilitation counselors generated to reduce unemployment among youth with disabilities.

The second role that special educators are likely to be asked to play is that of initiator of the transition process, both for a local community and for individual students. Initiation of transition planning requires special educators to loosen their hold on students, and to form partnerships with parents, adult service providers, and representatives from business and industry. Transition initiation includes the identification of students for transition planning, the development and coordination of individualized transition planning teams, and the implementation and coordination of identified goals once an individualized transition plan (ITP) is written. Table 8.2 lists responsibilities special educators must be willing to assume as part of the transition initiation role (Freagon et al., 1986; McCarthy, Everson, Inge, & Barcus, 1985; Pietruski, Everson, Goodwyn, & Wehman, 1985).

The responsibility for initiating transition is a task that many special educators and administrators are increasingly willing to accept (Freagon et al, 1986; Lambrou et al., 1986). However, a caveat is warranted here; transition planning is only a bridge between a secondary

Table 8.2. Transition initiation responsibilities assumed by special educators

Administrative responsibilities

Establish and participate in a local interagency task force or core team for transition into adulthood planning.

Designate agency liaison and define guidelines for local and building level transition planning.

Target names of students for transition planning and coordinate data management.

Attend ITP planning meetings for individual students.

Establish local interagency agreements with key agencies and organizations.

Direct service responsibilities

Organize and attend individualized transition planning meetings.

Coordinate the development and implementation of transition plans.

Identify referral needs and ensure that referrals will be made to appropriate adult services and agencies.

Ensure "optimal" parent, family, and student participation in the transition planning and implementation process.

program and employment including other adult opportunities. Transition planning can only be as good as the secondary program it uses as a foundation and the adult services it moves students into (Wehman, Kregel, & Barcus, 1985; Will, 1984b).

Vocational Rehabilitation

Historically, state and local rehabilitative services were designed to assist individuals reenter the work force and/or to regain independent living skills after injury or illness. The focus was on rehabilitative services rather than on habilitative services. Because of these limitations, vocational rehabilitation typically provided successful job placement services for high school graduates with less severe disabilities, but was less likely to serve young adults with minimal vocational preparation or prior job experiences.

Although rehabilitative services across the United States are beginning to respond to the habilitative needs of individuals with more severe developmental disabilities because of the mandates of the Rehabilitation Act of 1973 and amendments of 1986, many parents and educators still have questions about the role rehabilitation services can play in the transition from school to work process. The local department of rehabilitative services will be able to provide local core teams and individualized transition planning teams with information on the variety of vocational and independent living services provided by state and local agencies.

Applicants referred to rehabilitation services are first evaluated to determine eligibility for, and potential to benefit from, rehabilitation. If a referred client is deemed eligible, a vocational rehabilitation counselor may provide any or all of the following 15 services:

1. Guidance and counseling
2. Vocational evaluation
3. Physical and mental health and medical services
4. Vocational training
5. Financial maintenance
6. Transportation
7. Family services
8. Interpreter services
9. Reader services
10. Telecommunication aids and devices
11. Recruitment services in public service employment
12. Job placement, including supported employment placement
13. Postemployment services
14. Occupational licenses needed to enter an occupation or employment

15. Any other services that can be expected to assist an individual with a disability in obtaining employment.

Specific services vary from state to state depending upon the flexibility of the funding levels. However, all states receiving Title I monies under the Rehabilitation Act of 1973 must provide the services listed in the 15 categories above to eligible individuals. When a state cannot furnish services to all persons who apply, the state must arrange service provision to include individuals with severe disabilities. Rehabilitative services are also time-limited, whereas the services typically provided by or purchased by departments of mental retardation and mental health are generally provided on a long-term basis.

The inclusion of a vocational rehabilitation representative on a local core team and on transition planning teams for students in their final year of school is essential because of the important role the representative plays in the student's vocational evaluation, job placement, and supported employment. A special education teacher and vocational special needs teacher who have combined their resources to prepare a student for employment and to initiate comprehensive transition planning have provided the vocational rehabilitation counselor with the "proof" he or she needs to become involved with a student's ITP planning. A comprehensive transition plan can assist the rehabilitation counselor in assessing the needs of transition-age youth and in choosing the most appropriate services available in the locality. Working closely with a student and his or her transition planning team, the vocational rehabilitation counselor may provide job placement, supported employment, or any of the services listed above for a student with disabilities. Job placement must be seen as a joint effort between educators and vocational rehabilitation counselors, and not as the sole responsibility of any one person.

Traditionally, local vocational rehabilitation counselors working within a public agency have played a broad *case management role* through the purchase of services (Tooman, Revell, & Melia, 1986). As members of local core teams and transition planning teams, rehabilitation representatives may extend this role to ensure dissemination of accurate information to parents and educators. The information being disseminated would include behavioral and standardized vocational evaluations of a referred student's employment potential (Ditty & Reynolds, 1980; Everson & Moon, 1987). Table 8.3 lists the optimal responsibilities assumed by representatives of public rehabilitation agencies as they perform a case management role in transition planning and implementation.

Table 8.3. Case management responsibilities assumed by vocational rehabilitators

Administrative responsibilities

Develop vendorship (Hill, 1986) and purchase of service agreements with employment and supported employment service providers.

Establish and participate in a local interagency task force or core team for transition into adulthood planning.

Designate agency liaison for local transition coordination.

Provide inservice training to parents and school personnel on agency's criteria for eligibility and service provision.

Establish local interagency agreements with key agencies and organizations.

Direct service responsibilities

Attend ITP planning meetings for students during their final year of secondary program and/or at age students are at high risk for dropping out of school.

Serve as a consultant to ITP planning team throughout secondary years.

Gather and analyze vocational assessment data from a variety of sources for referred students.

Coordinate and monitor the vocational training, job placement, or supported employment placement of postsecondary students.

Identify referral needs and ensure that referrals will be made to appropriate adult services and agencies.

Increasingly, professionals with rehabilitation counseling backgrounds will be playing a *direct service role* as supported employment specialists or job coaches in the transition from school to work process (Szymanski, Buckley, Parent, Parker, & Westbrook, in press). Supported employment specialists may operate out of for-profit or not-for-profit organizations that provide supported employment services to individuals with severe disabilities. Vocational rehabilitation counselors from public agencies may purchase services from these organizations through a vendorship agreement (Hill, 1986). The role of supported employment specialist or job coach requires skills and responsibilities that are not unique to any one discipline or agency. Recent literature has suggested that supported employment specialists require technical skills and communication skills that cut across various disciplines (e.g., Moon et al., 1986; Poole, 1985; Wehman & Melia 1985). For example, vocational rehabilitation training is one of several disciplines that have become increasingly involved in direct provision of supported employment services.

Case Management Agencies and Organizations

Case management agencies generally handle a variety of services that are typically provided by state and local human service agencies such as the department of mental health, department of mental retardation, department of social services, and developmental disabilities planning councils. Population specific groups such as departments of the visually impaired, United Cerebral Palsy, and programs for individuals with autism may also provide such services. Eligibility criteria, referral procedures, and types of services provided vary across agencies and organizations as well as across states and localities.

Agencies and organizations providing case management services may assist transition-age youth in a variety of ways. First of all, they play an *information resource role* (O'Neill, personal communication, October, 1986) as members of local core teams and as members of individualized transition planning teams. In this role, case management agencies and organizations may assist in analyzing the impact of employment on social security and medical benefits, and in relaying this information to clients and their families. Case management agencies and organizations may also assist with residential placements, family support services, advocacy, and guardianship issues. Table 8.4 lists in further detail the various responsibilities that case management agencies or organizations may optimally play as information resource specialists in the transition from school to adult life process.

Table 8.4. Information resource and direct service responsibilities assumed by case management agencies and organizations

Administrative responsibilities

Establish and participate in a local interagency task force or core team for transition into adulthood planning.

Designate agency liaison for local transition coordination.

Provide inservice training to parents and school personnel on agency's or organization's eligibility information and service provision.

Coordinate data management of referral and service needs for local transition-age students.

Establish local interagency agreements with key agencies and organizations.

Direct service responsibilities

Attend ITP planning meetings for students during their final 2–3 years of school and/or at age students are at high risk for dropping out of school.

Share responsibility for assessment of student's needs and for referral procedures with other ITP team members.

Provide information to the team on available community resources that may be utilized by the family and student (e.g., residential, family support, medical, income support, therapy and counseling).

Conduct home visits as needed.

Provide follow-along services once student has been placed in employment and in other adult service programs.

The Developmental Disabilities Act of 1984 (PL 98-527) has added "employment related" activities as a new priority service by 1987 for all state agencies administering developmental disabilities funds. Additionally, the Omnibus Reconciliation Act of 1981 (PL 97-35) has enabled those states who currently have Medicaid waivers to use Medicaid monies for employment and supported employment services. The passage of the Employment Opportunities for Disabled Americans Act (PL 99-643) in November of 1986 provides permanent authorization of Section 1619 of the Social Security Act. Section 1619 enables individuals who receive Supplemental Security Income (SSI) to retain partial SSI and Medicaid coverage up to a certain employment level. Use of developmental disabilities funds by case management agencies and organizations will increasingly allow them to assume a *direct services role* or to purchase direct services in the implementation and follow-along of transition goals particularly in supported employment services.

Although these three legislative acts have reduced some barriers to redirecting funding toward supported employment and community living alternatives, there are still significant disincentives blocking the redirection of funds for case management services. Thus, administrators and direct service providers often have to rely on creativity and innovativeness to provide optimal case management services. O'Neill (personal communication, October, 1986) has suggested that funding coalitions between education and adult service agencies that make transition-age students and young adults a service priority need to be designed at the state and local level. Local interagency agreements outlining the goals of transition planning and the specific responsibilities case managers can assume will help to initiate and formalize the changing role process, and to redirect existing funds toward employment and other community-based transition outcomes.

Vocational Education

Vocational educators have been actively involved with vocational training and job placement programs for students since the passage of the first Vocational Education Act of 1963. Amendments in 1968 mandated, for the first time, that limited federal funds (10%) from the Act be used for special education students. It wasn't until 1976, however, that states were required to match the 10% of federal funds allocated for students with disabilities. Most recently, the Carl D. Perkins Act of 1984 argued for equal access to vocational education programs for students who have been traditionally underrepresented in vocational education programs. Under this act, the practice of matching federal and state funds would be continued. The language of the 1984 act has, for the first time, strongly supported the participation of individuals with moderate and severe disabilities in vocational education programs through the provision of supplemental staff, materials, and services such as adaptations to existing curricula (Conaway, 1986; Rezeghi, 1986). Vocational special needs teachers are available in many LEAs to provide assistance and support to students with disabilities in vocational education classes.

Charlotte Conaway (1986) has defined the role of vocational educators as *providers of occupational preparation*; this preparation is intended for secondary school students who have a wide range of abilities. Vocational educators are trained to teach specific occupational skills that will prepare students to be competitively employed. In the role of providers of occupational preparation, vocational educators may assume a variety of administrative and direct service responsibilities that will enhance the chances of obtaining employment for students with more severe disabilities. Responsibilities that are increasingly being assumed by vocational educators during the transition process for youth with moderate and severe disabilities are described in Table 8.5.

The combination of the special educator's skills in teaching individuals with disabilities and the vocational educator's skills in identifying and teaching vocational skills in a community can result in a comprehensive approach to vocational training and job placement that will benefit students with moderate and severe disabilities.

Parents and Families

Professionals often state that parents and family members are the most important elements in the transition from school to adult life process, because they are the only people to have continuous and stable contact with the student throughout the entire process (Everson & Moon, 1987). However, as many parents have pointed out (e.g., M. Brooks, personal communication, 1986), it is unfair for professionals to assume that parents are willing and able to assume an active case management role during a lengthy transition period that may last as long as 8–10 years. Brooks (1986) has commented, "We parents are not always 'optimal'. Flexibility in assigning parent roles is essential and professionals cannot make assumptions about where parents are coming from and what they should do. Parent involvement ranges from case management and chief advocate to no active involvement."

Individual transition planning teams need to encourage active participation by parents and other family members during the secondary school and late transition years. Professionals must be able

Table 8.5. Occupational preparation responsibilities assumed by vocational educators

Administrative responsibilities

Establish and participate in a local interagency task force or core team for transition into adulthood planning.

Designate agency liaison for local and building level transition planning.

Target names of students for inclusion in secondary vocational education program and coordinate assessment data.

Assure information dissemination on vocational education to parents and students no later than the beginning of the ninth grade.

Establish guidelines for equal access of students receiving special education services in vocational education programs through supplemental staff materials, services, and changes in curricula.

Establish a business advisory committee in cooperation with the special education administrator to obtain feedback and support from local employers on vocational curricula and community-based job sites.

Direct service responsibilities

Attend the ITP planning meetings of all students receiving special education services to provide input on appropriate vocational goals.

With the assistance of the special education and vocational rehabilitation counselor, collect and analyze evaluation data.

Consult with the ITP team on local employment trends, job outlooks, and specific skills required for jobs.

With the assistance of the special education teacher, identify and analyze community-based vocational training sites in the student's local community.

With the assistance of the special education teacher and other ITP team members, teach a variety of community-based vocational training skills to secondary students.

Assist with job placement and job-site training or postsecondary vocational preparation for students during their final year of school.

and willing to work with parents to assess the role they would like to assume and which of the associated responsibilities they would like to undertake. The transition of any child from adolescence to adulthood is a stressful time for most families (Olson et al., 1984), but these stresses are different and sometimes more intense for families with a disabled member (Brotherson, Backus, Summers, & Turnbull, 1986). Professionals serving on transition planning teams must be sensitive to a family's needs and expectations and must address these needs during the development and implementation of individualized transition plans.

The "optimal" role, therefore, that parents should assume during the transition planning years is simply that of a *participant*; however, additional parental responsibilities may be encouraged and nurtured

Table 8.6. Participant responsibilities that can be assumed by parents and families

Attend ITP planning meetings.

Provide input to the team on family's needs and the young adult's needs and the specific responsibilities the family is able and willing to assume.

Mobilize the team to develop a plan that integrates the young adult into the community and decreases his or her dependence on the family and on social service systems.

Focus the team's planning on the individual student's and family's needs.

Request information on the various issues that the family will need to address— for example, residential, recreational, guardianship, financial, medical, social, behavioral, or sexual issues.

Provide informal home and community skill training and provide behavioral intervention that compliments the secondary curricula.

by professionals who are sensitive to the individual family's needs. Professionals must be willing to work as a team with parents, and "optimal" transition planning needs to be set in place for every child regardless of the extent of parental involvement (Brooks, 1986).

Examples of responsibilities that parents can assume as participants in the transition process are outlined in Table 8.6 (Brooks, 1986; Brotherson et al., 1986; Goodall & Bruder, 1986).

Educationally Related Services and Medical Services

For many secondary students and young adults with moderate and severe disabilities, occupational therapists, physical therapists, speech therapists, audiologists, school psychologists, school nurses, and social workers will play an active and direct service role during the transition years. These professionals provide educationally related services under the guidelines of PL 94-142 to many students who have been targeted to receive special education services. As members of IEP/ITP planning teams, they may play a critical role in the vocational, recreation, and independent living preparation of secondary students with disabilities. Table 8.7 describes some of the responsibilities and services professionals may optimally provide in their roles as *transition preparation* personnel.

The assessment, training, and therapy provided by these professionals must be integrated into the curricula and written into the transition goals of all secondary students who require their services. This means that transition planning teams may, for example, seek the assistance of the targeted student's occupational therapist in helping the student eat more independently in the employee's lunchroom on a

Table 8.7.   Transition preparation responsibilities: Educationally related services and medical professionals

`dministrative responsibilities

`tablish cross-agency and transdisciplinary inservice training for profes-
`ls and parents.

`h procedures and policies to assist direct service providers in provid-
`nity-based therapy and training.

`rship to core teams in identifying ongoing medical, therapeutic,
`es for postsecondary youth.

`nsibilities

`l, therapeutic, and psychological expertise to the plan-
`development.

`ce of the other ITP team members, provide assessments and
`ormation related to their individual areas of expertise.

`n training and therapy in the community as students are placed in
`unity-based sites.

`sist parents and students in identifying ongoing needs for medical, social, and therapeutic services after graduation. Assist with securing referrals and funding for needed services.

Conduct home visits as needed.

job-site. The physical therapist may assist the student with stepping from sidewalk curbs onto public buses during travel training to and from the job-site. Or the speech therapist may work with the student to answer co-worker's questions more clearly and completely. These responsibilities will in many cases be the same responsibilities that these professionals are already assuming, but as transition-age students are increasingly moved into community sites for extended periods of time during the school day, therapy and training will need to be provided in the community sites instead of in the school building. Effective transition preparation by these professionals will also require a change in focus from a purely developmental approach to include the provision of support and training needed to maintain an individual in a community site. For example, an occupational therapist may determine that a particular student is currently unable to eat independently in the school cafeteria. Rather than considering this a prerequisite vocational need, the therapist may work with the other ITP planning team members to provide the student assistance and adaptations during lunch time at a community-based vocational training site. For example, instead of considering a student's body rocking a barrier to the student's placement on a community-based training site, the school psychologist may take another approach. He or she may assist the ITP team with the development and implementation of a behavior management plan that will permit the student's placement on job-sites and other community settings.

Students and Adults with Disabilities

The final members of a local transition core team or interagency task force are one or more adults with disabilities who can help to focus the team's planning efforts on outcomes for individual students and clients. An adult client who has made the transition from school to adult life can help the team identify gaps and duplications in service delivery. He or she can also assist the team with more accurate identification of the services most needed by transition-age youth in order to achieve employment and other adult outcomes. Perhaps most importantly, an adult client can assist core team members in teaching young adults with disabilities to be vocal advocates for themselves.

The student targeted for transition planning should always be an active member of his or her ITP planning team. It is difficult, if not unrealistic, for a 16- or 17-year-old adolescent to accurately plan what he or she would like to achieve as an adult, but it is even more unrealistic for a team of professionals to plan what job the young adult will do, where the young adult will live, and how he or she will spend leisure time without the active participation of the student in question. Even students with severe cognitive disabilities and limited speech can provide input to the ITP team members through their behavior and performance during various activities. Similarly, adolescents with sensory and motor disabilities can be encouraged to take responsibility for making their own decisions and being their own advocates.

However, preference for a janitorial job instead of a food service job, or for participation in an aerobics class instead of a crafts class can only be made if a student has had exposure to two or more activities from which a choice can be made. An adolescent's decision to accept or reject adaptive communication or visual aids during employment training can only be made if the ITP planning team has included the student in all aspects of transition planning and decision making.

CHARACTERISTICS OF EFFECTIVE INTERAGENCY AND TRANSDISCIPLINARY TEAMS

Interagency Approach

Comprehensive transition planning and implementation requires the adoption of both an interagency and a transdisciplinary approach by participating professionals. Figure 8.1 portrays the interagency ap-

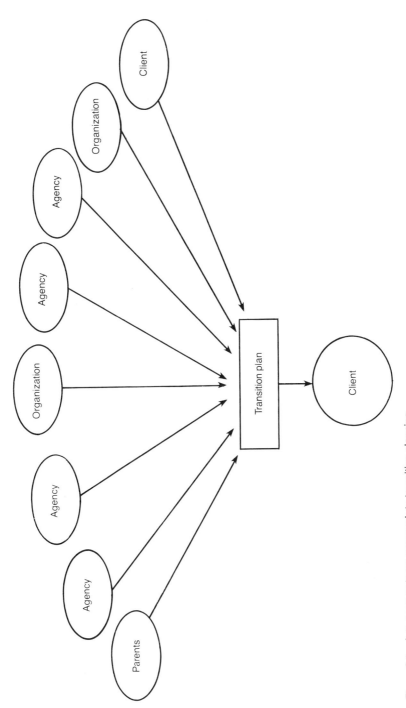

Figure 8.1.   Interagency team approach to transition planning.

proach. The interagency approach attempts to coordinate the resources and services of all local agencies and organizations in a core team or task force involved with transition planning. Interagency cooperation assumes that cooperation will enable agencies to: 1) provide higher quality services for their clients, 2) make more efficient use of their limited resources, and 3) increase their local political power (Hagebak, 1982). This model requires participating agencies and organizations to provide an agency liaison to participate as a member of an ongoing planning team or task force. Each team member brings his or her expertise to the meetings and contributes his or her agency's resources toward the development of a cooperative plan or local interagency agreement. When interagency teams include parents and client representatives as members, team members must ensure that clients and parents are granted the same power and participation privileges as other team members.

Transdisciplinary Approach

A transdisciplinary approach (McCormick & Goldman, 1979) is required by transition planning teams to develop and implement individualized transition plans. Figure 8.2 describes the transdisciplinary approach. During the transition planning phase, this model requires professionals from various disciplines and agencies to serve as both consultants and service providers. During the early secondary years, school and educationally related service professionals assume primary direct service responsibility with consultation from adult services providers. During the final secondary year, the team must ensure systematic transfer of direct service responsibilities from school providers to adult service providers. As adult service providers assume more and more direct service responsibilities, school providers must release their hold on students and assume a consultative role.

STRATEGIES FOR CHANGING ROLES AND TEAM BUILDING

Professionals and parents who agree to serve as members of both interagency and transdisciplinary transition teams come to meetings with their own unique agendas and expectations. They come representing their own agency's or organization's needs, as advocates for their own sons and daughters, and as individuals with their own experiences and professional backgrounds. In most cases, they have been chosen to participate on teams because they are leaders in their agencies and organizations. The one thing they may have in common

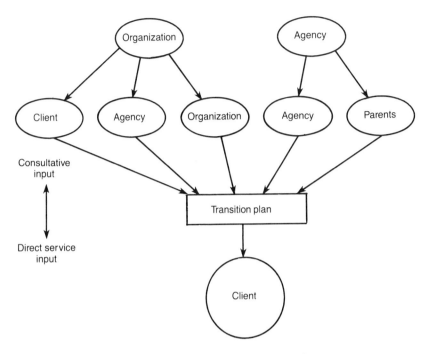

Figure 8.2. Transdisciplinary team approach to transition planning.

is that they are concerned about individuals with disabilities. Thus, it is not unusual for teams to experience territoriality and competitiveness as they begin to work together. The guidelines suggested below are strategies that teams may find useful as they begin to plan local systems change and to develop individualized transition plans.

Strategy 1:   Focus Transition Planning on Individual Clients

The involvement of parents of offspring with disabilities and adult clients who have lived through the transition years helps to focus agencies and organizations on the needs of individual students within a given locality. A stated goal of reducing local special education graduates' unemployment rate from 75% to 35% in 2 years may sound positive to local core team members, but is likely to be met with impatience from parents and clients, who may want to know what will happen to the remaining 35% of graduates. Core team members must know individual students in the community and be willing to address their unique strengths and needs during planning. Members who are familiar with local needs assessment data that target individual student needs will find it more difficult to accept the status of existing services when confronted with remaining service needs. "How will the decision to delay the development of mobile work crews affect Mary and other 20-year-olds?" is an example of the type of question team members should raise during planning and implementation efforts.

Strategy 2: Involve All Team Members in Role Release

Role release has been defined by Lyon and Lyon (1980) as a process transdisciplinary teams must go through to ensure maximum coordination of services for youth with disabilities. According to Lyon and Lyon (1980), there are three levels of interaction for team members involved in role release: 1) general information, 2) informational skills, and 3) performance competencies.

Level one, information sharing, requires team members to communicate with other team members the specific information their agency or discipline brings to transition planning. For example, much of the confusion experienced by Mary's ITP team in the beginning of this chapter was the result of other team members' lack of understanding of each other's mandates and services. Before a transdisciplinary or interagency team can effectively work together, they must have a clear and accurate understanding of the agencies and organizations involved. Sharing of basic information between team members builds a strong foundation for future meetings by acknowledging past misunderstandings and by increasing team members' awareness of the complexity of transition planning.

Level two, sharing skills, requires team members to assist each other in using basic information to make judgments and decisions. For example, vocational rehabilitation counselors, who have a basic understanding of supported work, can choose whether or not to purchase services from a provider. Parents who have a clear understanding of local residential programs can choose whether or not to select community-based residential services for their son or daughter. Special education teachers who have a basic understanding of vocational rehabilitation services can assist with community-based vocational training to enhance a student's chances of being evaluated positively for rehabilitation services.

Level three, sharing performance competencies, requires team members to communicate some of their expertise by training other team members to demonstrate new skills. A school psychologist may assist a special education teacher with developing a behavior management program in a community-based job-site. An occupational therapist may assist a vocational education teacher with teaching a student to use a number pad on a computer in a community-based job-site. A vocational evaluator may teach several other team members to collect job production data in a community-based job-site. Sharing performance skills with other team members may be the most difficult level of role release, because it requires professionals to share certain skills that they may have spent years learning themselves. In some cases (Lyon & Lyon, 1980), professionals may be legally prohibited from sharing expertise with nontrained and noncertified professionals. Certainly, these requirements should be described to members and respected, but these limited instances should not serve as barriers to other opportunities for shared skill training.

Strategy 3: Engage in Long-Range Strategic Planning

Change by individuals, by agencies, and by localities takes time. The recognition by team members that comprehensive transition planning requires a commitment to change is also a commitment to working together as a team for an extended period of time. Optimal transition planning for individual students cannot be completed in one IEP/ITP meeting: it must begin early in the secondary years and continue into formal follow-along services and responsibilities during the early adult years. Change in local services and programs cannot be planned and implemented by a time-limited task force. Core team members must be prepared to: 1) define a long-range mission, 2) set short-term objectives, 3) forecast and address potential "what ifs" and "yes, buts" that may arise, and 4) continuously reevaluate and reassess team objectives and progress.

Strategic planning by interagency and transdisciplinary teams is based upon the often quoted adage, "Local problems have local solutions". Strategic planning is also based upon two assumptions: first, a problem voiced by any one agency or discipline affects all team members; and second, any problem can be resolved if all team members are committed to cooperatively and creatively seeking solutions.

SUMMARY

Comprehensive and effective transition planning by professionals and parents requires a basic understanding of all involved agencies and disciplines. It also requires an interagency and transdisciplinary team approach to defining "optimal" roles and strategies for playing those roles. Defining roles and responsibilities for all participating professionals, parents, and clients is a crucial prerequisite for comprehensive transition planning.

Chapter 9   *Transition*

Local and State
Initiatives in
Action

To this point in the book, emphasis has been placed on transition planning and program development primarily at the individual level. In this final chapter, the focus expands to include an examination of strategies and leading illustrations of transition planning and related employment outcomes that are actually in practice. For meaningful transition to occur, it is clear that communication is necessary between the numerous disciplines that will ultimately be involved. Transforming a local school system or even an entire state school system from a vacuum of transition activity to an active and comprehensive transition planning network—such as the one described in this book—requires significant systems change. What follows is a list of the factors that are important to effecting successful transition from school to adulthood for students with disabilities.

FACTORS ASSOCIATED WITH PROMOTING
TRANSITION PLANNING AT THE LOCAL OR STATE LEVEL

There are several characteristics that are usually associated with successful transition programs. First, it is very helpful for one agency to take the responsibility for initiating planning activity. In most states either local education agencies, or, at the state level, departments of education are assuming this responsibility.

The initial responsibility involves bringing people or agencies together and helping to set realistic planning agendas. For purposes of initial referral, case management, and confidentiality, the schools generally have been viewed as the starting point for transition planning. Many of the states providing leadership in transition share in common the field of education as the locus for the initiation of transition planning. Unless one agency assumes this responsibility, no meaningful planning can begin.

A second characteristic associated with effective transition planning is the inclusion of the appropriate disciplines in the planning process. But successful planning is due to more than just grouping professionals together: participants should also share a mutual knowledge and respect for each participant's agency. A description of many of the disciplines was discussed in the last chapter. For example, assume a local meeting is taking place between representatives from the vocational rehabilitation office, the vocational education office, the special education, mental retardation and mental health offices, and the Joint Training Partnership Act office. The purpose of the meeting is to plan employment outcomes for 22 youth who have severe learning disabilities, who are severely retarded, and who have cerebral palsy. Assume further that most of the representatives have never heard of the Carl Perkins Act (vocational education), the Medicaid Waiver provisions (mental health/retardation Title XIX), or the Vocational Rehabilitation Act or Education for All Handicapped Children Act. If, in fact, more of the representatives would have taken the time to understand the statutory or regulation problems that some of the other participating agencies encounter, the entire process might be collaborative rather than only a mixed collection of individuals representing individual agencies and separate agendas.

The special educator will not understand why the vocational rehabilitation representative cannot easily pay for permanent long-term supported employment. Similarly, the mental health person will not understand why the vocational educator can only spend so many dollars on individuals labeled "handicapped." The vocational rehabilitation professional will not understand why the JTPA representative cannot ensure greater funding allocations for clients with severe handicaps. These limitations in communication and understanding will be major impediments to making transition occur.

It is also clear to those who have worked closely with transition-related programs that each participating agency needs to contribute some cash or "in-kind" resources. Contributions usually are not made unless there is a driving administrative force behind them, such as the endorsement of the state governor, a county board chairman, a strong school superintendent, or a legislative mandate. The collective contribution of funds will eventually overcome a longstanding obstacle to transition implementation, that is, long waiting lists for limited services.

A fourth characteristic of successful transition planning is represented by regular communication and frequent meetings between the participating agencies. The best way for agencies to become familiar with each other and with the operational problems that exist in most transition programs is to meet often. This solution works at both the state level and the local level.

A fifth characteristic that is associated with effective programs is a "custom-tailored," individualized client approach. (This success is reflected in the move toward individual transition plans discussed in Chapter 4.) Meeting the diverse needs of each disabled student may be time-consuming, but the individualized approach is essential.

Finally, the sixth important element of successful transition planning is the needs assessment; this is conducted within the community to determine what resources are available. The mechanism for conducting the needs assessment was discussed in Chapters 3 and 4. It should be noted that this type of needs assessment is necessarily ongoing. It will be continually updated by the frequent meetings of the representatives of the participating agencies.

TRANSITION INTO SUPPORTED COMPETITIVE EMPLOYMENT: FIVE SCHOOL SYSTEMS MAKING IT WORK

As has been noted throughout this book, one of the major goals of transition planning is preparing special education students for the world of work (Brolin, 1982; Hasazi et al., 1985; Kiernan, Smith, & Ostrowsky, 1986; Wehman, Moon, & McCarthy, 1986). However, much information is unavailable. Very few published reports actually chronicle how supported employment can facilitate ongoing competitive employment achievements for students labeled mildly, moderatly, or severely handicapped. Similarly, few reports give special attention to employment successes, problems, and overall outcomes of such students. To date, most papers have discussed transition as a process rather than as an employment outcome (Everson, 1986; Wehman, Kregel, & Barcus, 1985). Work experience reports do not usually reveal the use of unsubsidized wages paid directly from the employer to the student. Furthermore, much of the literature concerns cooperative education activities directed to regular education students or to handicapped or disadvantaged students who exhibit a high level of independence.

Therefore, it is the purpose of this section of the chapter to present an interim report on the progress of students with mental retardation in five school systems across three different geographical areas of Virginia. These areas are: Northern Virginia, Central Virginia, and

Southeast Virginia. The five participating schools played major administrative roles in implementing this program. The authors believe this is one of the few transition reports that demonstrate the competitive employment capabilities of students with mental retardation who have not yet formally left school.

Method of Collecting Employment Data

The data presented in this section were collected by professional service staff who work as industry-based employment specialists (also known as job coaches), under a federal project aimed at demonstrating vocational transition in five school systems. Most of the service staff have either Bachelors or Masters degrees in Special Education, Psychology, Rehabilitation, or Social Work. The data reported here were accumulated throughout a 24-month period from October 1984 to September 1986. These staff were trained in data collection and verification. This competitive employment program, which took place at Virginia Commonwealth University, has been widely regarded as unique for its exclusive focus on supported competitive employment (e.g., Rusch, 1986; Wehman, Kregel, & Barcus, 1985; Wehman, Hill, Hill et al. 1985).

As noted in Chapter 7, the supported competitive employment approach emphasizes vocational intervention directly at the job-site after the person is hired. This model requires the use of a skilled professional in human services who can provide specialized placement and training support. The major contrast between supported competitive employment and traditional job placement is that supported competitive employment offers students permanent follow-along support at the job-site by staff; without this support these students would fail to keep their jobs. The skills necessary by staff primarily include training the students and advocacy on his or her behalf in dealings with co-workers and employers. Most students would not be considered "job ready" and hence would need intervention almost immediately upon employment. Programs that do not provide this type of ongoing support have consistently failed to keep people with serious disabilities competitively employed.

All data collected were drawn only from placements of students for which the authors had direct contact. Students participated from five school districts in the greater Richmond area, in Virginia Beach, and in Alexandria, Virginia. Student selection for job placement was based on a variety of factors such as parental support, travel accommodations, and job availability. None of the students had ever worked before in a real job, and the majority of them did not have daily community-based vocational training in their curriculum (see Chapter 6).

Parents and teachers expected most students would be placed into an adult activity center or sheltered workshop. As noted earlier, there was less concern in this program about the entry-level skill of these students since the supported employment approach is used to overcome whatever individual vocational deficits are present.

All student data have been stored in a Franklin ACE 1000 computer along with data from many other adult clients who have been out of school for a longer period. These data are continually updated by a computer programmer and a data entry specialist.

The staff and school district personnel worked closely with local rehabilitation counselors and the post-21 agency representatives in their respective areas. Each school district provided one teacher to work with project staff. Hence, three direct service project teams were developed, each with five teachers drawn from the five school districts. A team approach to providing supported employment and a funding base was utilized in each of the five localities. A three-way interagency agreement identical to that described in Chapter 5 was constructed for each of the five school systems and was utilized to guide the involvement of each agency.

To summarize, the students in this report were referred for services into supported competitive employment. Consistent levels and amounts of data were collected for each student qualifying for the program. That data is presented in the following report.

Selected Outcome Data and Implications

Demographics   There are data on 34 persons listed in Table 9.1. The students ranged in age from 17 to 22 years old, and in measured intelligence from 24 to 61. The average age of this group was 20 years old, with the average measured intelligence of 42. Over half were functionally nonverbal or had severely impaired speech. All were ambulatory. None had independent travel skills prior to placement, and all students lived at home. Only 10 students of the 34 had attended an integrated school. As can be seen from Table 9.2, a number of persons were placed into second and third jobs as the need arose.

Virtually all of the individuals had worked in entry-level service, with most working in for-profit service companies (see Table 9.2). The ratio of handicapped to nonhandicapped persons was usually at least 1 to 6. Positive or social work behavior by a number of the individuals was observed. This behavior was regarded by staff and co-workers as a major asset. Slow work speed, poor endurance, and unacceptable work quality were major problems. In most cases students held part-time jobs since they were still in school. Most parents were eager to have their son or daughter stay in school until the age of 21. Parents

Table 9.1. Demographics and financial benefits

Student name	Age at placement	IQ	School type	Staff intervention time (in hours)	Cumulative months worked	Cumulative wages earned	Cumulative taxes paid
1. Ed	20	48	Segregated	298	2.66	1,114.45	256.32
2. Carolyn	22	45	Segregated	101	1.18	502.50	115.57
3. Connie	20	61	Segregated	638	21.36	9,970.65	2,293.25
4. Beetle	18	47	Integrated	196	19.02	12,031.20	2,767.18
5. Nathaniel	19	50	Segregated	101	4.86	1,175.15	270.28
6. Christine	17	47	Integrated	182	5.52	1,680.00	386.40
7. Fanny	20	39	Integrated	174	14.19	2,800.60	644.14
8. Nancy	20	45	Segregated	92	4.83	422.10	97.08
9. Kevin	21	57	Segregated	110	2.73	840.00	193.20
10. Mathew	17	67	Integrated	88	5.52	3,706.10	852.40
11. Nathan	21	46	Segregated	217	16.53	6,141.90	1,412.64
12. Willard	19	42	Segregated	324	9.23	2,914.50	670.33
13. Duke	18	44	Segregated	292	8.41	3,085.35	709.63
14. Lucy	20	39	Integrated	65	6.11	1,890.00	434.70
15. Frank	18	24	Segregated	487	13.57	2,581.36	593.71
16. Kim	21	47	Integrated	394	23.69	8,564.50	1,969.83
17. Alicia	21	34	Segregated	72	2.00	724.50	166.63
18. Peter	22	45	Segregated	60	6.54	1,381.50	317.74
19. Cody	18	62	Segregated	373	17.58	5,989.80	1,377.65
20. Cynthia	21	32	Segregated	286	3.84	1,329.40	305.76
21. Fraser	20	24	Segregated	290	2.37	847.55	194.94
22. Ralph	18	48	Segregated	118	23.92	7,966.20	1,832.23
23. Lonnie	19	49	Integrated	53	2.30	569.50	130.98
24. Loretta	20	57	Integrated	312	2.99	1,137.50	261.62

		X = 20.0		X = 44.6				
25.	Bob	21	Segregated	43	274	14.23	4,345.19	999.39
26.	Jill	22	Segregated	43	59	0.36	167.50	38.52
27.	Sandra	19	Segregated	49	75	4.90	1,474.00	339.02
28.	Ahab	21	Integrated	43	305	12.65	3,920.00	901.60
29.	Craig	21	Segregated	33	99	10.74	857.60	197.25
30.	Less	22	Segregated	36	57	5.16	462.30	106.33
31.	Montie	20	Segregated	36	206	1.77	670.00	154.10
32.	Andrew	21	Segregated	40	162	25.95	8,851.45	2,035.83
33.	Luke	20	Segregated	56	216	1.68	784.00	180.32
34.	Lloyd	17	Segregated	56	156	6.87	4,256.25	978.94
35.	Tony	21	Segregated	42	152	1.71	536.00	123.28
36.	Juan	21	Integrated	45	725	18.37	7,652.40	1,760.05
37.	Kostas	21	Integrated	43	243	2.89	1,654.90	380.63
38.	Melinda	19	Integrated	42	354	9.33	5,477.50	1,259.82
39.	Pepper	21	Segregated	54	206	23.92	2,351.70	540.89
40.	Dominique	20	Segregated	58	96	24.67	5,055.15	1,162.68
41.	Rita	22	Integrated	35	122	18.37	4,740.90	1,090.41
42.	Terrance	17	Segregated	52	64	5.22	1,733.35	398.67
43.	Rex	19	Segregated	61	56	4.80	813.90	187.20
44.	Jane	22	Integrated	27	311	3.81	639.00	146.97
45.	Felix	18	Segregated	40	383	8.08	3,208.50	737.95
46.	Dean	21	Segregated	41	141	6.11	1,447.20	332.86
47.	Taylor	20	Integrated	24	161	17.87	5,370.05	1,235.11
48.	Redd	20	Segregated	41	31	0.76	268.00	61.64
49.	Harding	23	Integrated	50	328	13.24	4,648.75	1,069.21
50.	Horace	22	Segregated	38	37	0.30	161.00	37.03
51.	Arnold	20	Integrated	32	200	7.26	2,936.00	675.28
52.	Janet	19	Integrated	59	344	16.33	5,071.90	1,166.54
		$\overline{X} = 20.0$		$\overline{X} = 44.6$	10,882	488.28	158,920.80	36,551.78

223

Table 9.2. Nature of employment

	Student name	Location	Company	Type of Job
1.	Ed	Richmond	O'Toole's Gay Nineties	Food-Front dining area
2.	Ed	Richmond	Marriott Corp.	Food-Back kitchen utility
3.	Carolyn	Virginia Beach	Great American Outlet Mall	Janitor/Housekeeper
4.	Connie	Alexandria	Rustler's Steak House	Food-Front dining area
5.	Connie	Alexandria	Popeye's Fried Chicken	Food-Preparation
6.	Beetle	Alexandria	Murry's Steaks–Alexandria	Stock clerk/Warehouse
7.	Beetle	Alexandria	Murry's Steaks–Arlington	Stock clerk/Warehouse
8.	Nathaniel	Virginia Beach	Red Lobster Restaurant	Food-Front dining area
9.	Nathaniel	Virginia Beach	Annabelle's Restaurant	Food-Preparation
10.	Christine	Alexandria	Wendy's Restaurant	Food-Back kitchen utility
11.	Fanny	Chesterfield	Wee Folks, Inc.	Food-Back kitchen utility
12.	Nancy	Virginia Beach	Respite Care Center	Janitor/Housekeeper
13.	Kevin	Alexandria	Wendy's Restaurant	Food-Back kitchen utility
14.	Mathew	Alexandria	Mark Winkler Management	Janitor/Housekeeper
15.	Mathew	Alexandria	Wendy's Restaurant	Food-Back kitchen utility
16.	Nathan	Richmond	Chi Chi's Restaurant	Food-Dish/pot washer
17.	Nathan	Richmond	SAGA Corp.	Food-Dish/pot washer
18.	Willard	Henrico	J. C. Penny Company	Janitor/Housekeeper
19.	Duke	Henrico	Western Sizzlin Rest.	Food-Front dining area
20.	Lucy	Chesterfield	Howard Johnson's Rest.	Food-Dish/pot washer
21.	Frank	Henrico	Chi Chi's Restaurant	Food-Dish/pot washer
22.	Frank	Henrico	Morrison's Cafeteria	Food-Dish/pot washer
23.	Kim	Alexandria	Popeye's Fried Chicken	Food-Front dining area
24.	Alicia	Richmond	Shoney's Restaurant	Food-Back kitchen utility
25.	Peter	Virginia Beach	Va. Beach Public Schools	Janitor/Housekeeper
26.	Cody	Virginia Beach	Pembroke Mall	Janitor/Housekeeper
27.	Cody	Virginia Beach	Kentucky Fried Chicken	Food-Front dining area
28.	Cynthia	Virginia Beach	Red Roof Inn	Janitor/Housekeeper
29.	Fraser	Richmond	Azalea Mall	Janitor/Housekeeper
30.	Ralph	Virginia Beach	Great American Outlet Mall	Janitor/Housekeeper
31.	Lonnie	Virginia Beach	Red Lobster Restaurant	Janitor/Housekeeper
32.	Loretta	Alexandria	Coffee Butler Services	Food-Dish/pot washer

#	Name	City	Company	Job
33.	Bob	Richmond	Chi Chi's Restaurant	Food-Dish/pot washer
34.	Bob	Richmond	Morrison's Cafeteria	Laundry
35.	Jill	Richmond	SAGA Corp.	Food-Dish/pot washer
36.	Sandra	Virginia Beach	Kentucky Fried Chicken	Food-Preparation
37.	Ahab	Alexandria	Magruder Grocery Store	Stock clerk/Warehouse
38.	Craig	Virginia Beach	Respite Care Center	Janitor/Housekeeper
39.	Craig	Virginia Beach	Placid Residence	Janitor/Housekeeper
40.	Less	Virginia Beach	Pancakes-N-Pickles	Food-Front dining area
41.	Montie	Henrico	Pizza Hut	Food-Dish/pot washer
42.	Andrew	Henrico	J. C. Penny Company	Janitor/Housekeeper
43.	Luke	Alexandria	Coffee Butler Services	Food-Dish/pot washer
44.	Lloyd	Henrico	Tobacco Company Rest.	Food-Dish/pot washer
45.	Tony	Virginia Beach	Pembroke Mall	Janitor/Housekeeper
46.	Juan	Alexandria	United Virginia Bank	Clerical
47.	Kostas	Chesterfield	Holiday Inn of Petersburg	Food-Back kitchen utility
48.	Melinda	Alexandria	Popeye's Fried Chicken	Food-Preparation
49.	Melinda	Alexandria	Coffee Butler Services	Food-Dish/pot washer
50.	Pepper	Richmond	St. Benedict School	Janitor/Housekeeper
51.	Dominique	Virginia Beach	Pancakes-N-Pickles	Food-Dish/pot washer
52.	Rita	Chesterfield	Bradlee's #570	Stock clerk/Warehouse
53.	Terrance	Virginia Beach	Morrison's Cafeteria	Janitor/Housekeeper
54.	Terrance	Virginia Beach	S. L. Nusbaum Realty Co.	Janitor/Housekeeper
55.	Rex	Virginia Beach	Va. Beach Public Schools	Janitor/Housekeeper
56.	Jane	Alexandria	Rustler's Steak House	Food-Back kitchen utility
57.	Felix	Virginia Beach	Miller and Rhoads	Janitor/Housekeeper
58.	Felix	Virginia Beach	Annabelle's Restaurant	Food-Dish/pot washer
59.	Dean	Virginia Beach	Oceana Naval Base-Civ Per	Janitor/Housekeeper
60.	Taylor	Chesterfield	Western Sizzlin/Chester	Food-Dish/pot washer
61.	Redd	Virginia Beach	Kentucky Fried Chicken	Food-Back kitchen utility
62.	Harding	Chesterfield	Safeway Grocery Store 361	Stock clerk/Warehouse
63.	Horace	Henrico	Western Sizzlin Rest.	Food-Front dining area
64.	Arnold	Chesterfield	Plata Grande Restaurant	Food-Dish/pot washer
65.	Arnold	Chesterfield	Holiday Inn-Koger Center	Laundry
66.	Janet	Alexandria	The Scott Shop	Assembler/Bench worker

were very skeptical about how successful their sons or daughters would be once they were placed in real jobs.

Financial Benefits and Costs   Table 9.1 also describes the number of months worked, wages accumulated, and taxes paid to date. None of the students had ever worked before or had earned wages. Most had been limited to school classroom activity, although some had been involved in community volunteer work or school prevocational sheltered workshop activity. Those students who worked less than 20 hours per week did so in order to stay in school for longer periods of time. The cumulative earnings of this group totaled over $158,000 in unsubsidized wages. Also reported were the average number of staff hours spent supervising students each month. A total of 10,882 hours of staff time on the job-site was reported across all persons for the 66 placements made to date. This figure reflects the total duration of the individual's employment. This was noted in order to determine the job retention cost per placement. A rate of $20.53 per hour was established for our job coach services by the Virginia Department of Rehabilitation Services (Hill, 1986). By multiplying the total staff intervention hours of 10,882 by the $20.53 per hour rate, an estimate of total costs incurred was obtained. This total was $223,407. The cost per person was $4,296, the cost per placement was $3,384.

One tangible result of this program was to show that persons with relatively limited measured intelligence ($\bar{x} = 44$) can work competitively if given the proper amount of job-site training and on-going support. The results also show that given a commitment to competitive employment and use of a supported employment approach, individuals can work competitively even if they are graduating from a segregated school program. Even further, the results show that outcome-oriented interagency agreements are very useful in transition planning, and that directing resources specifically toward graduate job placement and job retention is a highly successful approach.

Community-based nonpaid work experiences provided by several of the schools did tend to result in less follow-up training once a student was at the job-site. This tendency was apparent in several of the school programs, which reinforces the suggestions put forth in Chapter 6.

Finally, results indicated that after students had been employed for 24 months, parents gradually became more accepting of a competitive employment alternative. Parents who had for years believed that their child could not work required information to see that competitive employment is a truly viable option.

The benefits of initiating early transition planning and gainful employment for students before graduation are clearly evident. One advantage of fully involving the school staff in the employment process was that curriculum changes reflecting the demands of actual jobs in the community were developed and implemented. Another advantage of pre-graduation planning was that school personnel were available to identify individual student needs and to provide assistance with services or training while the student was still enrolled in school. In addition, a continuity of service provision from school to work was maintained, as well as a linkage between school, parents, and community services. This linkage, which has been one of the major positive results of transition planning to date, has reduced problems that were initially encountered, such as parent expectations, case management needs, and flexibility of school staff and student schedules. The logical flow of case management responsibility—for example, from school to adult services—has been ensured.

With early transition planning leading to gainful employment, parents can be better prepared for the commitment of a "real job versus school training." Such a commitment, for instance, requires adherence to company policy concerning sick leave and vacation time. Parents can also benefit from the support of school personnel demonstrating successful student placements, encouraging parent networking, and conducting inservice training sessions and job-site visits for parents.

The 10,882 hours of intervention reflect the amount of time staff spent providing students with job placement services, on-site training, and follow-along support services. These data were fundamentally consistent with the projected start-up costs for supported competitive employment programs, particularly for those programs involving individuals whose average measured intelligence level is just above 40. The authors' earlier work (Hill, Banks, Handrich, Wehman, Hill, & Schafer, 1987; Wehman & Hill, 1982) indicates that intervention hours, and thus costs, decline over time, while workers' wages and benefits continue to accumulate. Hence, the benefit-cost ratio markedly improves the longer an individual is employed.

Of the 52 students placed into competitive jobs over the 24 months of the project, approximately 55% continue to be employed. Based on the cumulative months worked, 74% of the students have remained in their jobs longer than 6 months. The mean length of employment for the 66 placements is 12.5 months. This figure compares favorably with the average length of employment for nonhandicapped individuals in the same type of entry-level service jobs; this figure, according to the National Hotel and Restaurant Association, is less than 5 months (Wehman, Hill, Hill, Brooke, Pendleton, & Britt, 1985).

Successful job retention beyond 6 months was achieved by 92% of the students attending an integrated school, as compared to only 64% of those students enrolled in a segregated school setting.

It is far too early to make definitive conclusions regarding the retention rates of students in these school systems, but several preliminary observations can be made. First, the students were placed in their competitive jobs while they were still enrolled in school. Such early placement provides work experience similar to that of nonhandicapped students, who may work in several jobs during their final years of school. These early job experiences will help them make informed career and employment choices following graduation from school. Second, parental support was a critical component of employment success (Goodall, Wehman, & Cleveland, 1983). The changes that occurred in parental expectations as graduates moved from sheltered placements to competitive settings and their increased confidence in the program may have been the result of their continuous participation in the transition process. Third, these preliminary results may not reflect the long-term impact on the service delivery system that will become more evident with the passage of time. Changes in policy procedures, funding sources, and staff and agency responsibilities are being developed and implemented with the ongoing coordinated planning between the service providers involved.

As a result of this program, post-21 adult agencies are cooperating with school systems to make transition plans for students with mental retardation prior to the students' graduation. Two additional results of the program were the development of a vocational transition process, and the delivery of supported employment services in the five school systems. There is little doubt that meaningful transition planning is more easily effected when there are already concrete illustrations of vocational competence. The schools who are participating in this study are making vocational transition a reality.

It should be noted that while the previous discussion pertained only to students with mental retardation who were in a supported employment setting, students with different disabilities will have different outcomes. For students with mild handicaps, for example, there are other ways of attaining effective transition to employment. Because of this variety of outcomes it will be beneficial to see how a number of states are implementing state-level transition planning for students with all types of disabilities. Several states have begun to either pass laws, to develop resolutions, to solicit planning grants, or to develop recommendations. Some of these ideas and recommendations are quite good. The next section is devoted to examining a selection of these state transition planning programs.

TRANSITION INITIATIVES AT THE STATE LEVEL

In virtually every state of the country some degree of transition planning is occurring at the state level. This planning has developed in response to the call for action by the U.S. Department of Education, Office of Special Education and Rehabilitation Services (Will, 1984a). This nationwide trend has been one of the most salient manifestations of mobilization ever seen in special education and rehabilitation. Although most states have only initiated activity in this area, several are quite advanced in their planning and development. Several of the principle recommendations developed by states to enhance transition are listed in the profiles below. In no way is this selection meant to suggest that these are the best programs or the most progressive states. Instead, the states that were included were those whose transition planning programs were the most clearly documented.

Transition in Illinois[1]

Spearheaded by the Governor's Planning Council on Developmental Disabilities under the very capable leadership of Carl Suter, Illinois has developed a formidable planning document (Bates, Suter, & Poelvoorde, 1986). This report provides information on the number of students "aging out" of school programs in the 1980s. The report also discusses the benefits of transition planning and, most importantly, makes a series of wide-ranging recommendations concerning transition implementation.

Figure 9.1 presents data from Illinois showing the cumulative costs of unemployment versus alternative employment costs for students leaving special education in 1989. Obviously, the gradient of increased state expenditures is much less for employment than for unemployment. These figures are provided as a concrete illustration of accrued taxpayers' savings that result from the expansion of more effective transition services.

Observations and Recommendations   In this section, 12 observations of the current system for providing school and postschool transition services are provided. These observations are followed by specific recommendations for action related to transition planning in Illinois. The recommendations identify a process that assures a longitudinal commitment to the improvement of existing services and to the development of more effective transition resources.

---

[1]We are grateful to Dr. Paul Bates for letting the authors use the information about Transition in Illinois from Bates, Suter, and Poelvoorde (1986).

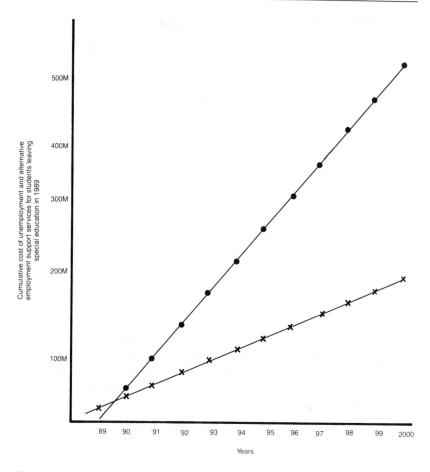

Figure 9.1. Cost comparison associated with existing system and recommended system of transition planning and expanded employment. (● = annual cost of unemployment estimated to be 45 million dollars annually for the 9,000 students projected to be unemployed. X = alternative model of employment support services, including transition planning for all students. Initial cost of over 22 million dollars is followed by an annual cost of approximately 16 million dollars for the 9,000 students leaving special education in 1989.)

Observation #1 The transition needs of persons with disabilities are complex. Thus, transition programs require the ongoing commitment of interagency resources for the purpose of expanding secondary service options, the development of more effective postsecondary services, and the promotion of individualized transition planning.

At present, each human services agency responsible for transition services operates independently, with no ongoing mechanism to promote interagency coordination. However, there are some notable exceptions to this trend. The Department of Rehabilitation Services

(DORS) has a cooperative agreement with the Illinois State Board of Education (ISBE) for providing the Secondary Work Experience Programs (SWEP) for several thousand special education students in Illinois. Also, the Department of Mental Health and Developmental Disabilities (DMHDD), DORS, and Governor's Planning Council on Developmental Disabilities (GPCDD) have combined resources in a concerted initiative to establish supported employment options for adults with severe disabilities.

Several reviews of existing transition services indicate that cooperative planning between school and adult service programs at the state or local level is virtually nonexistent (Brodsky, 1983; Hasazi et al., 1985; McDonnell, Wilcox, Boles, Bellamy et al., 1985; Wehman, Kregel, & Barcus, 1985). Effective transition services require the development of secondary and postsecondary programs and the coordination of state and local resources. Furthermore, the complex process of implementing such a program requires a long-term commitment of interagency resources.

Recommendation #1 Create a Transition Assistance Committee (TAC) within the Governor's Planning Council on Developmental Disabilities (GPCDD) for the purpose of implementing and coordinating an ongoing commitment of interagency resources for the improvement of school and postschool transition services.

The TAC should be chaired by a Transition Coordinator, administratively supervised by the Executive Director of the GPCDD, and consist of primary membership from the Illinois State Board of Education (ISBE), the Department of Rehabilitation Services (DORS), the Department of Mental Health and Developmental Disabilities (DMHDD), and the consumer groups. As determined by the TAC, additional state agencies, candidates, providers, and professionals will be invited to participate on selected topics. The TAC would function as the central contact point for questions from candidates, providers, agencies, and others regarding transition service issues. This council would also be responsible for developing interagency agreements and for orchestrating the systems change that would be a necessary part of an ongoing commitment to the development of effective transition services. Important activities of the TAX are as follows:

1. Develop state level interagency agreements between ISBE, DORS, and DHMDD regarding transition development and coordination activities (reviewed anually).
2. Develop a data system for collecting information regarding student characteristics, postschool goals, needed transition services, and postschool outcomes experienced by special education graduates, or drop-outs.

3. Develop a process for individualized transition planning, inter-agency involvement, and transfer of case coordination.
4. Develop a model for local transition planning and coordinating committees (TPCC's).
5. Develop interagency agreements that put into operation commitments to provide inservice or technical assistance to candidates and providers regarding effective transition services.
6. Develop a position paper on personnel required to provide effective transition services.
7. Conduct program evaluation studies for the purpose of developing specific recommendations regarding improvement of transition services.

Observation #2   The ability of the educational system, the local human service programs, and the state agencies to respond to the transition needs of young people with disabilities is dependent on their knowing who the candidates are and what program needs (if any) they have. Unfortunately, this information is not generally available. It is difficult to obtain information on the actual number of people who anually leave special education programs, and even more difficult to determine what the service needs of these people are. Even if these data were available on persons who were leaving special education programs in a particular year, the data would probably not be available until it is too late for effective planning and needed service development to occur.

A transition data system is therefore an essential component of this proposal. This sytsem must include information on students several years prior to their departure from the special education program, must identify individualized goals and service needs, and must be available for school and postschool service providers. At present, the Illinois State Board of Education is responding to requirements of PL 98-199 by having local school districts report individualized "exit" information on their students, including anticipated service needs and potential agencies involved. Unfortunately, this information is provided upon the students' graduation, thus hindering cooperative planning of needed services by the school and postschool agencies. The collection of this information has not been preceded by needed inservice training. Furthermore, no plan has been presented for using the obtained information to make program improvements.

Recommendation #2   The TAC, in consultation with ISBE, DORS, and DMHDD, should develop a transition planning and needs assessment data system that identifies student characteristics, projected employment and independent living goals, and needed secondary and postsecondary services.

If one is to promote meaningful systems change that results in more enriching postschool outcomes, one must know who the people are who will be served and what they will need well in advance of the students' graduation or exit from public education. Consistent with the requirements of the Carl Perkins Act (PL 98-524) and the Amendments to the Education for All Handicapped Children Act (PL 98-199), transition planning should be completed several years prior to the student's departure from public education, for example, during the year in which the student turns 14. The students' individualized transition plans should be updated anually until the student graduates or terminates his or her special education program. Obviously, considerably more development of this system is necessary before adoption would be recommended on a statewide level. However, the profile has been included to provide the reader with an example of the type of information that is necessary for effective transition planning.

The process for implementing this recommendation would include the following activities:

1. Identify content and format for the transition planning and needs assessment data systems.
2. Identify how the information will be used for program decision making on an individual and systems level.
3. Conduct inservice training on how the system should be implemented.
4. Solicit input on the data system from selected school districts.
5. Develop recommendations regarding adoption of the data system.

Observation #3 Human service professionals do not have follow-up data on persons who leave special education programs, and thus are unable to evaluate the effectiveness of specific services or to determine existing and future needs for service development. As a result, very little is known about the postschool life experienced by individuals who have participated in special education. The inadequacy of this information base limits the ability of the postschool systems to respond to the ongoing support service needs of persons with disabilities.

Recommendation #3 The TAC, in conjunction with ISBE, DORS, and DMHDD, should develop a postschool follow-up survey to be used in connection with the Transition Planning and Needs Assessment data system for persons who have graduated, completed, or terminated a secondary special education program. This follow-up assessment should be conducted 1 year following a person's exit from special education programs.

At present there is very little information in Illinois regarding the postschool employment and residential status of handicapped youth following high school. Follow-up studies in other states suggest that people with disabilities are not doing very well after leaving special education. These studies describe high levels of unemployment, underemployment, dependency, and minimal participation in community activities. Although there is no reason to question the veracity of these disturbing follow-up reports from Illinois, the absence of data is a major hindrance to the authors' efforts to develop policy and services that more effectively address the transition needs of people leaving special education programs. Hasazi and colleagues (1985) point out that follow-up information is needed as a basis for evaluating the appropriateness of the high school curriculum. McDonnell et al. (1986) emphasize that the lack of data prevents the systems change that is necessary to establish an array of transition services resulting in more successful postschool outcomes for disabled consumers.

By requiring a 1-year follow-up survey of all persons leaving special education programs, the state of Illinois could develop an information base from which it could continually evaluate the postschool status of special education students. This information should contribute to system change within ISBE, DORS, and DMHDD, and could facilitate interagency cooperative agreements. Activities that would be necessary to develop the information system include:

1. Identify content and format for postschool follow-up survey.
2. Identify how the information will be used for program decision making on an individual and systems level.
3. Solicit feedback regarding the postschool follow-up survey design.
4. Recommend process for determining responsibility for conducting follow-up.
5. Write recommendation for adoption of a statewide follow-up data system, list the resources necessary to implement and maintain the system.

Observation #4 Independent living and employment related objectives are not identified for all secondary special education students in the Illinois program. Also, formal transition planning with interagency involvement, as needed, is not done consistently. By failing to provide school experiences that correspond with the demands of postschool life, and by failing to engage in cooperative planning, schools deny students the opportunity to develop important social and vocational skills for postschool environments and may cause them to become dependent upon postschool services.

Recommendation #4 Formal transition planning should be initiated by the public schools in conjunction with the students' IEP meetings. Transition plans should be developed for students several years (2–6) prior to departure, for example, during the year in which the student turns 14. Plans should be updated annually.

The most logical point of responsibility for initiating the transition planning process for individual students is in conjunction with the IEP. Authorities in the field of transition services concur with this recommendation (Hasazi et al. 1985; McDonnell & Hardman, 1985; Wehman, Kregel, & Barcus, 1985; Wehman et al., 1986). According to Hasazi (1985), the necessary components of comprehensive transition planning include the identification of residential outcomes, identification of vocational outcomes, and specification of other goals necessary for living as independently as possible after graduation. McDonnell and Hardman (1985) further elaborate on the responsibility of public education for initiating the transition planning process by identifying the following three critical activities that must be completed by high school programs:

1. Initiate a planning process that sequences critical decisions across the students' high school career so that all potential service options and support needs may be identified and established prior to graduation. (p. 284)
2. Educate parents so that they may actively participate in the planning process and advocate for needed services. (p. 284)
3. Establish formal links between education and adult service agencies to allow comprehensive planning for youth with severe handicaps. (p. 283)

The TAC would be responsible for developing the procedural recommendations for formalized transition planning. In the first year of implementation the TAC would:

1. Identify the content of the transition plan and format for conducting formal transition planning.
2. Identify the process by which interagency cooperation will be requested and assured in formal transition planning.
3. Pilot the transition planning process and solicit input regarding content, format, and needed resources.
4. Develop recommendations regarding adoption of formal transition planning on a statewide basis.

Observation #5 There is little evidence at the local level of interagency planning and coordination of transition resources and services. Adult service agencies and providers are rarely involved in IEP discussions. The case management responsibilities of the IEP team are not shared with appropriate adult service agencies prior to the student's departure from public school. Furthermore, the private employment sector has not been actively involved in transition planning.

Recommendation #5   Transition Planning and Coordinating Committees (TPCCs) should be established in local communities. These committees will promote interagency coordination for the development of effective transition, special education, vocational education, community colleges, DORS, DMHDD, consumer groups, and private employment.

Virtually all recommendations for transition planning include a local planning unit. In most cases the local planning unit is conceptualized as being the individual transition team. Recommendation #4 of this proposal described the process by which individual transition teams would be developed according to a particular student's need for specific services. The TPCCs identified in Recommendation #5 would be the local counterpart to the state level TAC. Since many service coordination issues must be decided locally, the TPCC would have this responsibility.

Project TIE (Transition Into Employment) of the Rehabilitation Research and Training Center at Virginia Commonwealth University describes the need for a core transition team (see Chapter 3), a functional equivalent to the proposed TPCC. Composition of the core team includes representatives from local special education, vocational education, vocational rehabilitation, and local health/mental retardation agencies. Other potential core team members would be: a parent, consumer, employer, medical representative, and a rehabilitation engineer. The core transition team would function primarily in an advisory capacity to the various individual transition teams.

The core transition team or TPCC is an excellent coordinating unit within the comprehensive transition planning and service development initiative because it centralizes all planning activity. An important issue that would need to be resolved prior to establishing TPCCs would be the unit of organization. Since public schools and postschool service agencies are organized differently, it is difficult to determine the most useful area of responsibility for local TPCCs. Since a primary motivation for transition planning is to enhance gainful employment, the unit of organization for TPCCs should be related to vocational training and employment support services. Possibilities include service delivery areas of the Job Training Partnership Act and the 59 regional program areas that have been established as part of the Education for Employment initiative of ISBE's Department of Adult Vocational and Technical Education (DAVTE).

Observation #6   Parents of secondary special education students do not have information regarding school vocational services, adult service agencies, or postschool options from which to make informed decisions. Without this information, parents cannot fulfill their proper role as advocates for service options that will enhance their son or daughter's employability and community integration.

Recommendation #6 A statewide information campaign regarding transition related services (e.g., career and vocational services, adult service agencies, and postschool options) should be directed at the parents of persons with disabilities. This recommendation is consistent with requirements of the Carl Perkins Act (PL 98-524).

Parents must be actively involved in transition planning. This involvement must begin several years prior to a student's departure from public education and should be accompanied by information regarding the availability of independent living outcomes.

The TAC, with the cooperation of member agencies, should develop a plan to provide information to parents, advocates, and guardians of persons with disabilities regarding transition service options and desired program outcomes. The agencies participating in the TAC should then implement this plan. The effectiveness of parent awareness should be evaluated as part of an annual review. The responsibility for parent awareness must be shared by all agencies that provide transition services.

Observation #7 Secondary service options involving independent living and employment related outcomes are not available in all school districts for all categories or severity levels of disability. Some programs, for example, serve mildly handicapped students and not severely handicapped students. Some school districts offer a comprehensive array of vocational education experiences to a wide variety of special education students, while other school districts have more restrictive eligibility requirements that limit the number or persons qualified to receive services.

In Illinois, the Department of Rehabilitative Services is actively involved in many school districts through its Secondary Work Experience Program (SWEP). This program has increased the vocational preparation options that are available for several thousand secondary school students in Illinois. Although this is an example of interagency coordination, SWEP options are not available in all Illinois communities. Furthermore, within the DORS-sponsored SWEP programs, the criteria used to determine program eligibility for persons with more severe handicaps vary widely. Similar inconsistency exists across other public school programs in regard to availability of vocational education experiences, community training opportunities, and support services for employment and independent living training.

Recommendation #7 Technical assistance and inservice training activities should be initiated for the purpose of improving and expanding available program options for secondary special education students.

Each secondary special education district should allocate a sizable portion of its inservice or staff development resources for the development of transition services. Effective transition services must then be identified and service delivery issues addressed in an effort to increase the availability of program options.

The TAC should assume a leadership role in effecting the systematic changes that are required to increase the availability and effectiveness of transition service options. Each participating member of the TAC would document internal efforts to identify, expand, and improve upon the delivery ot transition services.

Observation #8 Postsecondary service options involving independent living and employment are inconsistently available across disability categories, severity levels of disability, and communities. Supported work and supported employment services are available in some communities and not in others. Similarly, residential support services that promote greater community integration and participation are available only in some communities for some people.

Recommendation #8 Technical assistance and inservice activities should be undertaken by postsecondary agencies (e.g., community colleges, DORS, DHMDD) for the purpose of improving and expanding the transition service options available to young adults with disabilities. Specifically, adult services for persons with disabilities should demonstrate a concerted effort to expand support services for employment and independent living.

In Illinois a cooperative venture by the GPCDD, DORS, and the DHMDD has established several supported work programs for adults with disabilities. The support services provided through these program options have enabled many persons with severe disabilities to succeed in competitive job situations.

The TAC would be responsible for identifying postsecondary transition service options that would be expanded to permit people with disabilities to participate with increasing independence in community employment and residential situations. This council would assume primary leadership in an ongoing effort to promote the development, expansion, and effectiveness of postsecondary service options.

Observation #9 Personnel are not being adequately trained to provide secondary and postsecondary transition related services. The responsibilities of special education have expanded to include the preparation of students for employment and independent living; however, many special education teachers are still being prepared to assume more traditional classroom teaching responsibilities. These teachers are not being trained to provide vocational and independent living instruction in more realistic settings. In fairness to existing special education personnel, it should be noted that the ranking of transition-related services as a top priority is a relatively recent development.

As people with more severe disabilities become involved in employment preparation programs, a new set of skills must be acquired by teachers and other service providers. Unfortunately, most vocational educators, postsecondary educators, and rehabilitation personnel have not been trained to adapt curriculum and instructional materials for students with severe handicaps. Also, adult service personnel in sheltered workshops, vocational settings, and in developmental training programs have not been prepared to provide training in integrated community environments.

Recommendation #9 Professional qualifications need to be identified for professionals and paraprofessionals associated with school and postschool transition services. Community colleges, universities, and appropriate state agencies should be provided recommendations regarding specific skills, coursework, and certification requirements for personnel providing transition services.

An expansion of secondary and postsecondary transition service options will require a radical change in existing personnel preparation practices. The TAC must provide guidance to training institutions regarding needed inservice and preservice training practices. Since the success of new and expanded transition services options are ultimately dependent on the effectiveness of staff training practices, improvements in personnel preparation must be a top priority of the TAC.

Observation #10 Very few program evaluation studies of transition services and outcomes have been conducted. As a result, we have little data from which to judge the effectiveness of specified program options and from which to make determinations about resource allocation. The exception to this rule has been the technical assistance and evaluation project of the Department of Special Education at the University of Illinois. This project has provided assistance to several supported employment programs in the state of Illinois. The evaluation component of this project is designed to obtain information regarding the effectiveness of the program options with particular client populations.

Recommendation #10   Program evaluation studies should be conducted to investigate specific relationships between student characteristics, program components, and transition-related outcomes.

The Transition Planning and Needs Assessment data, in combination with follow-up information on all students leaving special education school programs, provide an excellent base for conducting more extensive program evaluation. If the characteristics of effective transition services can be identified, support services can be directed toward those areas most likely to result in successful postschool outcomes. Program evaluations studies would enable the TAC to make informed decisions about needed system change.

Observation #11   Most secondary and postsecondary services for persons with disabilities do not define measures by which their effectiveness should be judged. This lack of data reduces accountability within the field of human services, and does little to promote program improvement.

Recommendation #11   The TAC agencies should identify transition evaluation measures and should design a system for evaluating their effectiveness in accomplishing stated objectives. These outcome measures should be included in the postschool follow-up evaluation.

Recommendation #11 is closely related to Recommendation #10. The effectiveness of transition services is the measure against which programs should be evaluated. Since informed policy development is a goal of the TAC, the data-gathering and evaluation procedures advocated in Recommendations #10 and #11 are extremely important.

Observation #12   Many young people with disabilities are not provided access to the opportunities or experiences that would maximize their ability to live independently and be economically self-sufficient. Observations #7 and #8 point out that progressive secondary and postsecondary service options are not widely available in the state of Illinois. For example, the Department of Rehabilitation Services determines service provision eligibility on the basis of the individual's potential for gainful employment. These eligibility decisions are highly dependent on the availability of support services in specific communities. The supported employment initiative in the state of Illinois has increased the availability of support service options in many communities. Also, by easing eligibility restrictions, the initiative has made services available to persons previously judged to be ineligible. The practice of excluding people from service eligibility by DORS is understandably unpopular with clients and their families, especially when those services are viewed as essential for an individual to attain desired employment and independent living objectives. Although DORS was singled out in the above example, other agencies and services similarly restrict program eligibility. To DORS' credit, they have been very active in developing transition services that enable them to more effectively serve people with severe disabilities.

Recommendation #12   Services that focus on enhanced employment outcomes and increased community participation should be available to all Illinois residents. Necessary code and statute changes, in addition to interagency agreements, should be established to ensure residents' access to needed community services.

All persons should be given the opportunity to experience meaningful employment and to participate in community activities. Support services must be developed by school and postschool agencies that enable people to attain maximum levels of independence in employment and community living. A person's ability to perform meaningful work and to participate in the community is restricted more by inadequate service options than by severity of disability.

From these recommendations it is clear that the Illinois approach is ambitious and comprehensive. An especially attractive feature of this model is the heavy emphasis on personnel training, leadership development, and technical assistance outreach. These recommendations should be very appealing to a number of other states.

The Transition Planning Process in Florida

A state that has been exemplary in its planning for transition has been Florida. A uniquely positive feature of this state's legislature has been its support for a special study on transition that was presented to the Florida School Boards Association (Project Transition, 1986). Unquestionably, when school board involvement is substantial, any educational issue has a better chance of taking hold locally. In Florida, a long study was undertaken to determine the extent of need among students leaving special education programs. Particular attention was paid to graduation requirements for exceptional students and to the high dropout rate for handicapped students.

Florida also made a series of substantial recommendations that are now being implemented. These recommendations are similar to those made by Illinois but Florida places more emphasis on the vocational and adult education services. What follows are the eight specific recommendations made to the Florida legislature.

Recommendations

1. Enact additional legislation requiring the implementation of a transition process within each school district by July 1, 1987. Each district will have an interagency organization that will strengthen the transition from school to community for all students with

handicaps by utilizing components identified throughout this report. In addition, a transition plan will be required as part of the IEP process. Transition planning will begin when the student is 14; the plan will include parents, appropriate agency, and post-secondary or private sector representatives, and will be reviewed annually. Responsible agent: Department of Education.

2. Have state transition responsibilities assumed by certain targeted staff who will work closely with the Florida Interagency Transition Council and with local interagency councils. These groups will advise other agencies of names and further services needed by exceptional education students. Each local interagency council is charged with implementing a model transition process and with developing strategies to involve potential employers in the private sector in providing employment for persons with disabilities. Responsible agents: Florida Legislature and Department of Education.

3. Form a statewide task force that will address the needs of students wtih disabilities and will make recommendations on the problem of dropouts in exceptional education. Each local school district will be required to provide data on dropouts from all exceptional education programs. Responsible agent: Local education agencies.

4. Strengthen coordination efforts between exceptional education and vocational education in each county, and emphasize the need for more vocational work experience and workstudy classes for students with handicaps. Responsible agent: Florida Department of Education.

5. Implement the recommendations made in the Auditor General's report that call for increased numbers of sheltered workshops and increased day training opportunities leading to competitive employment. Supported employment should be made available for disabled residents throughout Florida. Responsible agents: Florida Legislature and Department of Health and Rehabilitative Services.

6. Develop standards for adult basic education programs to determine skills needed to complete the program within a specified period of time. Build on the existing components within these programs to make them viable options in the continuum of services available for handicapped adults. Advocate for additional staff at the state level for exceptional adult basic education programs; develop programs in counties not offering adult education programs and provide weighted funding for students of these pro-

grams. Responsible agents: Florida Legislature and Department of Education.

7. Develop vocational education as another viable option in the array of services available for handicapped students and adults. This can be done by expanding specialized vocational education programs with adaptive equipment, by increasing personnel responsible at state and local levels for exceptional vocational education and exceptional adult vocational education, and by providing weighted funding for specialized adult vocational education. Responsible agents: Florida Legislature and Department of Education.

8. Increase substantially the funding level for Health and Rehabilitative Services Developmental Service programs. A transition process will have little meaning without appropriate services such as case management as a way for handicapped individuals to achieve independence. Numerous reports have documented the tremendous need for additional Developmental Services funding. Responsible agents: Florida Legislature and Department of Health and Rehabilitative Services.

The follow-through and comprehensiveness of the Florida program has been outstanding. It appears that this state is well on its way to statewide transition programming.

Indiana and Transition

The key force in Indiana's commitment to transition has been the Governor's Planning Council on Developmental Disabilities. In a very short time, Indiana has been able to bring transition from being merely a "buzzword" to being a successful interagency program, with planning in several Indiana communities.

The Governor's Planning Council on Developmental Disabilities sponsored a statewide "Strategies for Change" conference on transition and supported employment in the spring of 1985. From the beginning, key policymakers, advocates, and administrators have viewed transition as inseparably linked to supported employment outcomes leading into competitive employment. Following the "Strategies for Change" conference, the Governor's council sponsored three followup "From School to Life" regional conferences on transition and supported employment in November. State and national leaders were brought in to share their experiences. In each region, parents, teachers, social workers, agency personnel, and administrators attended in large numbers. Most significant was the overwhelming attendance by vocational rehabilitation counselors.

At the regional conferences, the Governor's council introduced the recently passed Indiana Public Law 28. This law established a mechanism for persons who are disabled to gain entry into the adult service delivery system. It "requires school corporations to identify handicapped students who may benefit from ongoing adult services, provide information of ongoing adult services to student or student's parent, and facilitate transfer of student information to appropriate ongoing adult service agency." Rules and regulations were written that detailed how PL 28 is to be instituted. Through the rules and regulations that are the guidelines for carrying out the law, interagency collaboration resulted in a requirement that individual transition planning conferences would be held for every student with handicaps "who may benefit from ongoing adult services after their last year of school attendance." (Summary of PL 28)

Before November 1, in the identified student's last school year, the following actions should be undertaken by the following parties:

The School Corporation:

1. At a Case Conference/Annual Case Review Meeting, identifies students who are likely to benefit from adult services
2. Invites a local rehabilitation counselor to attend the Case Conference/Annual Case Review Meeting
3. Gives written materials concerning adult services to student and parents
4. Gives student and parents "consent to release information" form

If consent form is signed and received by the school corporation, The School Corporation:

1. Transfers necessary information to the local vocational rehabilitation counselor before February 1 each year

The Vocational Rehabilitation Agency:

1. Receives information from school corporation
2. Determines elgibility
3. Transfers information to local Department of Mental Health

The Department of Mental Health:

1. Receives information from vocational rehabilitation agency
2. Determines eligibility
3. Returns information and eligibility decision to vocational rehabilitation counselor

The Vocational Rehabilitation Agency:

1. Notifies student, parent, and referring school corporation of eligibility decision within 180 days of receipt of information.

Due to the leadership efforts of the Governor's council, schools, local rehabilitation agencies, and related state employees were requesting more information in order to successfully administer transition projects that would dovetail with supported employment outcomes at regular worksites. The Governor's council addressed this need by contacting the Training Division of the Rehabilitation Research and Training Center of Virginia Commonwealth University. The Training Division provided a "How-to" workshop for employment specialists, job coaches, and job developers who were training themselves to become employment specialists. This March 1986 workshop in Indianapolis provided much of the content for transition efforts in Indiana, and has helped them to be successful.

The work of the Governor's Planning Council on Developmental Disabilities continues through 1987 as its Transition and Supported Employment Committee assists the Governor's Supported Employment Policy Steering Committee. The following Executive Order was passed:

> In Executive Order No. 16–85 Indiana's Governor Orr states: IT IS HEREBY ORDERED that there is established the Governor's Supported Employment Policy Steering Committee, the members of which shall be appointed by and serve at the pleasure of the Governor. Only those persons appointed by the Governor may serve in a membership capacity on this Supported Employment Policy Steering Committee, and only Committee members may vote on any matter involving the Committee. The Committee is encouraged to seek counsel and input from any person or group with knowledge and expertise in matters concerning the developmentally disabled, most especially the Governor's Planning Council on Developmental Disabilities.

The key to Indiana's beginning efforts in transition has been interagency collaboration. Concurrent with the state-level developments by the Governor's committee and council, local interagency transition and supported employment projects have been successful. The Transition and Supported Employment Project of Washington Township (Indianapolis) is an example of this success. The combination of Chapter I innovative grant funding, PL 94-142 discretionary funding, and the support of a local Association for Retarded Citizens, Noble Centers, has evolved as an alternative to day activity center placements. An advisory council was formed from members of the following state and local agencies to support and advise the project:

1. The Department of Mental Health
2. Indiana Rehabilitation Services

3. The Department of Education
4. Washington Township Schools
5. The Marion County Association for Retarded Citizens
6. The Hollis Adams Foundation (parents)

In 9 months this cooperative effort had placed seven individuals who, without the benefit of transition or supported employment efforts, would have continued attending full-time segregated school facilities or would have remained on waiting lists for adult day activity center placement.

With the project's demonstrated success during the grant period, Indiana Rehabilitation Services and the Department of Mental Health are now funding the project and its expansion county-wide. Other transition projects are taking place in Columbus, South Bend, Johnson County and in other Indiana communities.

The Virginia Approach to Transition

Due to the groundwork and planning of Dr. Patricia Poplin at the Virginia Department of Education, and Mr. Thomas Bass from the Virginia Department of Rehabilitative Services, the State of Virginia has embarked upon a broad-scale approach to transition. With the aid of some special federal project funds, cooperative interagency planning has occurred. This planning is aimed at development, implementation, and refinement of a model that ensures disabled students will receive transition services upon leaving special education. Transition services include employment, independent living, and successful life adjustment. Case management tracking of the student from school to the adult service system with the aid of computer technology is a major part of this model.

There are many positive features to what Virginia is in the process of doing, some of these features have already been implemented by the three previously mentioned states. One noteworthy aspect of Virginia's approach, as can be seen below, is a substantial emphasis on program implementation rather than just program planning. Major aspects of the Virginia model of transition include:

1. Interagency planning for delivery of transition services at state and local levels among the following agencies:
   —the Division of Special Education and Vocational and Adult Education within the Virginia Department of Education
   —the Virginia Department of Rehabilitative Services
   —The Employment Committee of the Virginia Board for Rights of the Disabled

     —the Virginia Department of Mental Health and Mental Retardation
     —the Virginia Community College System
     —the State Council of Higher Education for Virginia
     —the Governor's Employment and Training Division (which administers the Job Training and Partnership Act)
     —the Virginia Department for the Visually Handicapped
     —the Department for the Deaf and Hard of Hearing

2. The establishment of a State Interagency Transition Task Force (SITT) to develop a transition planning process that integrates and develops case management procedures among service providers
3. The implementation and evaluation of the transition planning process and service delivery procedures developed by the SITT occurring at the local level in pilot sites representing four distinct geographic and demographic entities that have applicability across the Commonwealth of Virginia, as well as across the nation
4. The provision of transition programs and services using the coordinated interagency case management procedures developed by the SITT for up to 240 youth and young adults representing all categories of disabilities
5. The development of a computerized transition resource information system for the state that identifies resources necessary to meet the transition needs of students with disabilities
6. The development of a computerized tracking and follow-up system that will assist state agencies in tracking disabled individuals through the state's service delivery system and will provide follow-up information on the status of each individual
7. To implement and evaluate the effectiveness of the transition information resource system and the tracking and follow-up system in each pilot site
8. The involvement of candidates and their parents, employers, and human service professionals in the development and implementation of a formal transition planning process
9. The commitment by all cooperating agencies to the development and implementation of formal interagency agreements that define roles, responsibilities, service delivery components, and funding sources for transition planning and case management services.

This model is very ambitious in scope, and has the full authority of the State Department of Education behind it. The challenge being faced by Virginia and other states is how to effect change at the local

Table 9.3. Virginia transition model: Case management examples

Case 1:   A physically disabled student with good intellectual abilities and aca-
          demic skills may find college and university programs within the state
          providing modifications in undergraduate curriculum offerings based
          on student needs identified through the Virginia transition model.

Case 2:   A high school dropout who had been classified as emotionally handi-
          capped by the public schools has the potential of receiving a more effi-
          ciently and effectively planned program in a private industry council
          (JTPA funded) administered training program as a result of record and
          information transfer coordinated through the state transition planning
          and case management procedures.

Case 3:   A 22-year-old moderately mentally retarded student who "aged-out" of
          the secondary special education program in the public schools would
          have better access to the coordinated employment services of DRS
          and MHMR, as well as assistance in obtaining community residential
          and transportation services through the VAST transition process. In
          addition, early transition planning for this individual would result in a
          secondary special education program being specifically designed to
          prepare the student for community transition and adjustment.

level, when resources and services are very limited, and graduating
students are continually being placed on waiting lists.

The Virginia model presents three different illustrations of how
disabled youth would be served through the case management system. Table 9.3 shows how this system could positively affect persons
with three different disabilities.

TRANSITION ACTIVITIES IN SELECTED STATES

While we have been very impressed with the way Illinois, Florida,
Virginia, and Indiana have developed their transition programs, it is
clear that many other states have made significant strides as well in
planning and legislation. For example, Massachusetts was the first
state in the country to pass a law (House Bill No. 688) mandating individual transition planning and agency coordination. Long waiting
lists and lack of funds have troubled the implementation of this law.

Another state that has new transition legislation is Kansas. To the
authors' knowledge, this is the only state that legislatively mandates
vocational rehabilitation to take the lead in pulling all agencies together. The Kansas law (HB 2300) became effective in the 1986–1987
school year. This legislation provides for transition planning in two
pilot sites, Salina, Kansas, and Hayes, Kansas. A student may be referred to the Department of Social and Rehabilitative Services any
time in the final 6 months of school by his or her transition planning

team. The plan is to eventually expand the service period so that planning begins in the final 3 years of school. Populations to be served in the pilot sites are those persons with mental retardation, autism, deafness, or blindness; other SSI recipients are also eligible. This legislation entitles disabled persons to receive a transition plan, but not necessarily to receive services.

The states of California, West Virginia, Tennessee, and Idaho are four other states that have active interagency planning committees. In West Virginia, for example, statewide conferences were held in March, 1986, and in November, 1986 to review and pull together the best thinking on transition implementation. William Phelps and Ivan Dean Cook, leading figures in the field, have significantly influenced the direction of transition activity in this state. The March 21, 1986 conference document provides their workscope, tasks, and plans for long-term implementation.

In California, beginning June 25, 1986, the Transition Model Program was initiated. A total of one million dollars was appropriated. The transition program offers opportunities and services for a broad range of individuals with exceptional needs. This includes but is not limited to:

1. Employment and academic training
2. Strategic planning
3. Interagency coordination
4. Parent training

The program will build on existing resources and knowledge and will include, but not be limited to:

1. The development and provision of inservice training programs, resource materials, and handbooks that include the major components of an effective school-based transition program
2. The development of the role and responsibilities of special education in the transition process
3. The development and implementation of systematic and longitudinal vocational educational curriculum
4. The development of materials, resource manuals, and inservice training programs to support the active participation of parents in the planning and implementation of transition-related goals and activities
5. The development of resources and inservice training that will support the implementation of individualized transition planning for all individuals with exceptional needs
6. A research and development program that will support the major features of the model transition program

SOME CONCLUDING THOUGHTS

The previous discussion has highlighted reports from some of the more progressive state transition planning programs. Again, it should be reiterated that in no way does this review wish to suggest that these are the only states engaged in successful programs. In fact, very few states are not involved to some extent in meaningful transition planning activity.

What are the basic elements of these successful programs? One element consistently found in successful programs is comprehensiveness, that is, the wide-spread involvement of all possible agencies that might make a difference. Such commitment, while logistically difficult, may in the long run provide the sustaining momentum of the entire transition movement in any given state. The concerted involvement of many groups, if well orchestrated, gives new vitality and authority to problem solving that one organization alone,—special education, for example, could never provide.

Another consistent feature of these state programs is that, with the exception of Kansas, it is the Department of Education in each state that must initiate planning and implementation activities. This element is highly consistent with the recommendations made to Congress by the National Council on the Handicapped (1986):

1. Congress should direct the Department of Education to designate the state educational agency as the lead agency to start, develop, and carry out the transition planning process. . . (p. 22).
2. Congress should direct the Department of Education to strengthen regulations requiring the involvement of education coordinators and vocational rehabilitation counselors in the transition process. . . (p. 23)

Attention to inservice training and other personnel preparation activities was another feature present in successful programs. Without technical assistance and continuing staff development it is likely that the challenge of properly training personnel can never be met. New staff must be recruited and, even more than that, existing staff must be retrained. Vocational educators and special educators need to better understand each other's roles. Rehabilitation counselors and special educators must more fully understand the limitations as well as the potential of their respective positions. Illinois in particular seems to have taken the lead here with the help of the Secondary Effectiveness and Transition Institute, based at the University of Illinois.

What perhaps is the most interesting feature about each of these reports is that, other than Florida, most states did not recommend soliciting more money as their highest possible priority. While there is general acknowledgment that new funds will have to be forthcoming in order to sponsor additional students, the general focus of these reports was on the coordination of existing resources and on increased efficiency and collaboration in the sharing of resources.

SUMMARY

This book addresses methods of planning and implementing meaningful transition programs. The authors have focused on the individual, local, and state planning levels. Research has been reviewed, models were presented, successful practices were described, and training programs were outlined. The authors have endeavored to ground this book in practicality, while at the same time providing a state-of-the-art approach to program development. There is a major challenge ahead: for professionals from many disciplines to work together more than ever for effective transition planning as we move toward the end of the decade.

Appendix A
Guidelines for Parent Involvement in Vocational Training

THE FOLLOWING GUIDELINES HAVE BEEN USED BY MANY FAMILIES WHO ARE interested in actively participating in the vocational training and school-to-work transition of their son or daughter. Teachers, counselors, and case managers may want to provide these guidelines to parents as an initial, concrete way to become involved in the transition process. Of course, there are many more suggestions than those provided here. The ones that follow are adapted from Moon and Beale (1985).

IF YOU ARE THE PARENTS OF AN ELEMENTARY-AGE CHILD WITH A DISABILITY, YOU CAN:

1. Become aware of your child's eventual need to enter the world of work. Speak positively about working and supporting oneself.
2. Be sure your child's current IEP addresses employment awareness and training.
3. Be aware of the employment training opportunities available in the upper grades.
4. Point out workers to your child when you go out in the community. Discuss what the worker is doing and encourage your child to think about what job she or he might like.
5. Give your child specific responsibilities around the house. Insist

that she or he perform all duties thoroughly and on time. Give
your child an allowance for completing duties.
6. Encourage school teachers to include in their daily lesson plans
work-related concepts, such as money, employer-employee relationships, staying on-task, moving from one area to another, and
keeping a work station clean.
7. Emphasize physical fitness and appropriate use of free or play
time.
8. Encourage your child to dress and groom appropriately.
9. Familiarize yourself with state and federal regulations concerning education and employment of persons with handicaps.
10. Find out about the services available to adults with handicaps in
your community. Also, learn about the "state-of-the-art" vocational and residential options available in other areas and compare these to the options in your locale.

IF YOU ARE THE PARENTS OF A
MIDDLE SCHOOL–AGE CHILD WITH A DISABILITY, YOU CAN:

1. Actively support the school's efforts to provide job training in
community-based sites.
2. See that your child's IEP addresses specific vocational training
and functional social and community access skills that are to be
taught in a variety of actual work settings.
3. Make sure that job training in the community is available in the
high school program your child will enter.
4. See that educators are formally communicating with local vocational rehabilitation agency representatives and residential case
managers.
5. Start meeting adult service providers to sort out what options
your child should have access to.
6. Find work outside the home for your child to do during vaca-
tions, weekends, and after school.
7. Continue to work with your child on appearance, health maintenance, and physical fitness.
8. Teach your child to budget money and use banking facilities by
providing a small allowance or pay for performing certain jobs.
9. Continue to discuss the importance and benefits of working and
earning wages.
10. Get your child involved in community-based leisure activities
and teach him or her to use the public transportation system.

IF YOU ARE THE PARENTS OF A
HIGH SCHOOL-AGE CHILD, YOU CAN:

1. Make sure that your daughter or son has a formal ITP that specifies job placement and residential options and includes deadlines for the achievement of both goals. Training sites, methods, and persons responsible should be part of this ITP.
2. See that a team is formed composed of human services professionals, the student, and the student's family to develop the ITP as part of the formal IEP process. The professionals in the team could be the special and vocational education teachers, the rehabilitation counselor, the developmental disabilities case manager, or others.
3. Encourage the school to find, place, and train your child in a full- or part-time job that pays a wage while he or she is still in school.
4. If job placement has not previously been arranged, make sure that some sort of adult service program is clearly in place for your child before he or she graduates. (This should be part of the ITP.)
5. Continue to work with the student on matters of appearance, grooming, physical fitness, budgeting, completing chores, staying on schedule, and use of community-based facilities.

Appendix B *Knowing Work and Residential Options*

IT IS IMPORTANT THAT PARENTS AND ADVOCATES BECOME AWARE EARLY IN a child's education of the employment and living options that may or may not be available in a particular community. The following lists indicate the range of residential and employment options ranked in a hierarchy of "least to most restrictive" that exist throughout the country. Several of the residential options, such as large residential facilities, hotels, or workshop dormitories, may not be desirable for persons with severe handicapping conditions.

Residential Options

1. Independent living
   Single-family homes
   Shared homes
   Individual or shared
     apartments
   Groups of individual
     apartments
   Dwellings in new
     apartment buildings
   Residential hotels
2. Natural or adoptive home
   (with in-home services)
3. Other relative's home
4. Friend's home
5. Foster family care

Employment Options

1. Competitive employment
2. Supported employment
   Unsubsidized wages
   May or may not be paid
     minimum wages
   Located in integrated
     worksites in the com-
     munity with the op-
     portunity to interact
     with nonhandicapped
     workers
   Examples: Supported
     competitive employ-
     ment; Specialized in-
     dustrial program

257

Residential Options

6. Developmental foster home
7. Group homes
   Small group home
   Medium group home
   Large group home
   Mixed group home
   Group home for older adults
8. Nursing homes
   Community care facility (ICF)
   Convalescent home
   County home
9. Boarding homes
10. Hotels
11. Sheltered villages
12. Public residential facilities
13. Private residential facilities
14. Workshop-dormitories

(Adapted from Heal, Novak, Sigelman, and Switzky [1980].)

Employment Options

(small business); Sheltered enclave; Mobile work crew

3. Employment training programs
   Subsidized wages
   May or may not be paid minimum wage
   May or may not take place in integrated work settings
   Supervision and training may be provided by industry or by professional staff
   Examples: Transitional Employment Program (TEP); Job Training Partnership Act (JTPA); Projects With Industry (PWI); On-the-Job Training (OJT); School sponsored job training stations
4. Evaluation and training in specialized facility
5. Sheltered workshop
6. Work activity center/adult service center
7. Rehabilitation center/ developmental center/ adult day program
8. Health care maintenance program

(Adapted from Goodall and Bruder [1986].)

Appendix C

Federal Initiatives, Legislative Mandates, and Employment Incentive Programs

DUE TO THE EFFECTIVENESS OF PL 94-142 IN IMPROVING THE GENERAL education of students with handicaps, there are now large numbers of students leaving school who do not have appropriate work or community living options arranged for them. As a result of this gap in services, federal initiatives have been proposed and laws have been enacted mandating the human service agencies to provide assistance to young people as they move from school to adult life. In addition, there are new sources of money available as a result of these initiatives and laws, and programs have been established by the business community that can assist in the transition from school to work.

Parents and professionals need to understand the impact that these new initiatives and laws will have on vocational training programs and adult work and living options for their child with disabilities. Several of the more salient federal priorities, initiatives, and legislation are outlined below.

1. Education for All Handicapped Children Act of 1975 (PL 94-142) (Amended 1983 & 1986)

— All handicapped children, regardless of the severity of their disability, will receive a free, appropriate education at public expense.
— Education of handicapped children will be based on a full and fair evaluation and assessment of the unique needs of each child.
— Individualized education programs (IEPs) will be drawn up for every child found to be eligible for special education, stating precisely what kinds of special education and related services each child will receive. Related services for handicapped children include recreation, industrial arts, *vocational education*, counseling, and transportation. Also included are other specific activities that meet individual needs, such as speech pathology services and physical and occupational therapy.
— Parents have the right to participate in every decision related to the education of their handicapped child.
— Parents must give consent for any change in the child's program being considered; parents and teachers must be included in conferences held to draw up individualized programs; parents must approve these plans before they go into effect.
— The right of parents to challenge and appeal any decision related to identification, evaluation, and placement of their child must be fully protected by due process procedures that are clearly spelled out.

2. Transition of Youth with Disabilities Priority—Office of Special Education and Rehabilitation Services: U.S. Department of Education (1984)
   — Establishes as a national priority the availability of services effecting transition from school to working life for all individuals with disabilities.
   — Maintains that the goal of education and transition is sustained employment. An array of services are available to help the student achieve this goal:
     a) high school foundation offering an integrated, community-based, functional curriculum
     b) coordinated efforts among school and adult service providers to assure a smooth transition
     c) combination of work options with the support necessary for employment retention

3. Supported Employment Initiative—Office of Special Education

and Rehabilitation Services: U.S. Department of Education (1984)

— Defines supported employment as being characterized by four elements:
    a) It is designed for individuals typically served in day activity programs who, because of the severity of the disability, are not served by vocational rehabilitation.
    b) It involves the continuing provision of training, supervision, and support services
    c) It is designed to produce the same benefits received by nonhandicapped workers as manifested by indicators considered to be normal measures of employment quality: income level, quality of working life
    d) It incorporates flexibility in support strategies to assist individuals in obtaining and performing work
— Provides funding to assist states in converting traditional day activity programs to alternative supported employment programs.

4. Employment Initiative—Administration on Developmental Disabilities, U.S. Department of Health and Human Services: Office of Human Development Services
    — Establishes employment of persons with developmental disabilities as a funding priority.
    — Supports the concept of the private sector as the primary source of competitive jobs for persons with developmental disabilities.
    — Provides for a national public awareness campaign to increase interest in employing persons with developmental disabilities.

5. Education of the Handicapped Act Amendments of 1983 (PL 98-199)—Section 626
    — Provides for secondary education and transition services for handicapped youth ages 12–22.
    — Authorizes funding for research and training for the following:
        a) development of strategies and techniques for transition to independent living
        b) establishment of demonstration models emphasizing vocational, transitional, and job placement services
        c) provision of demographic studies on numbers and types of handicapping conditions of students and on services required by these students

        d) initiation of collaborative models between education agencies and adult service agencies

        e) development of procedures for evaluation of transition programs

6. Carl D. Perkins Vocational Education Act of 1984 (PL 98-524)
   — Maintains that 10% of State's formula grant allotment under Part A should be used to provide vocational education to handicapped individuals as additional costs over regular vocational education expenditures.
   — Mandates that every student with disabilities and his or her parents should be informed of vocational education opportunities available in the school 1 year before vocational education services are provided, or by the time the student reaches ninth grade.
   — Ensures that students with disabilities have equal access to services through vocational education when appropriate, as indicated in the IEP. Services may include:
       a) vocational assessment
       b) special services with adaptation of curriculum to meet needs
       c) guidance counseling and career development
       d) staff and counseling services to facilitate transition

7. Developmental Disabilities Act of 1984 (PL 98-527)
   — Adds "employment related" activities as a new priority service to administering agency of developmental disabilities funds. This area will be mandated priority by fiscal year 1987.
   — Drops nonvocational social developmental services as a priority service.
   — Provides $10,000 supplement to UAFs for activities related to raising public awareness of employment of persons with developmental disabilities

8. Employment Opportunities for Disabled Americans Act (PL 99-643) (1986)
   — Permanently authorizes section 1619(a) and (b) of the Social Security Act.
   — Section 1619(a) authorizes cash benefits to be paid to working social security beneficiaries as long as their earnings are below the federal break-even point.
   — Section 1619(b) authorizes the continuation of Medicaid coverage to social security recipients whose earnings, minus medical costs, do not equal the total of SSI and Medicaid benefits.

— Once an individual "earns out" of 1619(b), there will be a 12-month period during which he or she may automatically move back into either 1619(a) or (b).

9. Social Security Act, Title XVI, 1974 Amendments (Supplemental Security Income *SSI*)
   — Authorizes SSI on an as-needed basis for blind, aged, or disabled.
     a) disability prevents person from substantial gainful activity for continuous period of 12 months
     b) must show low income and possess few assets to qualify for benefits
     c) under Section 1615, adult beneficiaries must be referred to state vocational rehabilitation agency

10. Social Security Act, Section 202 of Title II, 1972 Amendments (Social Security Disability Insurance *SSDI*)
    — Provides Social Security benefits to children of workers receiving SS retirement or disability benefits or of workers who died and were insured for SS benefits at time of death.
      a) benefits to age 18
      b) after age 18, adult disabled children can receive benefits if disability began before age 22
      c) adult disabled children must be referred to state vocational rehabilitation agency

11. 1965 Amendments to the Social Security Act (Grants to states for Medical Assistance and Medicaid)
    — Authorized grants-in-aid to states for Medicaid programs.
      a) eligibility based on financial need
      b) most individuals with handicaps are eligible

12. Social Security Disability Amendments of 1980, Sections 1619(a) and (b) (Public Law 96-265)
    — Section 1619(a) authorizes the payment of cash benefits to working Social Security beneficiaries as long as their earnings fall below the federal eligibility level.
    — Section 1619(b) authorizes the continuation of Medicaid coverage to Social Security recipients with earnings exceeding the break-even point if recipients continue to qualify for benefits.
    — allows for a 15-month reentitlement period following the 9-month trial period for SSI and SSDI beneficiaries if recipient loses a job because of his or her disability.

13. Title XIX of Social Security Act, 1971 Amendments (PL 92-223) (ICF/MR)

— Authorizes Medicaid reimbursement for intermediate care facilities (ICF).

14. Omnibus Budget Reconciliation Act of 1981 (PL 97-35) (Community-Based Care Waivers)
    — Permits states that obtain a waiver to finance, through the federal-state Medicaid program, noninstitutional services for individuals who would otherwise require institutional care.

15. Rehabilitation Act (PL 99-506) (1986)
    — Provides for supported employment services in all states by 25 million dollar authorization.
    — Authorizes supported employment as a viable rehabilitation option.
    — Provides new emphasis on rehabilitation engineering for persons with severe physical disability.
    — Expands personnel preparation and demonstration activities in supported employment for persons with the most severe handicaps.

TARGETED JOBS TAX CREDIT

The Targeted Jobs Tax Credit (TJTC) program, initiated by President Carter, was signed into law on November 6, 1978. The operation of the TJTC program has been altered many times since it was initiated; the most recent change occurred under the Tax Reform Act of 1986, which was signed into law on October 22, 1986. This legislation reauthorized the TJTC program for a 3-year period through December 31, 1988.

The TJTC program is managed and operated jointly by the Departments of Labor and Treasury. The Department of Labor administers the eligibility determination and certification provisions through its Employment and Training Administration. The Department of the Treasury administers the tax credit provisions of the program through its Internal Revenue Service. The IRS is responsible for granting the tax credit to employers and for enforcement of the provisions.

Congress intended in TJTC to open up work opportunities for certain disadvantaged groups of people. The program is a tool to help eligible persons move into unsubsidized employment in the private sector, thereby helping to ease the chronically high unemployment rates among these groups.

The TJTC program is an incentive to employers to make more and better job opportunities available to workers from the nine targeted groups and to retain these workers in the critical first months of employment.

The TJTC program is based on the following principles: 1) work is a way for the disadvantaged to gain the skills, training, and experience they need to suceed; 2) employment in the private sector is the best solution to unemployment; and 3) resources should be targeted toward those most in need.

The economic incentive is in the form of a sizable reduction in a company's federal income tax liability based on the amount of wages paid to each worker who qualifies an employer for the credit. The program is also appealing because there is little paperwork involved, and the burden of proving a worker's eligibility is completely handled by outside agencies.

State employment agencies act as the program managers at the state and local levels to oversee certification procedures. Employers may contact the job service division and request only TJTC eligible candidates for their job openings. Companies can also refer potential job applicants to the job service office, which will then determine the individual's eligibility.

Employers claim the tax credit by filing IRS Form 5884 along with federal income tax forms. The TJTC applies to qualified wages that a company pays to eligible members of targeted groups.

TJTC FACTS

The Targeted Jobs Tax Credit, or TJTC, is a tax break in the form of credits that are subtracted from the federal income tax payment owed by a business to the government. All private employers engaged in trade or business can take advantage of this tax credit. An employer is eligible for this tax credit by hiring workers who qualify as members of one of the "targeted" groups.

The tax credit is computed by using the wages paid to each qualifying employee during the first 2 years of employment with the company. The credit, subject to certain limitations, is 40% of the first $6,000 the worker is paid in wages during the first year of employment (maximum credit allowed is $2,400 per worker).

Certifying agencies in the community determine worker eligibility and issue "vouchers" to eligible target group members. When a business hires an eligible worker, a small amount of paperwork (a few lines on the bottom of the voucher) must be completed by the company and mailed to the TJTC unit on or before the first day the person begins work.

The TJTC unit will usually mail back a certification for the worker within 3 working days. This certification, along with the dollar amount of wages paid to certified employees, is the only documentation the company needs to claim the credit.

There is a minimum employment or retention period an employer must satisfy in order to claim any portion of the tax credit for a worker. A worker who is hired under the TJTC program must be employed for at least 90 days for 120 hours of paid employment before the employer can claim the tax credit.

Employers claim the credit by filing IRS Form 5884 with their federal income tax return. The certification is retained in the company's tax files as proof of entitlement.

There are certain limitations (such as the company's tax bracket) that affect the actual amount of the net tax reduction. Employers with questions can refer to IRS Publication 906 for detailed TJTC information, or they may contact the IRS.

Employers can also contact the local employment commission job service to find out how to locate qualified workers, or to obtain information on certification procedures and eligibility determination.

VOCATIONAL REHABILITATION ON-THE-JOB TRAINING

There are currently 15 mandated services that state vocational rehabilitation (VR) agencies must offer under federal regulations. Within these guidelines, on-the-job training is a legitimate training service that every state VR has the potential to provide.

Vocational rehabilitation on-the-job training is a wage subsidy program in which employers are reimbursed for the additional training costs borne by the employer of a worker who is disabled. (Employers should not be remunerated for regular orientation training that is given to any new employee.) The reimbursement is based on the reasoning that the trainee will not usually exhibit 100% productivity during the first few weeks or months of training. The decreasing amount of reimbursement payments over the period of training acknowledges that the trainee will perform at higher levels of productivity as training progresses.

On-the-job training gives an individual the opportunity to learn a specific occupation or to acquire skills necessary to perform certain duties under actual employment conditions. This employment training can be arranged by a vocational rehabilitation agency if the work experience provided by an employer is an effective means of attaining an individual's vocational objective. There should be a reasonable expectation that the trainee will acquire skills adequate to maintain the job position, and that the trainee will be hired by the employer at the end of the designated training period.

In most cases, the OJT agreement is formalized as a written contract between the VR agency and the employer. There is no typical OJT agreement: the specific terms of an OJT arrangement may vary from state to state, as well as within a state.

Employers who accept trainees for on-the-job training programs must pay at least minimum wage (or the going rate for a particular position), and must agree to provide full coverage for Worker's Compensation, unemployment insurance, and Social Security. Also, the trainee should be eligible for any benefits that other employees receive.

One important note needs to be mentioned. Employers who participate in an on-the-job training program involving financial reimbursements are still eligible for the federal Targeted Jobs Tax Credit. However, the TJTC will not go into effect until after the OJT funds are no longer being received by the employer. The employer must still apply for certification from the state TJTC unit *on or before the day a worker is hired.*

ASSOCIATION FOR RETARDED CITIZENS OF THE UNITED STATES'S ON-THE-JOB TRAINING PROJECT

The Association for Retarded Citizens (ARC) On-The-Job Training Project encourages businesses throughout the United States to provide job opportunities for mentally retarded persons. The program operates through a contractual agreement between an employer and the ARC. The employer agrees to provide a job and 320 hours of intensive on-the-job training to a person with mental retardation. The ARC agrees to reimburse 50% of the entry wage for the first 160 critical hours (4 weeks) of employment and 25% of the wages during the second 160 hours of employment.

This financial reimbursement is made to offset the additional costs that sometimes occur when providing training to a worker who is mentally retarded. The reimbursement is paid at the end of the training period.

Any organization involved in the job placement and training of individuals with mental retardation can apply for ARC/OJT reimbursement funds if the trainee and the employer are eligible.

An individual is eligible for OJT services if he or she is mentally retarded; at least 16 years old; and unemployed for at least 7 consecutive days, or unofficially enrolled in school, or working only part-time.

On-the-job trainees are considered regular employees right from the start. The participating employer must pay the trainee at the same rate of pay as other nondisabled employees in the same position. The employer retains absolute right of employee selection and termination.

An employer is eligible for OJT reimbursement funds if he or she pays the trainee at least minimum wage; hires the trainee for at least 35 hours per week; intends to continue the trainee as a regular employee after the training period (there is no obligation if employee is unable to meet work requirements); does not hire an immediate family member; and does not hire a trainee when a layoff status exists for the same or equivalent job.

The following types of business cannot be reimbursed under the ARC project: federal agencies, any facility used for sectarian instruction or as a place for religious worship (including church-affiliated elementary and secondary schools), sheltered workshops or other agencies that habilitate persons with mental retardation, businesses that operate only during certain seasons of the year, and apparel manufacturers (for power sewing machine operator positions).

The completion of an application form asking 15 questions about the job training site and of a record of wages paid to the trainee during the first 320 hours of employment is the only paperwork required of the employer—a small investment of time and effort by a company for a big return!

JOB TRAINING PARTNERSHIP ACT (JTPA)

For the first time, the private sector, in equal partnership with the government, is determining the nature and direction of federally funded job training programs through the Job Training Partnership Act (JTPA). The identification of training needs and work skills by local business and industry and the funding of appropriate training programs is the hallmark of JTPA programs.

Ensuring that education and training are geared toward the acquisition of skills valuable to private sector companies is the basis for the active participation of employers in employment training programs. Each state has a job training coordinating council composed of individuals representing service providers, local government, and business and industry. This council is responsible for general administration of the program and contributes to the design of local training activities in service delivery areas.

Each service delivery area within a state has a Private Industry Council (PIC). The members of the PIC must be representatives of education, labor, rehabilitation, and private sector business. This council determines which local programs are funded and generally oversees the activities and policies implemented at the local level. The PIC determines the local job training program and selects the entity to administer the program; this could be the PIC, the unit of local government, or a nonprofit organization.

There are 28 services that may be provided under JTPA, although additional job training services can be provided by local plan administrators. Some of the services listed are job counseling, on-the-job training, programs to develop work habits, work experience, and customized job training or the Projects With Industry model.

For additional information on the Job Training Partnership Act refer to *Job Training Partnership Act, PL 97-300: An Analysis and Guide* prepared by the National Association of Rehabilitation Facilities, Washington, D.C.; *Using the Job Training Partnership Act to Further Local Economic Development; Job Creation Through Economic Development: The Role of Private Industry Councils;* and *Economic Development and Job Creation* from the National Alliance of Business, Washington, D.C. For information on how to get involved with JTPA, contact the state job training coordinating council.

PROJECTS WITH INDUSTRY (PWI)

Projects With Industry (PWI) are federally financed cooperative arrangements that may be made with employers for the establishment of projects that prepare individuals, especially severely handicapped individuals, for competitive employment. These projects may include training exclusively, or training in combination with employment, depending on need.

The PWI program brings together business, industry, and rehabilitation services in a cooperative effort to meet the employment needs of the private sector with qualified disabled workers. Although PWI funding arrangements allow for creativity and flexibility, there are three broad requirements to which PWI agencies or organizations must adhere:

1. It must have as its ultimate objective the placement of disabled people into competitive jobs.
2. It must have a Business Advisory Council made up primarily of employers in management positions.
3. It must include a training program that aids in the qualification of disabled people for competitive employment. (In a few instances, projects that do not have a training component have been funded and supported by PWI.)

There is no typical applicant for PWI funds. Projects with Industry grants have been awarded to rehabilitation facilities, national labor organizations, industrial or community trade organizations, nonprofit and for-profit businesses, industries, and commercial enterprises. PWI grants have also been awarded to other agencies or organizations that have demonstrated their capacity to provide employment training, job placement services, and other assistance to individuals with disabilities.

In the first 10 years of PWI funding, 50,000 disabled persons were placed into employment with 15,000 corporations. A survey of a sample of companies employing PWI graduates reports a solid retention rate of 75%–80%. Currently, there are approximately 100 Projects with Industry in operation throughout the country.

For further information on PWIs, refer to the *Federal Register* for notification of Requests for Proposals; the *Projects With Industry International Directory* prepared by The Menninger Foundation in cooperation with Project Independence in Topeka, Kansas; the *National Director of Rehabilitation Services Administration Funded Projects with Industry*, published in Washington, D.C. by the National Association of Rehabilitation Facilities; the *Projects With Industry Rehabilitation-Industry Advisory Council*, prepared by the National Association of Rehabilitation Facilities; and *Projects With Industry: A Public/Private Partnership that Works*, published by the Arkansas Rehabilitation Research and Training Center.

Appendix D   *Employment Information Resources*

THE FOLLOWING ORGANIZATIONS CAN PROVIDE FURTHER INFORMATION ON legislation and on incentives available to employers who hire individuals with disabilities:

Architectural and Transportation Barriers Compliance Board
330 C Street, S.W., Room 1010
(202) 245-1591
(Architectural Barriers Act of 1968; accessibility complaints)

Association for Retarded Citizens of the United States
On-The-Job Training Project
2501 Avenue J, P.O. Box 6109
Arlington, Texas 76011
(817) 640-0204

Berkeley Planning Associates
3200 Adeline Street
Berkeley, California 94703
(415) 652-0999
(Job accommodation studies)

Department of Health and Human Services
Administration on Developmental Disabilities

200 Independence Ave., S.W.,
    Room 348F
Washington, D.C. 20201
(202) 245-2888

Mainstream, Inc.
1200 15th Street, N.W., Suite 403
Washington, D.C. 20005
(202) 833-1136 Voice/TTY
(Rights and responsibilities under federal law for employers and persons with disabilities; accessibility information; barriers survey, "The Cost of Accessibility")

National Association of Rehabilitation Facilities
P.O. Box 17675
Washington, D.C. 20041
(703) 556-8848
(Projects With Industry; Job Training Partnership Act)

National Restaurant Association
Handicapped Employment
  Programs
311 1st Street, N.W.
Washington, D.C. 20001
(202) 638-6100
(Projects With Industry pro-
  grams in food services)

E. I. duPont de Nemours & Company
Graphics Communication Division (A-15124)
Wilmington, Delaware 19898
(800) 527-2601
(1981) (duPont survey of employment of the handicapped)

Human Resources Center
Albertson, NY 11507
(516) 747-5400
(Projects With Industry; affirmative action; accessibility)

Internal Revenue Service
Legislation and Regulations
  Division
1111 Constitution Avenue, N.W.
Washingon, D.C. 20224
(202) 566-4473
(Tax deducation for barrier
  removal)

Job Accommodation Network
President's Committee on Em-
  ployment of the Handicapped
P.O. Box 468
Morgantown, WV 26505
1-800-JAN-PCEH

Office of Special Education and Rehabilitative Services
U.S. Department of Education
400 Maryland Avenue, S.W.
Washington, D.C. 20202

President's Committee on Employment of the Handicapped
1111 20th Street, N.W.
Washington, D.C. 20036
(202) 653-5044 Voice/TTY

U.S. Department of Labor
Employment Training
  Administration
601 D Street, N.W.
Washington, D.C. 20210
(202) 523-6871
(Job Training Partnership Act;
  Targeted Jobs Tax Credit)

U.S. Department of Labor
Office of Federal Contract
Compliance Programs (OFCCP)
200 Constitution Avenue, N.W.
Washington, D.C. 20213
(202) 523-9368
(Affirmative action and ac-
  cessibility compliance)

Contact the following agencies in each state for information and
  assistance:

State Employment Commission or Job Services
(Targeted Jobs Tax Credit)

Private Industry Councils
(Job Training Partnership Act)
**State (or Governor's) Committees on Employment of the
   Handicapped**
(Job Training Partnership Act)
State Department of Labor
(Targeted Jobs Tax Credit)
State Departments of Vocational Rehabilitation
(On-The-Job Training Funds)
State Industrial Commissions
(Worker's compensation; second injury clause)
State Job Training Coordinating Councils
(Job Training Partnership Act)

Appendix E   *Annotated Bibliography on Supported Employment and Transition*

SUPPORTED EMPLOYMENT

Anthony, W. A., & Jansen, M. (1984). Predicting the vocational capacity of the chronically mentally ill: Research and policy implications. *American Psychologist, 39*(5), 532–544.

In response to the growing recognition that adequately trained personnel and appropriate intervention techniques were not available to meet the rehabilitation needs of psychiatrically disabled persons, the first Rehabilitation Research and Training Center in Mental Health was established in August, 1979. Because the Center's mandate is to focus on problems of national scope, and because the chronically mentally ill have been severely and adversely affected by the recent Social Security Administration actions that have terminated disability benefits, a review of the research literature surrounding the vocational capacity of psychiatrically disabled persons was undertaken. This article details results of that review, identifies needed research in the area of employability of the chronically mentally ill, and notes implications for policy.

Bellamy, G. T., Rhodes, L. E., & Albin, J. M. (1986). Supported employment. In W. E. Kiernan & J. A. Stark (Eds.), *Pathways to employment for adults with*

This annotated bibliography was developed by Paul Wehman, M. V. Morton, Cheri Stierer, Wendy Wood, and Jane Everson.

275

developmental disabilities (pp. 129–138). Baltimore: Paul H. Brookes Publishing Co.

Supported employment was proposed as an alternative to traditional prevocational programs. The authors cited federal legislation and regulations, lack of movement from more-to less-restrictive vocational settings, and inadequate wages as reasons for the increased desirability of supported employment programs. Other problems with traditional vocational programs were listed as inefficient client training techniques, distorted services objectives, and insufficient funding of coordination programs. The key features of supported employment were addressed as: 1) serving a population of individuals who need ongoing support in order to work, 2) placing these individuals in paid community employment, and 3) offering ongoing support to maintain these individuals in employment. Implementation issues were: 1) the creation of new criteria and programs to provide supported employment, 2) changes in eligibility criteria for federal funding, and 3) development of outcome measurements for supported employment and personnel preparation.

Brickey, M. P., Campbell, K. M., & Browning, L. J. (1985). A five year follow-up of sheltered workshop employees placed in competitive jobs. *Mental Retardation, 23*(2), 67–73.

This study followed 53 former sheltered workshop employees placed in competitive employment during 1978. the mean age was 28, mean IQ was 56 (range 32–101), and levels of retardation included severe (3), moderate (23), mild (25). Two workers were not mentally retarded. Follow-up consisted of graduate site visits and phone contacts. Results showed as of January 1, 1983, 34% of participants were employed and 11% were unemployed. Of those employed, wages ranged from $3.62 to $5.46. Some part-time employees reported wages lower than their previous Social Security Disability and sheltered workshop wages. These results were limited to food service positions with McDonalds. The parents of all competitively employed workers wanted their sons or daughters to work, and 11 competitively employed workers said their parents significantly influenced them. Findings showed 65% of participants who lived with their parents were employed, while 41% of participants in other residential arrangements were employed. The authors stated that if more follow-up services had been provided, a higher percentage of participants would have been working.

Cho, D. (1984). An alternate employment model for handicapped persons. *Journal of Rehabilitation Administration, 8,*(2), 55–63.

This article described a Japanese model factory system that originated with Center Industries in Sidney, Australia. The same model is also utilized in Wichita, Kansas. The model factory system of Japan consists of a number of small businesses employing a large number of handicapped persons along with nonhandicapped persons. A survey of 10 model factories in 1977 showed the average number of employees was 57, and that 56% of those employees were handicapped. The average annual earnings for physically handicapped workers was $4,300; the average annual earnings for mentally handicapped workers was $5,590. The average earnings of handicapped workers in sheltered workshops was ⅓ the earnings of physically handicapped model factory workers. The Japanese model included the following features: 1) the cost of hiring one severely handicapped person was equivalent to employing two mildly handicapped persons; 2) model factories were for-profit private enterprises that could return profits to the owners and directors of the company; 3) quota-levy grant systems that set quotas for hiring handicapped workers, charging, for example, a levy for businesses that hire below this quota, and using these funds as cash grants to reward employers who hire handicapped workers in excess of the quota standard. The most distinctive feature of the Japanese model was the balanced mixture of handicapped and nonhandicapped workers in an employment model that uses a business rather than a service orientation.

Edgerton, R. B., Bollinger, M., & Herr, B. (1984). The cloak of competence: After two decades. *American Journal of Mental Deficiency, 88*(4), 345–351.

The study follows 15 participants of an original 48-participant study begun in 1960; follow-up studies were conducted in 1972 and again in 1982. The mean age of participants was 56 and mean IQ was 61. Information was gathered through interviews, phone contacts, and direct observation. Participants were asked the same questions as in previous follow-up surveys, and researchers' data were checked for reliability. Questions concerning the stability of participants' lives, responses to life stressors, personal and social resources, and quality of life were asked. Results showed chronic stressors for the sample were poverty, illness, and fear of loss of social supports. Acute stressors were physical injury, loss of a job, and loss of a spouse, lover, or benefactors. Social resources included friends, relatives, social workers, employers, or other benefactors. No participant in the 1982 survey was receiving any service from the mental retardation services system. Aside from drawing on personal coping mechanisms such as optimism and flexibility, the ways in which participants dealt with life stressors depended not only on the social support system around them, but also on their knowledge of where to look for help, and their perseverance and ingenuity in locating new resources. Competence in the area of social behavior, styles of coping, and communication also contributed significantly to participants' success at coping.

Gersten, R., Crowell, F., & Bellamy, G. T. (1986) Spillover effects: Impact of vocational training on the lives of severely mentally retarded clients. *American Journal of Mental Deficiency, 90*(5), 501–508.

The effects of vocational training on the lives of 22 severely mentally retarded adults were examined. Although no training time was devoted to social skills or to independent living skills, the authors hypothesized that the work experience would have some impact on how the clients were perceived by careproviders and on how clients behaved in social settings. Three instruments were used: a naturalistic observation of leisure behavior, the Becker Adjective Checklist, and the Adaptive Behavior Scale (ABS). No significant growth was observed for the entire sample on any of the dependent measures; however, secondary analyses revealed significant growth on three measures (perceived competence on the Becker Adjective Checklist and the ABS factor scores of Independence and Social Responsibility) for those clients who were most successful in vocational training.

Goodall, P. A., Wehman, P., & Cleveland, P. (1983). Job placement for mentally retarded individuals. *Education and Training of the Mentally Retarded, 18*(4), 271–278.

Job placement was defined as matching a client's abilities to the requirements of a specific job that results in competitive employment for that client. The necessary attributes of successful job placement specialties were listed as: 1) thorough knowledge of the clients to be served, 2) awareness of current trends in vocational opportunities for the moderately and severely retarded, and 3) a strong commitment that handicapped workers do make valuable employees. The specific skill areas needed in the client placement process were: job development, client assessment, and placement. The article provided a table outlining each of these areas. Problems in the placement process were also listed as they included attitudinal barriers, locating cooperative employers, client specific problems such as behavior or transportation, and client's family and living situation. A separate table was included that outlined specific problems and solutions to barriers to employment.

Hill, M., Hill, J., Wehman, P., Revell, G., Dickerson, A., & Noble, J. (in press). Time limited training and supported employment: A model for redistributing existing resources for persons with severe disabilities. *Journal of Rehabilitation.*

A model for improving employment services to persons who are severely disabled utilizing existing state and local financial and personnel resources is described. The model services are based upon the supported work model of competitive employment used successfully with severely disabled persons from 1978 to 1985 in the State of Virginia. These services included job placement, direct job-site training and advocacy, ongoing assessment, and, when needed, extensive follow-along services. The article advocates the use of this model in any location utilizing vocational rehabilitation time-limited funds and services from the initial intensive training stage to job stabilization. The provision of critical long-term follow-along services would then be shifted to state and local agencies such as developmental disabilities, mental retardation services, social services, and private organizations.

Hill, J., Wehman, P., Hill, M., & Goodall, P. (1986). Differential reasons for job separation of previously employed persons with mental retardation across measured intelligence levels. *Mental Retardation, 24*(6), 347–351.

Reasons for job terminations of persons with mental retardation who were competitively employed during a 6-year study period were analyzed. Of the 107 terminations that occurred, 50% were caused by employee-related reasons (e.g., attitude, skill, or behavior problems). The other half were caused by environmental forces beyond the control of the employee or of the job trainer supplying the supported work services. Analysis of variance yielded highly significant differences in the mean IQs for the employee-caused termination group versus the environmentally-caused termination group (55 vs. 48, respectively). Implications of these findings for appropriate program efforts with individuals who are mildly and moderately retarded were discussed.

Kraus, M. W., & MacEachron, A. E. (1982). Competitive employment training for mentally retarded adults: The supported work model. *American Journal of Mental Deficiency, 86*(6), 650–653.

Competitive nonsubsidized employment was stated as the goal of all supported work programs. Work Opportunities for the Retarded, a pilot program, trained and assessed the individual work behaviors and performance necessary for the competitive employment of 26 participants. Participants' average age was 33, average IQ was 62, and highest grade completed was ninth grade. Results showed a 50% placement rate for the sample. The average hourly wage was $3.16, and 65% of the participants had a commitment from the company to be hired based on company standards. Placement was significantly related to task performance, positive work behavior, and the ability to perform to maximum ability at a rate that is comparable to a regular worker's productivity. Placement was also significantly related to attendance, ease of supervision, and job reinforcement. The supported work model consisted of the following: graduated stress, close supervision, and on-the-job training. The study also proposed the practices of matching the worker's abilities to the requirements of the job, and of providing job reinforcements within the employment setting.

Mank, D. M., Rhodes, L. E., & Bellamy, G. T. (1986). Four supported employment alternatives. In W. E. Kiernan & J. A. Stark (Eds.), *Pathways to employment for adults with developmental disabilities* (pp. 139–153). Baltimore: Paul H. Brookes Publishing Co.

The four employment models presented were supported jobs, enclaves, work crews, and benchwork. These models represented options of supported employment appropriate for a variety of organizational arrangements, working conditions, and business specializations. A chart was included that compared organizational set up, number of workers, program cost, level of implementation, integration, employment benefits, severity of workers' disability, and environmental obstacles to employment for each of the models. Similarities between the models included size, the teaching of nonvocational behaviors, the inclusion of meaningful wages, long-term support, immediate employment rather than preparation for work, opportunities for integration, and a common mission of employment for people with severe disabilities. Personnel similarities included staff whose jobs required management, direct services, and business skills. The authors included a chart of program outcomes for assessment of each program's effectiveness.

Martin, J., Schneider, K., Rusch, F., & Geske, T. (1982). Training mentally retarded individuals for competitive employment: Benefits of transitional employment. *Exceptional Education Quarterly, 3*(3), 58–66.

Data presented in this article suggest that competitive employment is an efficient use of society's resources. Data clearly indicate that traditional placement of an individual into extended employment, work activity, or day care results in a fixed cumulative cost to society. Presently, there are sufficient disincentives associated with Supplemental Security Income (SSI) and similar welfare programs for disabled individuals to discourage their use. This suggests that competitive employment programs will continue to be underutilized and largely unavailable options to mentally retarded and other developmentally disabled persons. Familiarity with the rules and regulations associated with Supplemental Security Income alone would point out that persons who are not participating in transitional employment training often earn more money than those receiving training. It is safe to project that until disincentives such as this are minimized, and until the benefits of competitive employment and community participation are realized, the mentally retarded person earning less than minimum wage in a sheltered workshop will continue to absorb a disproportionate share of our society's resources, and will contribute little to our national economy.

Nicholson, J. R., Nailen, P. M., & Tobaben-Wyssam, S. (1984). Competitive employment for sheltered and work activity clients: A national study. *Vocational Evaluation and Work Adjustment Bulletin, 17*(3), 103–107.

Three hundred seven workshops answered a survey designed by the Jackson County Board of Services for Developmentally Disabled and The Helping Hand of Goodwill, Kansas City, Missouri. The survey was designed to determine current attitudes regarding competitive placement of workers and to ascertain the problems encountered in attempting such placements. Results showed an average of 106 clients were employed in the responding workshops, and that these workshops had an average of 14 clients on waiting lists. Eighty-six percent of the workshops had attempted to secure competitive employment for their clients and had successfully placed 60% of the cases. (Subsequent longevity on the job was not noted.) Attempts were made to place an average of 15 clients. Of the responding workshops, 45% of the facilities stated that the average length of competitive placement was over 12 months. Of the surveys returned, 66% included optional additional comments: the four most frequently cited problems were difficulties with parents, economy, motivation, and loss of SSI benefits. The four most successful areas of employment were custodial (66%), food service (59%), factory work (45%), and clerical (22%). Recommendations included securing employment in areas other than these four, obtaining information regarding employer benefits, soliciting client's input as to job interests, and commitment to a transitional employment program. Overall, placement efforts were viewed as sporadic.

Revell, W. G., Wehman, P., & Arnold, S. (1984). Supported work model of competitive employment for persons with mental retardation: Implications for rehabilitation services. *Journal of Rehabilitation, 50*(4), 33–38.

A list of problems associated with traditional sheltered workshop placements included: 1) lack of movement to competitive employment, 2) benefits and wages resulting in client's financial dependency, and 3) workshop dependence on public subsidy that limits clients' employment options and benefits. The authors stated that the supported work model should compliment and not supplant VR services, and that the goal of VR services should be competitive employment. The supported work model for the VR system called for: redirecting VR money to supported competitive employment, restructuring programs and retraining VR staff, and expanding VR services to include persons with severe disabilities. Suggested funding options for supported employment included redirecting funds used to purchase services into programs that offer competitive employment. Additional funding options included: 1) incorporating the cost of services into a fee-for-service agreement and into payment to community service providers for the provision of supported employment services, 2) using JTPA and PWI to provide funding for supported employment, and 3) utilizing multiple funding sources. Current case expenditures, agency staffing patterns, supplementary funding, and public and private agency cooperative programming were suggested areas for review for those instances when VR agencies experience difficulties in providing employment services to persons with severe disabilities.

Rhodes, L. E., & Valenta, L. (1985). Industry based supported employment: An enclave approach. *Journal of The Association for Persons with Severe Handicaps*, 10(1), 12–20.

A supported employment model was used by a nonprofit organization (Trillium Employment Services) to place a group of individuals with moderate to severe retardation in a community-based industry (Physio Control). After 1 year, six of the eight workers were employed, and all were working at 50% or above the standard production performance. Workers were employed for the same hours (10) and days per week (4) as regular employees; total yearly wages earned were $20,207.00, and total taxes paid were $2,425.00. These figures represented a sevenfold wage increase for the clients who had previously worked. The total public cost for the program's first year was $15,945.00. The article described the coordination between the nonprofit agency and industry regarding manufacturing and personnel procedures, training and supervision, and hiring policies. Also addressed were employers' concerns about workers' compensation, failure to meet set productivity levels, attendance, and benefits to industry. The enclave approach was considered a cost effective supported employment alternative for clients with moderate to severe mental retardation.

Rusch, F. R. (1979). A functional analysis of the relationship between attending and producing in a vocational training program. *The Journal of Special Education*, 13(4), 399–410.

This study evaluates the relationship between attending to task and speed of task completion in a vocational training program. Results show that subjects who spent more time completing tasks also spent an appreciable percentage of their time attending to task, by comparison with baseline measures. The article suggests that reinforcing facilitative responses may reduce observed variability in responses associated with speed of task completion.

Rusch, F. R. (1979). Toward validation of social/vocational survival skills. *Mental Retardation, 17*(3), 143–145.

As vocational employment training programs for mentally retarded adults continue to spread, the need to identify skills separate from the performance of specific job tasks becomes crucial. This paper suggests there are social and vocational behaviors that contribute to long-term maintenance of employment. The authors also discuss the training of social and vocational survival skills.

Rusch, F. R. (Ed.). (1986). *Competitive employment issues and strategies.* Baltimore: Paul H. Brookes Publishing Co.

This book is a comprehensive nationwide compilation of successful competitive employment demonstrations. Leading professionals describe components of successful programs and methods for implementing these programs. Issues frequently cited as barriers and concerns are also discussed. These issues include social behaviors, parent/professional partnerships, personal training, quality of life measures, and cost benefits of competitive employment for persons with disabilities.

Rusch, F. R., & Chadsey-Rusch, J. (1985). Employment for persons with severe handicaps: Curriculum development and coordination of services. *Focus on Exceptional Children, 17*(9), 1–8.

This article emphasizes: 1) employment as a meaningful outcome for the severely handicapped, and 2) the vocational preparation and education necessary for the handicapped to enter and remain in the working world (sheltered and competitive employment). Preparation for employment should take place when the student is between the ages of 13–21; school personnel need to assume a leadership role in effecting the students' meaningful transition from school to work. This paper provides curriculum guidelines that will enable school personnel to assume such roles. In addition, the paper emphasizes the need for coordinated services so that the transition from school to work process is effective and efficient.

Rusch, F. R., Connis, R. T., & Sowers, J. (1978). The modification and maintenance of time spent attending using social reinforcement, token reinforcement and response cost in an applied restaurant setting. *Journal of Special Education Technology, 2*(1), 18–26.

The purpose of this investigation was to evaluate a series of program variables used to modify the time a subject spent attending to task in an experimental restaurant setting. Selective behaviors of a mildly retarded, female young adult were evaluated based on the effect of three treatment variables upon time spent attending to task. Furthermore, the addition of an intermittent schedule of cost contingency, delayed token exchange, delayed performance feedback, and a final weekly paycheck were evaluated, resulting levels of response maintenance were investigated. Combinations of social reinforcement, token and response cost were found to be less effective in increasing percent of time spent attending to task than the simultaneous application of all treatment variables. Relationships were established between maintenance of appropriate attending to task behavior and the selective withdrawal of both token reinforcement and cost contingency. The collected data suggested that an intermittent schedule of response cost, weekly token exchange, weekly paychecks, and minimal feedback on performance earning were effective in maintaining response gains. Follow-up measures indicated that treatment gains were maintained after all contingencies were removed. Limitations of the present investigation and future areas of research were outlined.

Rusch, F. R., Martin, J. E., & White, D. M. (1985). Competitive employment: Teaching mentally retarded employees to maintain their work behavior. *Education and Training of the Mentally Retarded, 20*(3), 182–189.

Representative work behavior literature was reviewed in this article. The authors reviewed two kinds of studies: those using externally generated cues and those using externally and self-generated cues to maintain work/production behavior. The authors found that externally generated cues, although effective in the acquisition of specific skills, had limited value for generalization of skills. The incorporation of external and self-generated cues were found to offer beneficial results for both the acquisition and maintenance of work behaviors in competitive employment settings. The combination of self-monitoring, self-reinforcement, and antecedent cue regulation were three strategies thought to be the most effective for the training and maintenance of work behaviors.

Rusch, F. R., & Menchetti, B. M. (1981). Increasing compliant work behaviors in a non-sheltered work setting. *Mental Retardation, 19*(3), 107–111.

The training of one competitively employed person to cooperate with fellow co-workers in a nonsheltered work setting is attempted. A multiple-baseline design across different groups of co-workers was employed to evaluate the effectiveness of practice plus warnings in producing compliant responses. Results indicate practice and warnings are successful methods of drastically increasing positive compliant responding. Sending the person home, once, also results in generalized cooperation with a third, untreated group of fellow co-workers. Future areas of research are indicated.

Rusch, F. R., & Schutz, R. P. (1979). Non-sheltered competitive employment of the mentally retarded adult: Research or reality? *Journal of Contemporary Business, 8*(4), 85–98.

In this article, four major areas related to incorporating mentally retarded adults into nonsheltered competitive employment settings are reviewed. A profile of the mentally retarded adult as an individual striving to acquire competencies is presented, and selected research efforts in both sheltered and nonsheltered settings are examined. Two programs set up to train persons for employment are also reviewed. The research and model service programs presented show that mentally retarded adults are capable of becoming contributing members of society.

Wehman, P., & Hill, M. (1983). Cost benefit analysis of placing moderately and severely handicapped individuals into competitive employment. *Journal of The Association for the Severely Handicapped, 8*(1), 30–39.

Ninety clients were placed in 123 positions over a 47-month period. The study examined the financial benefits of competitive employment (without earned wages), and provided a cost basis for a trainer-advocacy intervention model. The method used clients who wanted to work and who had disabilities severe enough that the assistance of a trainer-advocate was required to gain competitive employment. In addition, clients were eligible for SSI, and most attended some type of day program. Fourteen factors including work duration, ratio of service quotient, estimated program expenditure, estimated program cost, and subsequent costs to the taxpayer were included in the procedure. Results showed that the financial benefits outweighed the costs in this job placement model. Implications from the study were that within 2–3 years, the benefits of a supported work program outweighed the costs. The financial benefits to moderately or severely disabled employed workers should encourage day programs to expand their services and to develop more effective computer technology for data management.

Wehman, P., Hill, M., Hill, J., Brooke, V., Pendleton, P., & Britt, C. (1985). Competitive employment for persons with mental retardation: A follow-up six years later. *Mental Retardation, 23*(6), 274–281.

During the period 1978–1984, 167 persons with mental retardation were hired in both full- and part-time competitive employment. Individuals were placed in a total of 252 janitorial and food service positions. All workers received wages of $3.35 or above, and no wages were subsidized. The mean age of workers was 30, the mean IQ was 50, and the median IQ was 49. Fifty-nine percent of the workers were in the moderate-severe mental retardation range. Eighty-one percent earned less than $200.00 annual salary during the year prior to competitive employment. Workers were placed into competitive employment using a supported work model that utilized individualized job placement, on-site job training and advocacy, ongoing assessment, and long-term follow-up. Using this method, the mean months employed were 19, total earnings were $1,069,309.00 and total taxes paid were $245,941.00. The mean number of staff hours spent per worker was 195 for the entire intervention process. Results of the study reveal needs for: 1) supported work demonstration programs, 2) financial incentives to day programs for providing supported competitive employment services, 3) greater demands placed on local service providers for supported employment programs, 4) increased funding and leadership for organizing competitive employment programs, 5) greater federal and state leadership for vocational transition services, and 6) increased efforts by school and vocational personnel to place students into actual, unsubsidized jobs.

Wehman, P., Hill, J., & Koehler, F. (1979). Placement of developmentally disabled individuals into competitive employment: Three case studies. *Education and Training of the Mentally Retarded, 14*(2), 269–276.

The article describes the job training and placement strategies used to employ three clients whose IQs ranged from borderline to severely retarded and who had previously not worked competitively. The program, Project Employability, was coordinated by Virginia Commonwealth University and initially funded by the Virginia Department of Rehabilitative Services. In order to evaluate the job performance of each client, data were collected on absenteeism, on-task behavior, amount of trainer assistance required, employer evaluations, and wages earned. Key elements cited in successful placement included positive parent attitudes, access to transportation, and employer cooperation. On-site trainer-advocates were also considered essential for the achievement of sustained employment.

Wehman, P., & Kregel, J. (1985). A supported work approach for competitive employment of individuals with moderate and severe handicaps. *Journal of The Association for Persons with Severe Handicaps, 10*(1), 3–11.

This article describes a supported work model for competitive employment including job placement, job-site training and advocacy, ongoing monitoring, and job retention and follow-up. Each component of the supported work model is described and suggestions are made concerning implementation of the model in public school and adult service programs. Suggested changes for public schools included commitments to competitive employment, curriculum design, and personnel preparation. The proposed adult services are related to policy and financial commitments, vendorship, reallocation of funds, and personnel preparation. The authors use data drawn from 170 clients placed in competitive employment over a 6-year period as the foundation for a supported work approach to competitive employment. The model is proposed for clients with moderate and severe handicaps.

Wehman, P., & Moon, M. S. (1987). Critical values in employment programs for persons with developmental disabilities. *Journal of Applied Rehabilitation Counseling, 18*(1), 12–16.

The purpose of this article is to delineate values that are essential elements of effective employment programs for persons with developmental disabilities. With the many efforts occurring nationally to create new vocational programs for disabled persons it is important to articulate the key aspects of meaningful employment programs. In this paper the following nine values were identified: 1) employment in integrated settings, 2) decent pay, 3) the need for vocational choices, 4) the importance of avoiding "charity" work, 5) vocational training to reflect local labor needs, 6) parent involvement in planning, 7) parent education concerning social security laws, 8) community-based vocational training, and 9) systematically planned transition. These values are described and examples are given of each.

TRANSITION PROCESS

Brolin, D. (Ed.). (1986). *Transition from school to work and life*. Columbia, MO: Division on Career Development, Council for Exceptional Children.

Brolin's text is a proceedings manual from the 1985 Council for Exceptional Children (CEC) Division on Career Development (DCD) conference. The book includes more than 80 abstracts on projects, curricula, teaching methods, and models on career development and transition for youth with disabilities. The manual is useful as a resource guide for professionals and parents interested in career development and transition for youth with mild to moderate disabilities.

Brown, J. M. (1984). A model for enhancing the transition of mildly handicapped youth into postsecondary vocational education. In J. Chadsey-Rusch (Ed.), *Conference proceedings from: Enhancing transition from school to the workplace for handicapped youth*. Champaign, IL: National Network for Professional Development in Vocational Special Education.

A four-stage transition model including assessment, planning, implementation, and evaluation is proposed by Brown. Activities that are combined with secondary education to facilitate transition are suggested within each of these stages. Brown suggests that students with disabilities experience difficulties during the transition process when their individual characteristics do not meet the demands of their environments; strategies are presented for educators to use to decrease this disjunction.

D'Alonzo, B., Owen, S., & Hartwell, L. K. (1985, October). Transition models: An overview of the current state of the art. *Techniques: A Journal for Remedial Education and Counseling, 1*(16), 429–436.

The purpose of this article is twofold: first, to describe nine models currently being used throughout the United States, and second, to provide a detailed description of a transition model currently being developed by the authors, Project INTERFACE. Critical components are described for each of the models. The authors summarize by describing six elements that are present in all of the models: 1) a cooperative interagency and individual referral network; 2) the interdisciplinary assessment, evaluation, and planning of skills required by the individual in order to function successfully within the community and on the job; 3) career development and education experiences; 4) job skills training coupled with community survival skill training; 5) linkage with business or industrial employers; and 6) supervised on-the-job-training.

Drake, G., & Witten, B. (1985). Facilitating learning disabled adolescents' successful transition from school to work. *Journal of Applied Rehabilitation Counseling, 17*(1), 34–37.

The authors state a need for public schools and rehabilitation services to develop cooperative programs. An emphasis is placed on the need for functional secondary education programs. Suggestions are given both for secondary teachers and rehabilitation counselors.

Halpern, A. S. (1985). Transition: A look at the foundations. *Exceptional Children, 51*(6), 479–486.

Halpern's article presents a critical examination of the transition model proposed by the Office of Special Education and Rehabilitation Services (OSERS), U.S. Department of Education. Specifically, the author questions OSERS' position that employment is the critical outcome of transition, and argues instead that the most important result of transition is community adjustment. Halpern describes community adjustment as an umbrella outcome that encompasses residential outcomes, employment outcomes, and social and interpersonal outcomes. The article includes recommendations for changes in existing secondary programs.

McCarthy, P., Everson, J. M., Inge, K. J. & Barcus, J. M. (1985, October). Transition from school to work: Developing the process for individuals with severe disabilities. *Techniques: A Journal for Remedial Education And Counseling, 1*(6), 463–472.

The authors describe a model for developing and implementing a transition from school to adult life that emphasizes supported employment outcomes. The authors envision a sequence wherein community planning is initiated by a local core team followed by the implementation of an individualized transition plan for a specific student by his or her transition team. Specific steps are outlined for each team of professionals and parents to follow.

McCarthy, P., Everson, J. M., Moon, S., & Barcus, J. M (Eds.). (1985). *School-to-work transition for youth with severe disabilities.* Richmond: Virginia Commonwealth University, Project Transition Into Employment.

This is an excellent monograph of articles that describes step-by-step procedures for developing and implementing transition from school to work services for youth with severe disabilities. The articles were written by various authors and include such subjects as secondary special education programming for youth with severe disabilities, coordinating interagency transition planning, developing and managing supported employment outcomes, and including parents in the transition planning process.

McDonnell, J. J. (1983). *Transition from school to work and adult services: A procedural handbook for parents and teachers.* Unpublished manuscript, University of Oregon, Eugene.

A manual designed for school personnel, adult service personnel, and parents to use in developing school to work transition plans for youth with disabilities. The manual was designed and field-tested in localities in Oregon.

McDonnell, J. J., & Hardman, M. (1985, December). Planning the transition of severely handicapped youth from school to adult services: A framework for high school programs. *Education and Training of the Mentally Retarded, 20*(4), 275–286.

This article provides a procedural framework for local school systems, adult service providers, and parents to plan and coordinate transition services. The procedures in this article outline specific steps and schedules for: 1) developing transition plans, 2) preparing parents, and 3) coordinating services between school and community service agencies.

McDonnell, J. J., Wilcox, B., & Boles, S. M. (1986). Do we know enough to plan for transition? A national survey of state agencies responsible for services to persons with severe handicaps. *Journal of The Association for Persons with Severe Handicaps, 11*(1), 53–60.

The authors used mail surveys and telephone interviews with state administrators of educational, vocational, and residential services across all 50 states and the District of Columbia for the purpose of predicting the scope of services needed by transition-age youth on a national level. Administrators in 44 of 51 state education agencies (86%) participated in the interview; 34 administrators of 51 state vocational programs (67%) participated in the interview; and 35 administrators of 51 residential programs for adults with severe handicaps (69%) participated in the interview. In 33 states 64% of administrators from all three programs participated in the interviews. The data suggest that there will be approximately 9,000 students with severe disabilities across the nation leaving school programs annually for the next 3 years. These students will face lengthy waiting lists for both vocational and residential services upon leaving their school programs. Where states indicated that expansion of current services is being planned, the expansion is not expected to meet the predicted needs of graduating students over the next 3 years.

McDonnell, J. J., Wilcox, B., Boles, S. M., & Bellamy, G. T. (1985). Transition issues facing youth with severe disabilities: Parents' perspective. *Journal of The Association for Persons with Severe Handicaps, 10*(1), 61–65.

The article presents data collected from 163 written questionnaires distributed to parents of severely disabled students. Parents were asked to identify the anticipated service needs of their offspring 5 years after leaving school and 10 years after leaving school. The results indicated that parents projected vocational services as the most important service need not only at graduation, but also 5 and 10 years after graduation. Income support and residential services were identified as the second and third most important needs at graduation. At 5 and 10 years after graduation, the order of anticipated needs was reversed, with the result that residential services was second most important and income support was ranked third most important.

McKinney, L., Vreeberg, M., & West, K. (1986). *Extending horizons*. Columbus, OH: The National Center for Research in Vocational Education.

The authors present a guide proposing a model for effecting the transition of youth with disabilities from vocational education into employment. The guide contains: 1) procedures for preparing and coordinating school and community teams, 2) materials for inservice training workshops, 3) career exploration information, and 4) instructional strategies. The guide was field-tested in Ohio.

Nettekoven, L., & Ramsey, E. (1985). Entitlements: One solution to the transition dilemma? In M. Gould & G. T. Bellamy (Eds.), *Transition from school to work and adult life*. Eugene: University of Oregon, Specialized Training Programs.

This article begins by describing the historical use of entitlements to ensure the provision of services for individuals with disabilities in the United States and Europe. The authors describe laws in four states and the District of Columbia that entitle students with disabilities to some type and degree of transition assistance upon leaving public school programs. Current federal entitlement services providing income support and health care support are also described. The authors question the appropriateness of using entitlement services and adult services for individuals with disabilities to achieve normalization.

Schumaker, J. B., Hazel, J. S., & Deshler, D. D. (1985, October). A model for facilitating postsecondary transition. *Techniques: A Journal for Remedial Education and Counseling*, (1), 437–446.

The authors describe a model for facilitating the transition of youth with learning disabilities from school to work and adult life. A seven-step Life Planning Program is described that provides students with instruction in motivational skill development, decision making, use of resources, and generalization of skills from the classroom to adult life.

U.S. Department of Education. (1985). *Cooperative programs for transition from school to work*. Washington, DC: U.S. Department of Education, Office of Special Education and Rehabilitative Services.

The results of a federally funded project that reviewed nine statewide and locally based transition from school to work programs. Detailed descriptions and data from each program are presented. Particular attention is given to the type and level of interagency cooperation evidenced by each program.

Wehman, P., Kregel, J., & Barcus, J. M. (1985). From school to work: A vocational transition model for handicapped students. *Exceptional Children*, 52(1), 25–37.

The authors present a three-stage vocational transition model that targets employment goals for youth with severe disabilities. The authors envision a model that moves a student from an integrated community-based secondary special education program, through a formal and interagency planning process, into an employment or supported employment setting. Data from 55 transition-age youth are presented for the purpose of comparing their employment status with their secondary special education programs.

Wehman, P., Moon, M. S., & McCarthy, P. (1986). Transition from school to adulthood for youth with severe handicaps. *Focus on Exceptional Children*, 18(5), 1–12.

The authors define transition from school to adult life as a process that results in employment alternatives and community living alternatives for youth with severe disabilities. The authors propose that formal transition planning should begin when the student is 16 and should target community living goals and employment goals as part of the student's secondary special education program. A sample Individualized Transition Plan (ITP) is provided that outlines sample employment and community living goals, targets appropriate individuals or agencies to be responsible for implementation of the goals, and provides a sample schedule for completion of the goals.

Will, M. C. (1984). OSERS *programming for the transition of youth with disabilities: Bridges from school to working life.* Washington, DC: U.S. Department of Education, Office of Special Education and Rehabilitative Services.

A position paper from the Office of Special Education and Rehabilitative Services (OSERS), this text defines transition as an outcome-oriented process that targets services for all students with disabilities. The OSERS model presents three types of service arrangements available to help the student move from a high school program into employment. The type of service arrangement most appropriate for a particular student varies according to his or her needs: 1) no special services, 2) time-limited services, and 3) ongoing services.

INTERAGENCY COLLABORATION

Ashby, S., & Bensberg, G. J. (1981). *Cooperative occupational preparation: Exemplary models.* Lubbock: Research and Training Center, Texas Tech University.

This manuscript discusses in-depth the necessity of interagency cooperation for bringing about the effective transition of students with disabilities from school to work. The primary service providers presented are vocational rehabilitation and special and vocational education agencies. A thorough discussion of federal laws and policy is provided along with legislative history for all three service providers. Specific legislation under discussion are: the Vocational Rehabilitation Act, the Education for All Handicapped Children Act, and the Vocational Educational Act. Components of state and local interagency agreements are provided. Statements on philosophy, federal statutes, and responsibilities of each department are a few of the components listed as necessary for cooperative agreements between agencies. Twenty-two exemplary programs are reviewed. The rationale for selection of the programs was also provided.

Fenton, J., & Keller, R. A., Jr. (1981). Special educational-vocational rehabilitation: Let's get the act together. *American Rehabilitation,* May-June, 6(5), 26–30.

The importance and logic of collaboration between special education and vocational rehabilitation are discussed. Historical precedents and relevant legislation that have provided the impetus for interagency cooperation are outlined. Some past models are briefly discussed and problems still evident in the successful implementation of interagency agreements are delineated.

Commitment of leadership, the development of a written document, degree of commitment, and the support system for implementation are listed as necessary components to developing a statewide initiative for interagency collaboration. Following the formalization of a state level commitment, agreements at the local level will need to be developed with specific plans for implementation at the service delivery level. Important to successful implementation at the local level is inservice training of personnel to provide for a better understanding of the cooperating agencies; for example, rehabilitation counselors will better understand the public education system and special education teachers will better understand vocational rehabilitation.

Freagon, S., Ahlgren, C., Smith, B., Costello, D., & Peters, W. M. (1986). *A system for successful interagency collaboration in the transition process: Movement through school to adulthood for students with moderate and severe handicaps.* Unpublished manuscript, Northern Illinois University, DeKalb.

This paper describes a longitudinal transition programming and planning process that includes a schedule for involvement of adult service agencies. At the elementary level, agencies already involved and those expected to become involved are noted on a student program planning record. For the secondary school level, a calendar is provided that delineates the times that adult service agencies will become involved to help the student achieve postschool employment, residential, recreation, and community living goals. Once the "level of support" needed by each student is established, agency representatives develop a plan for service provision appropriate for that student.

Hasazi, S. B. (1985). Facilitating transition from high school: Policies and practices. *American Rehabilitation, 11*(3), 9–16.

This article discusses transition planning as a process that takes place during the high school years, graduation, and the initial years after graduation. Local interagency agreements that feature collaboration between professionals in the fields of vocational education, special education, vocational rehabilitation, and developmental disabilities are discussed; employment and training agencies are recommended. The author argues that negotiated agreements should specify services to be provided by each agency, and should spell out referral procedures, procedures for interagency inservice training, and agreement monitoring and evaluation procedures.

Additional discussion subjects in the article include: course work important for transition, access to vocational education, work experience training, and the collection of follow-up data.

Illinois Governor's Planning Council on Developmental Disabilities. (1981). Illinois transition project: Transition planning and development for special education students in Illinois public schools.

The Illinois state plan for transition planning relies on the development first of state and then local interagency agreements. Interagency coordinating committees at the local level and a transition assistance council at the state level are suggested as the leading administrative bodies for planning and coordination of transition planning activities. Professionals from the fields of vocational rehabilitation, education, mental health, and developmental disabilities are all listed as critical participants in the cooperative planning and implementation of transition activities.

The specific transition plan to be coordinated with the IEP process is referred to as an individual interagency agreement. This document delineates the responsibilities of each agency for achieving the desired outcomes of the transition planning process.

Leadership Training Institute: Vocational and Special Education. (1980). *Interagency cooperation and agreements: Policy paper series: Document 4.* (James P. Greenan, Ed.). Urbana-Champaign: University of Illinois.

This monograph identifies and elaborates on several major issues that relate to the development of effective interagency cooperation. The primary agencies discussed are Vocational Education, Special Education, and Vocational Rehabilitation. Procedures for state planning and for the establishment of effective linkages to local level services are both described. Also, major attention is given to the subject of training education personnel to develop and implement effective interagency agreements. The manual is designed for use as a reference.

Martinson, M. C. (1982). Interagency services: A new era for an old idea. *Exceptional Children, 45*(5), 389–394.

This article discusses the interorganizational dynamics that can hinder interagency cooperation. For example, laws, regulations, and organizational structures specific to the participating agencies are viewed as possible obstructions to effective collaboration between agencies. Additionally, technical and political forces within organizations can make it difficult for agencies to interact cooperatively. Even further, territorial issues, self-interest, and competition for resources are all potential roadblocks to the achievement or smooth operation of interagency agreements.

A planning model that provides flexibility to "accommodate the diversity of needs identified by the respective agencies" is offered (p. 392). Problems associated with interagency collaboration, and current deficits in the areas of research, model demonstration, and development are discussed.

Porter, M. E., & Varty, J. (1980). *Building linkages with the rehabilitation agency: Development and implementation of a model program.* Paper presented at the Annual Conference on the Disabled Student on American Campuses.

This document, produced by the Educational Reproduction Information Center (ERIC), describes a model cooperative agreement between Macomb County Community College (MCCC), the legislature of Macomb County, Michigan, and the Bureau of Rehabilitation. A needs assessment that was conducted on services for the handicapped identified a lack of cooperation between the college and outside agencies, a lack of understanding between the faculty and rehabilitation personnel, and lack of individualization of transition plans for handicapped students.

Liaisons were assigned, and referral and release of information procedures were written and implemented along with interagency inservice training programs. Service delivery models were developed for individuals with visual, hearing, or mobility impairments.

Threet, S., & Nutringer, P. (1981). *Interagency coordination: A necessity in rural programs: Making it work in rural communities.* Macomb, IL: Western Illinois University.

This monograph contains six papers on interagency coordination of services for young handicapped children living in rural areas. The authors provide illustrations of how communication and coordination can be improved in order to limit the overlapping of services and the inefficiency that can result from agencies operating in isolation. Subjects of discussion include: improved quality of services, other collaborative efforts around the U.S., and the need for service providers to be knowledgeable of various agencies. The text places emphasis on service coordination for early childhood programs.

Tindall, L. W., Crowley, C. B., Getzel, E. E., & Gugerty, J. J. (1981). *Interagency linkages at the federal level: Descriptions of agencies and organizations.* Madison: University of Wisconsin-Madison.

This manual describes the policies and activities of the various federal agencies regarding interagency cooperative agreements. The leadership initiatives establishing cooperation of four key federal agencies are provided. The four agencies discussed are: 1) Office of Vocational and Adult Education, 2) Office of Special Education and Rehabilitative Services, 3) Office of Elementary and Secondary Education, 4) Office of Educational Research and Improvement. Sample agreements are provided in the appendices to assist state and local agencies in developing interagency agreements. The manual is designed for use as a reference.

Vogelsberg, R. T., Williams, W., & Ashe, W. (1981). Improving vocational services through interagency cooperation. In C. L. Hansen (Ed.), *Severely handicapped persons in the community.* Seattle, WA: Program Development System.

Vogelsberg's chapter describes the Vermont interagency model of comprehensive vocational services. Five major options of vocational or employment services are discussed. The process of developing the interagency agreement is described; the authors point out that funding and delineation of service responsibilities are the most delicate points in the negotiation process. The agencies and service providers included in this cooperative arrangement include vocational rehabilitation, the department of mental health, and an advisory board comprised of representatives from transportation, adult basic education, and employment agencies. Agreements at state, regional, and local levels are recommended to effectively implement vocational services. A case history of a model project in Vermont is described to illustrate the process established by one state in order to develop and implement statewide interagency linkages.

Wehman, P., Wood, W., Everson, J. M., & Parent, W. (1985). A supported employment approach to transition. *American Rehabilitation, 11*(3), 12–16.

The purpose of this paper is to discuss the role of special education in promoting community-based vocational instruction, transition planning, and competitive employment. The text includes an outline of methods for developing individualized transition plans for handicapped youth who are soon to leave special education. Two case studies of significantly mentally retarded persons who typically would not gain employment because of the severity of their handicaps are presented. Each case study describes how a supported work approach to competitive employment was used. The authors note that vocational rehabilitation played a major role in making these successful transitions occur—through referral, case management, and purchase of service. This research is drawn from a 7-year program in Virginia that used the supported employment model.

COMMUNITY-BASED TRAINING

Baumgart, D., & Van Walleghem, J. (1986). Staffing strategies for implementing community-based instruction. *Journal of The Association for Persons with Severe Handicaps, 11*(2), 92–102.

The authors present eight staffing strategies that can be utilized in implementing community-based instruction for disabled students. Examples and descriptive information about each strategy are presented, and advantages and disadvantages of each staffing option are discussed. Recommendations for the implementation and coordination of community-based training are summarized.

Browder, D., & Shapiro, E. (1985). Application of self-management to individuals with severe handicaps. *Journal of The Association for Persons with Severe Handicaps, 10*(4), 200–208.

The authors review and discuss research on self-management of behaviors for severely handicapped persons. Each intervention strategy is defined and is followed by a discussion of both antecedent and consequent strategies. Application suggestions and future research needs are presented in a summary fashion.

Brown, L., Nisbet, J., Ford, A., Sweet, M., Shiraga, B., York, J., & Loomis, R. (1983). The critical need for nonschool instruction in educational programs for severely handicapped students. *Journal of The Association for the Severely Handicapped, 8*(3), 71–86.

The authors present a brief historical review of education service delivery models for severely handicapped students. Six learning and performance characteristics are discussed. Implications for education are also presented. The advantages and disadvantages of four instructional location strategies are also addressed.

Davies, R., & Rogers, E. (1985). Social skills training with persons who are mentally retarded. *Mental Retardation, 23*(4), 186–196.

The authors present a review of research in social skills training for mentally retarded persons. Tables are included displaying author names, information regarding the study, and results of the research. The research is divided into three categories: motoric-physical social skills, social skills and behaviors, and social cognitive skills and behaviors. Suggestions are offered concerning the process of implementing social skills training programs.

Fine, A., Welch-Burke, C., & Fondario, L. (1985). Integration of leisure skills training in special education career education programs. *Mental Retardation, 23*(6), 289–296.

The authors examined five major techniques for augmenting leisure skills. Advantages and disadvantages of each technique are presented in the context of current research. A five-stage development model for the integration of leisure programming into career education for the mentally retarded is also included.

Ford, A., & Mirenda, P. (1984). Community instruction: A natural cues and corrections decision model. *Journal of The Association for Persons with Severe Handicaps, 9*(2), 79–88.

The authors present a decision model for teachers that should allow teachers to intervene more systematically when students fail to respond to relevant cues and corrections. Methods for identifying natural cue-related errors, the decision process, selection of natural cues, types of teaching and reinforcement procedures, intervention points, accentuation of natural cues, reinforcement, phasing out of services, and performance rates are addressed.

Hamre-Nietupski, S., Nietupski, J., Bates, P., & Maurer, S. (1982). Implementing a community-based educational model for moderately/severely handicapped students: Common problems and suggested solutions. *Journal of The Association for the Severely Handicapped, 7*, 38–43.

The authors present six barriers to implementing community-based educational models for moderately and severely handicapped students. The barriers include: 1) limited staff, 2) limited transportation, 3) scheduling, 4) cost, 5) negative reactions to curriculum change, and 6) applicability to multiply handicapped persons. Each obstacle is discussed and solutions are presented based on Iowa's attempt to implement such a model.

Nietupski, J. A., Hamre-Nietupski, S., & Ayres, B. (1984). Review of task analytic leisure skill training efforts: Practitioner implications and future research needs. *Journal of The Association for Persons with Severe Handicaps, 9*(2), 88–97.

A thorough review of training programs in the recreation and leisure domain through 1984 is presented. The studies involve severely handicapped individuals. Data-based analytic instructional efforts and recent curriculum volumes and position papers are the main focus of the text. A table is presented listing the authors, purpose, participants, and findings of the studies reviewed. Future research needs for recreation and leisure, as well as implications for the practitioner, are discussed.

Nietupski, J. A., Hamre-Nietupski, S., Clancy, P., & Veerhusen, K. (1986). Guidelines for making simulation an effective adjunct to in vivo community instruction. *Journal of The Association for Persons with Severe Handicaps, 11*(1), 12–18.

This article discusses the view of using in vivo instruction concurrently with simulation formats when total community instruction is not feasible. The authors define both simulated and in vivo instruction and present research validating both approaches. Five guidelines are presented for making simulation more effective. Future research needs were also identified.

Nietupski, J. A., Hamre-Nietupski, S., Welch, J., & Anderson, R. J. (1983). Establishing and maintaining vocational training sites for moderately and severely handicapped students: Strategies for community vocational trainers. *Education and Training of the Mentally Retarded, 18*(3), 169–175.

The authors suggest four strategies that may be utilized by community vocational trainers in establishing community-based vocational training sites. Also, six additional strategies are presented for maintaining these community-based sites. Interpersonal approaches and recommended procedural steps for each are discussed.

Snell, M., & Broder, D. (1986). Community-referenced instruction: Research and issues. *Journal of The Association for Persons with Severe Handicaps, 11*(1), 1–11.

The authors review the current literature on the application of community-based instruction. The text addresses such procedural issues as: environmental assessment, task analysis, trial sequencing, control, empirical and social validity, and measurement. Eleven guidelines for research in the area of community-based instruction are listed. Unresolved issues and problems with implementation of the model are presented.

Spooner, F., & Spooner, D. (1984). A review of chaining techniques: Implications for future research and practice. *Education and Training of the Mentally Retarded, 19*(2), 114–123.

The authors review research on forward chaining, backward chaining, and total task presentation in teaching the severely handicapped. A table of this research is presented displaying authors, studies, and results from studies conducted from 1966 through 1984. Research methods are examined to evaluate their effectiveness, and to determine optimal learning standards for persons with severe handicaps.

Voeltz, L., & Evans, I. (1983). Educational validity: Procedures to evaluate outcomes in programs for severely handicapped learners. *Journal of The Association for the Severely Handicapped, 8*(1), 3–15.

The authors present discussion of program development, monitoring, and evaluation efforts in education programs. Existing concerns for research on single-subject design and for developmentally based assessments are addressed. Three major criteria for evaluating programs are presented; cost effectiveness and issues of validity are also discussed.

Wershing, A., Gaylord-Ross, C., & Gaylord-Ross, R. (1986, June). Implementing a community-based vocational training model: A process for systems change. *Education and Training of the Mentally Retarded, 21*(2), 130–137.

Wershing's article describes the procedures necessary to implement a community-based instructional model for vocational training.

Issues involved in facilitating systems change are addressed. Strategies for programming, gaining administrative support, community site selection and development, parent involvement, and employer participation are provided. Benefits of community-based vocational training for disabled youth in preparation for transition to employment are illustrated through presentation of a case study.

References

Accommodating the spectrum of individual abilities. (1983). U.S. Commission on Civil Rights. Washington, DC: U.S. Government Printing Office.

Anderson, W., Beckett, C., Chitwood, S., & Hayden, D. (1986). *Next steps: Planning for employment*. Alexandria, VA: Parent Educational Advocacy Training Center.

Anthony, W. A., & Jansen, M. A. (1984). Predicting the vocational capacity of the chronologically mentally ill: Research and policy implications. *American Psychologist, 39*(5), 537–544.

Ashby, S., & Bensberg, G. J. (1981). *Cooperative occupational preparation: Exemplary models*. Lubbock: Research and Training Center, Texas Tech University.

Ballantyne, D., McGee, M., Patton, S., & Cohen, L. (1984). *Report on cooperative programs for transition from school to work* (Contract No. 300–83–0158). Waltham, MA: Harold Russell Associates.

Bates, P., Renzaglia, A., & Wehman, P. (1981, April). Characteristics of an appropriate education for the severely and profoundly handicapped. *Education and Training of the Mentally Retarded*, 140–148.

Bates, P., Suter, C., & Poelvoorde, M. (1986). *Illinois transition project*. Springfield, IL: Governor's Planning Council on Developmental Disabilities.

Baumgart, D., & Van Walleghem, J. (1986). Staffing strategies for implementing community-based instruction. *Journal of The Association for Persons with Severe Handicaps. 11*(2), 92–102.

Beer, M. (1980). *Organization change and development: A systems view*. Pacific Palisades, CA: Goodyear Press.

Bellamy, G. T., Horner, R., & Inman, D. (1979). *Vocational training of severely retarded adults*. Baltimore: University Park Press.

Bellamy, G. T., Mank, D. M., Rhodes, L. E., Borbeau, P., & Mank, D. (1986). Mental retardation services in sheltered workshops and day activity programs: Consumer benefits and policy alternatives. In F. R. Rusch (Ed.), *Competitive employment issues and strategies*. Baltimore: Paul H. Brookes Publishing Co.

Bellamy, G. T., Rose, H., Wilson, D. J., & Clarke, J. (1982). Strategies for vocational preparation. In B. Wilcox & G. T. Bellamy (Eds.), *Design of high school programs for severely handicapped students*. Baltimore: Paul H. Brookes Publishing Co.

Bellephant, E. (1986). Project Transition Into Employment (TIE) Tennessee State Action Plan. Richmond: Virginia Commonwealth University, Project Transition Into Employment.

Belmore, K., & Brown, L. (1978). Job skills inventory strategy for use in a public school vocational training program for severely handicapped potential workers. In N. Haring & D. Bricker (Eds.), *Teaching the severely handicapped* (Vol. 3). Seattle, WA: American Association for the Education of the Severely and Profoundly Handicapped. Vol. 3.

Benz, M. R., & Halpern, A. (1986). Vocational preparation for high school students with mild disabilities: A statewide study of administrator, teacher, and parent perceptions. *Career Development for Exceptional Individuals, 9*(1), 3–15.

Brodsky, M. M. (1983). *A five year statewide follow-up of the graduates of school programs for trainable mentally retarded students in Oregon.* Unpublished doctoral dissertation, University of Oregon, Eugene.

Brolin, D. E. (1973). Career education needs of secondary educable students. *Exceptional Children, 39,* 619–629.

Brolin, D. E. (1982). *Vocational preparation of persons with handicaps.* Columbus, OH: Charles E. Merrill.

Brolin, D. E. (1985). Career education material for exceptional individuals. *Career Development for Exceptional Individuals, 8*(1), 62–64.

Brotherson, M. J., Backus, L. H., Summers, J. A., & Turnbull, A. P. (1986). Transition to adulthood. In J. A. Summers (Ed.), *The right to grow up: An introduction to adults with developmental disabilities.* Baltimore: Paul Brookes.

Brown, L., Branston, M. B., Hamre-Nietupski, A., Pumpian, I., Certo, N., & Gruenewald, L. (1979). A strategy for developing chronological age–appropriate and functional curricular content for severely handicapped adolescents and young adults. *Journal of Special Education, 13,* 81–90.

Brown, L., Nietupski, J., & Hamre-Nietupski, S. (1976). The criterion of ultimate functioning. In: M. A. Thomas (Ed.), *Hey don't forget about me!* Reston, VA: CEC Information Center.

Brown, L., Pumpian, I., Baumgart, D., Van Deventer, L., Ford, A., Nisbit, J., Schnider, J., & Gruenwald, L. (1981). Longitudinal transition plans in programs for severely handicapped students. *Exceptional Children, 47,* 624–630.

Buckley, J., & Bellamy, G. T. (1984). *National survey of day and vocational programs for adults with severe disabilities: A 1984 profile.* Unpublished manuscript, Johns Hopkins University, Baltimore, MD. and University of Oregon, Eugene.

Certo, N., Haring, N., & York, R. (1983). *Public school integration of severely handicapped students: Rational issues and alternatives.* Baltimore: Paul H. Brookes Publishing Co.

Cho, P., & Schuerman, A. (1980). Economic costs and benefits of private gainful employment of the severely handicapped. *Journal of Rehabilitation, 46*(3), 17–22.

Colloster, L. (1975). *A comparison of the long range benefits of graduation from special vs. mainstream school for mentally handicapped students.* Seattle: Seattle Public Schools, Washington, Department of Planning, Research and Evaluation.

Conaway, C. (1986). Vocational education's role in the transition of handicapped persons. In J. Chadsey-Rusch & C. Hanley-Maxwell (Eds.), *Enhancing transition from school to the work place for handicapped youth: Personnel preparation implications.* Urbana-Champaign: University of Illinois.

Cook, I. (1986). *Project Transition Into Employment (TIE) West Virginia State Action Plan.* Richmond: Virginia Commonwealth University, Project TIE.

Crites, L. S., Smull, M. W., & Sachs, M. L. (1984). *Demographic and functional characteristics of respondents to the mentally retarded community needs survey: Persons living at home with family.* Unpublished manuscript, University of Maryland, School of Medicine, Baltimore.

Deloach, C. P., Wilkins, R. D., & Walker, G. W. (1983). *Independent living: Philosophy, process, and services.* Baltimore: University Park Press.

Dinger, J. D. (1973). *A follow-up study of the post school employment success of graduates from four high school special education programs in the midwestern intermediate unit IV in Pennsylvania for the school years 1969–1970. A final report.* Harrisburg: Pennsylvania State Department of Education.

Ditty, J. A., & Reynolds, K. (1980). Traditional vocational evaluation: Help or hindrance? *Journal of Rehabilitation,* 46(4), 22–25.

Drogin, R. (1985, March 16). Success in workplace. *Los Angeles Times.*

Dunn, D. J. (1979). What happens after placement? Career enhancement services in vocational rehabilitation. In D. Vandergoot & J. D. Worrall (Eds.), *Placement in rehabilitation* (pp. 167–196). Baltimore: University Park Press.

Edgar, E., & Levine, P. (1986). *Washington State follow-up studies of post-secondary special education students.* Seattle: University of Washington.

Elder, J. (1984). Job opportunities for developmentally disabled people. *American Rehabilitation,* 10(2), 26–27.

Elder, J. O., & Magrab, P. R. (1979). *Coordinating services to handicapped children: A handbook for interagency collaboration.* Baltimore: Paul H. Brookes Publishing Co.

Everson, J. (1986, June). *Local interagency transition planning.* Presentation made in doctoral seminar on transition from school to work, Rehabilitation Research and Training Center, Virginia Commonwealth University, Richmond.

Everson, J. & Moon, M. S. (1987). Transition services for young adults with severe disabilities: Defining professional and parental roles and responsibilities. *Journal of The Association for Persons with Severe Handicaps,* 12(2), 87–95.

Falvey, M. A. (1986). *Community-based curriculum: Instructional strategies for students with severe handicaps.* Baltimore: Paul H. Brookes Publishing.

Fardig, D. B., Algozzine, R. F., Schwartz, S. E., Hensel, J. W., & Westling, D. L. (1985). Postsecondary vocational adjustment of rural, mildly handicapped students. *Exceptional Children,* 52(2), 115–121.

Federal Register (May 27, 1987). Washington, D.C. U.S. Government Printing Office.

Fenton, J., & Keller, R. A., Jr. (1981). Special education-vocational rehabilitation: Let's get the act together. *American Rehabilitation,* May–June, 26–30.

Forbes Magazine. (1986, December). *Are we spending too much on education?*

Freagon, S., Ahlgren, C., Smith, B., Costello, D., & Peters, W. M. (1986). *A system for successful interagency collaboration in the transition process: Movement through school to adulthood for students with moderate and severe handicaps.* Unpublished manuscript, Northern Illinois University, DeKalb.

Freagon, S., Wheeler, J., Brankin, G., McDannel, K., Costello, D., & Peters, W. M. (1983). *Curriculum processes for the school and community integration of severely handicapped students age 6–21: Project replication guide*

(Monograph). DeKalb: Northern Illinois University, DeKalb County Special Education Association.

Goodall, P., & Bruder, M. B. (1986). Parents and the transition process. *The Exceptional Parent, 16*(2), 22–28.

Goodall, P. A., Wehman, P., & Cleveland, P. (1983). Job placement for mentally retarded individuals. *Education and Training of the Mentally Retarded, 18*(4), 271–278.

Greenan, J. P. (1980). *Interagency cooperation and agreements: Policy paper series: Document 4.* Champaign: University of Illinois.

Hagebak, B. A. (1982). *Getting local agencies to cooperate.* Baltimore: University Park Press.

Halpern, A. S. (1973). General unemployment and vocational opportunities for EMR individuals. *American Journal of Mental Deficiency, 28*(2), 123–127.

Halpern, A. S. (1985). Transition: A look at the foundations. *Exceptional Children, 57*(6), 479–486.

Halpern, A. S., Close, D., & Nelson, L. (1986). *On my own.* Baltimore: Paul H. Brookes Publishing Co.

Hamre-Nietupski, S., Nietupski, J., Bates, P., & Maurer, S. (1982). Implementing a community-based educational model for moderately/severely handicapped students: Common problems and suggested solutions. *Journal of The Association for the Severely Handicapped, 7,* 38–43.

Hanley-Maxwell, C. (1986). Curriculum development. In F. R. Rusch (Ed.), *Competitive employment issues and strategies.* Baltimore: Paul H. Brookes Publishing Co.

Harold Russell Associates. (1985). *Supported and transitional employment personnel preparation study.* Boston, Massachusetts.

Hasazi, S. B. (1985). Facilitating transition from high school: Policies and practices. *American Rehabilitation, 11*(3), 9–16.

Hasazi, S. B., Gordon, L. R., & Roe, C. A. (1985). Factors associated with the employment status of handicapped youth exiting high school from 1979-1983. *Exceptional Children, 51*(6), 455–569.

Hasazi, S. B., Gordon, L. R., Roe, C. A., Finck, K., Hull, M., & Salembier, G. (1985). A statewide follow-up on post high school employment and residential status of students labeled "mentally retarded." *Education and Training of the Mentally Retarded, 14,* 222–234.

Heal, L. W., Novak, A. R., Sigelman, C. K., & Switzky, H. N. (1980) Characteristics of community residential facilities. In A. R. Novak & L. W. Heal (Eds.), *Integration of developmentally disabled individuals into the community* (45–56). Baltimore: Paul H. Brookes Publishing Co.

Hill, M. (1986). *Outline and support materials to assist in the preparation of proposals to provide time-limited and on-going services within a program of supported employment.* Unpublished manuscript, Rehabilitation Research and Training Center, Virginia Commonwealth University, Richmond.

Hill, M., Banks, P. D., Handrich, R., Wehman, P., Hill, J., & Shafer, M. (1987, January). Benefit-cost analysis of supported competitive employment for persons with mental retardation. *Research in Developmental Disabilities, 8*(1), 71–89.

Hill, M., Hill, J., Wehman, P., Revell, G., Dickerson, A. & Noble, J. (in press).

Supported employment: An interagency funding model for persons with severe disabilities. *Journal of Rehabilitation.*

Hill, M., Wehman, P., Banks, P. D., & Metzler, H. (1987). *Benefit-cost analysis of competitively employed persons with moderate and severe handicaps.* Unpublished manuscript, Virginia Commonwealth University, Rehabilitation Research and Training Center, Richmond.

Hill, J., Wehman, P., Hill, M., & Goodall, P. (1984). Differential reasons for job separation of previously employed persons with mental retardation. *Mental Retardation, 24*(6), 347–351.

Horner, R. H., Meyer, L. H., & Fredericks, H. D. (1986). *Education of learners with severe handicaps: Exemplary service strategies.* Baltimore: Paul H. Brookes Publishing Co.

Horton, B., Maddox, M., & Edgar, E. (1983). *The adult transition model: Planning for post school services.* Seattle: University of Washington.

Hutchins, M., & Talarico, D. (1985). Administrative considerations in providing community integrated training programs. In P. McCarthy, J. Everson, S. Moon, & M. Barcus (Eds.), *School to work transition for youths with severe disabilities* (Monograph). Richmond: Virginia Commonwealth University, Project Transition Into Employment.

Kiernan, W. E., Smith, B. C., & Ostrowsky, M. B. (1986). Developmental disabilities: definitional issues. In W. E. Kiernan & J. A. Stark (Eds.), *Pathways to employment for adults with developmental disabilities* (pp. 11–20). Baltimore: Paul H. Brookes Publishing Co.

Klinger, B. Handicapped youth facing employment. *Alexandria Gazette,* March 16, 1985.

Kregel, J., Wehman, P., Seyfarth, J., & Marshall, K. (1985). Community integration for youth with mental retardation: Transition from school to adulthood. *Education and Training of the Mentally Retarded, 21*(1), 35–42.

Kusserow, R. (1984). *A program inspection on transition of developmentally disabled young adults from school to adult services* (U.S. Government Printing Office, 1984, 754021/4548). Washington, DC: Department of Health and Human Services.

Lacour, J. A. (1982). Interagency agreement: A rational response to an irrational system. *Exceptional Children, 49*(3), 265–266.

Lambrou, J., Lowder, M., Leslie, J., Jensen, L., Heidelberger, J., Zeller, D., Moure, C., & Steirer, J. (1986). *Transition! School to community.* Boise: Idaho State Department of Education.

Louis Harris Poll. (1986, February). *A survey of the unemployment of persons with disabilities.*

Lyon, S. L., & Lyon, G. (1980). Team functioning and staff development: A role release approach to providing integrated educational services for severely handicapped students. *Journal of The Association for the Severely Handicapped, 5*(3), 250–263.

Mank, D. M., Rhodes, L. E., & Bellamy, G. T. (1986). Four supported employment alternatives. In W. E. Kiernan & J. A. Stark (Eds.), *Pathways to employment for adults with developmental disabilities.* (pp. 139–153). Baltimore: Paul H. Brookes Publishing Co.

Massachusetts Department of Education. (1982). *The after 22 study.* Boston: Division of Special Education, Department of Education.

McCarthy, P., Everson, J. M., Inge, K. J., & Barcus, J. M. (1985, October). Transition from school to work: Developing the process for individuals with severe disabilities. *Techniques: A Journal for Remedial Education and Counseling, 1*(6), 463–472.

McCarthy, P., Everson, J. M., Moon, S., & Barcus, J. M. (Eds.). (1985). *School-to-work transition for youth with severe disabilities* (Monograph). Richmond: Virginia Commonwealth University, Project Transition Into Employment.

McCormick, L., & Goldman, R. (1979). The transdisciplinary model: Implications for service delivery and personnel preparation for the severely and profoundly handicapped. *AAESPH Review, 47*(2), 152–161.

McDonnell, J. J., & Hardman, M. (1985, December). Planning the transition of severely handicapped youth from school to adult services: A framework for high school programs. *Education and Training of the Mentally Retarded,* 275–286.

McDonnell, J. J., Wilcox, B., & Boles, S. M. (1986). Do we know enough to plan for transition? A national survey of state agencies responsible for services to persons with severe handicaps. *Journal of The Association for Persons with Severe Handicaps, 11*(1), 53–60.

McDonnell, J. J., Wilcox, B., Boles, S. M., & Bellamy, G. T. (1985). Transition issues facing youth with severe disabilities: Parents' perspective. *Journal of The Association for Persons with Severe Handicaps, 11*(4), 53–60.

McGee, J. (1975). *Workstations in industry.* Omaha: University of Nebraska.

McLeod, B. (1985, March). Real work for real pay. *Psychology Today, 14*(3), 42, 44, 46, 48–50.

Mithaug, D. E., Horiuchi, C., & Fanning, P. N. (1985). A report on the Colorado statewide follow-up survey of special education students. *Exceptional Children, 51*(5), 397–404.

Moon, M. S., & Beale, A. (1984). Vocational training and employment: Guidelines for parents. *The Exceptional Parent, 14*(8), 35–38.

Moon, M. S., Goodall, P., Barcus, M., & Brooke, V. (1986). *The supported work model of competitive employment for citizens with severe handicaps: A guide for job trainers* (2nd ed.). Richmond: Virginia Commonwealth University, Rehabilitation Research and Training Center.

National Council on the Handicapped. (1986, February). *Travel independence.* Washington, DC: Government Printing Office.

Nietupski, J. A., Hamre-Nietupski, S., Welch, J., & Anderson, R. J. (1983). Establishing and maintaining vocational training sites for moderately and severely handicapped students: Strategies for community/vocational trainers. *Education and Training of the Mentally Retarded, 18*(3), 169–175.

Noble, J. R. (1985, July). *A comparative cost-benefit analysis of adult day programs, sheltered workshops, and competitive employment.* Paper presented at UAF Leadership Seminar. Richmond: Virginia Commonwealth University.

Olson, D. H, McCubbin, H. I., Barnes, H., Larsen, A., Muren, M., & Wilson, M. (1984). *One thousand families: A national survey.* Beverly Hills, CA: Sage Publications.

O'Neill, C. (1983). *Report on State of Washington job placement of developmentally disabled individuals.* Seattle, Washington: Division of Developmental Disabilities.

O'Neill, C. (1986, October). Written response to authors' questionnaire on transition rules and responsibilities.

Paine, S. C., Bellamy, G. T., & Wilcox, B. (Eds.). (1984). *Human services that work: From innovation to standard practice*. Baltimore: Paul H. Brookes Publishing Co.

Pietruski, W., Everson, J., Goodwyn, R., & Wehman, P. (1985). *Vocational training and curriculum for multihandicapped youth with cerebral palsy*. Richmond: Virginia Commonwealth University, Rehabilitation Research and Training Center.

Poole, D. L (1985). *Social work and the supported work services model. A position paper*. Richmond: Virginia Commonwealth University, Supported Work Services Employment Project, School of Social Work.

Porter, M. E., & Varty, J. (1980). Building linkages with the rehabilitation agency: Development and implementation of a model program. Paper presented at the Annual Conference on the Disabled Student on American Campuses. (ERIC Document Reproduction Service, ED 187394).

Pumpian, I., Shepard, H., & West, E. (1986). *Negotiating job training stations with employers*. Unpublished manuscript, San Diego State University, San Diego.

Razeghi, J. (1986). Word from Washington. *The Journal for Vocational Special Needs Education, 8*(3), 35–37.

Rehabilitation Act Amendments (1986). PL 99-506. Washington, DC: U.S. Government Printing Office.

Rhodes, L. E., & Valenta, L. (1985). Industry based supported employment. *Journal of The Association for Persons with Severe Handicaps, 10,* 12–20.

Rhodes, S. R. (1986). *Interagency cooperative/collaborative agreements*. Washington, DC: National Association of Developmental Disabilities Councils.

Ricklefs, R. (1986). Faced with shortages of unskilled labor, employers hire more retarded workers. *Wall Street Journal*, October 21, 35.

Rogers, C., & Farrow, F. (1983). *Effective state strategies to promote interagency collaboration. A report of the Handicapped Public Policy Analysis Project*. The Center for the Study of Social Policy.

Rollin, J. (1986) *Project Transition in Florida*. Tallahassee: Florida School Board Association.

Rubin, S. E. & Roessler, R. T. (1978). *Foundations of the vocational rehabilitation process*. Baltimore: University Park Press.

Rusch, F. R. (Ed.), (1986). *Competitive employment issues and strategies*. Baltimore: Paul H. Brookes Publishing Co.

Rusch, F. R., & Chadsey-Rusch, J. (1985). Employment for persons with severe handicaps: Curriculum development and coordination of services. *Focus on Exceptional Children, 17*(9), 1–8.

Rusch, F. R., Chadsey-Rusch, J., & Lagomarcino (1986). Preparing students for employment. In M. E. Snell (Ed.), *Systematic instruction of persons with severe handicaps*. Columbus, OH: Charles E. Merrill, 471–490.

Rusch, F. R., & Mithaug, D. E. (1980). *Vocational training for mentally retarded adults. A behavior analytic approach*. Champaign, IL: Research Press.

Rusch, F. R., Mithaug, D. E., & Flexer, R. W. (1986). Obstacles to competitive employment and traditional program options for overcoming them. In F. R. Rusch (Ed.), *Competitive employment issues and strategies*. Baltimore: Paul H. Brookes Publishing Co.

Rusch, F. R., Schutz, R. P., & Agran, M. (1982). Validating entry-level survival skills for service occupations: Implications for curriculum development. *Journal of The Association for the Severely Handicapped.*, *7*, 32–41.

Sailor, W., Halvorsen, A., Anderson, J., Goetz, L., Gee, K., Doering, K., & Hunt, P. (1986). Community intensive instruction. In R. H. Horner, L. H. Meyer, & H. D. Fredericks (Eds.), *Education of learners with severe handicaps: Exemplary service strategies* (pp. 251–288). Baltimore: Paul H. Brookes Publishing Co.

Schindler-Rainman, E., & Lippitt, R. (1977). *Toward interagency collaboration, volunteer administration, 10*(2).

Seyfarth, J., Hill, J., McMillan, J., Orelove, F., McMillan, J., & Wehman, P. (in press). Factors influencing parents' vocational aspirations for their mentally retarded children. *Mental Retardation.*

Shafer, M., Hill, J, Seyfarth, J., Wehman, P., & Banks, P. D. (in press). A survey of employers experiences with supported employment. *American Journal of Mental Deficiency.*

Snell, M. E. (1986). *Systematic instruction of persons with severe handicaps.* Columbus, OH: Charles E. Merrill.

Snell, M. E., & Grigg, N. C. (1986). Instructional assessment and curriculum development. In M. E. Snell (Ed.) *Systematic instruction of persons with severe handicaps* (64–109) Columbus, OH: Charles E. Merrill.

Sowers, J., Thompson, L., & Connis, R. (1979). The food service vocational training program: A model for training and placement of the mentally retarded. In G. T. Bellamy, G. O'Connor, & O. C. Karen (Eds.), *Vocational rehabilitation of severely handicapped persons.* Baltimore: University Park Press.

Stainback, S., & Stainback, W. (1984). *Integration of students with severe handicaps into regular schools.* Reston: The Council for Exceptional Children.

Stanfield, F. (1973). Graduation: What happens to the retarded child when he grows up? *Exceptional Children*, *6*, 1–11.

Stodden, R., Browder, P., Boone, R., Patton, J., Hill, M., Fickens, J., Lau, R., Nishimoto, J., & Shirachi, S. (1986). *Overview of transition and the Hawaii transition project.* Honolulu: University of Hawaii at Manoa, The Hawaii Transition Project.

Szymanski, E. M., Buckley, J., Parent, W. S., Parker, R. M., & Westbrook, J. D. (1988). Rehabilitation counseling in supported employment: A conceptual model for service delivery and personnel preparation. In S. Rubin & N. Rubin (Eds.), *Contemporary challenges to the rehabilitation counseling profession.*

Tichy, N. M. (1983). *Managing strategic change: Technical, political, and cultural dynamics.* New York: John Wiley & Sons.

Titus, R., & Travis, J. (1973). Follow-up of EMR program graduates. *Mental Retardation*, *11*, 24–26.

Tooman, M. L., Revell, G. W., & Melia, R. P. (1986). *The role of the rehabilitation counselor in the provision of transition and supported employment programs.* Unpublished manuscript, ARCA Task Force on Supported Employment Subcommittee on Role, Richmond.

U.S. Department of Labor. (1977). *Sheltered workshop study: Workshop survey: Volume I.* Washington, DC: U.S. Department of Labor.

Vandergoot, D., & Worrall, J. D. (Eds.). (1979). *Placement in rehabilitation: A career development perspective.* Baltimore: University Park Press.

Venn, J. J., Dubose, R. F., & Merbler, J. B. (1977). Parent and teacher expectations for the adult lives of their severely and profoundly handicapped children. *The American Association for the Education of the Severely/Profoundly Handicapped Review, 2*(4), 223–238.

Wehman, P. (1981). Training for competitive employment. In P. Wehman, *Competitive employment: New horizons for severely disabled individuals* (pp. 45–75). Baltimore: Paul H. Brookes Publishing Co.

Wehman, P. (1983). Toward the employability of severely handicapped children and youth. *Teaching Exceptional Children,* Summer, 219–223.

Wehman, P. (1986). Supported competitive employment for persons with severe disabilities. *Journal of Applied Rehabilitation Counseling, 17*(4), 24–31.

Wehman, P., & Hill, J. (1982). Preparing severely handicapped students for less restrictive environments. *Journal of The Association for the Severely Handicapped, 7,* 33–39.

Wehman, P., Hill, M., Hill, J., Brooke, V., Pendleton, P., & Britt, C. (1985). Competitive employment for persons with mental retardation: A follow-up six years later. *Mental Retardation, 23*(6), 274–281.

Wehman, P., Hill, J., Wood, W., & Parent, W. A report on competitive employment histories of persons labeled severely mentally retarded. *Journal of The Asssociation for Persons with Severe Handicaps, 12*(1), 11–17.

Wehman, P., Kregel, J., & Barcus, J. M. (1985). From school to work: A vocational transition model for handicapped students. *Exceptional Children, 52*(1), 25–37.

Wehman, P., Kregel, J., & Seyfarth, J. (1985a). Employment outlook for young adults with mental retardation. *Rehabilitation Counseling Bulletin, 29*(2), 91–99.

Wehman, P., Kregel, J., & Seyfarth, J. (1985b). Transition from school to work for individuals with severe handicaps: A follow-up study. *Journal of The Association for Persons with Severe Handicaps, 10*(3), 132–136.

Wehman, P., & McLaughlin, P. (1980). *Vocational curriculum for developmentally disabled persons.* Austin, TX: PRO-ED.

Wehman, P., & Melia, R. (1985). The job coach: Function and roles in transitional and supported employment. *American Rehabilitation, 11*(2), 4–7.

Wehman, P., Moon, M. S., & McCarthy, P. (1986). Transition from school to adulthood for youth with severe handicaps. *Focus on Exceptional Children, 18*(5), 1–12.

Wehman, P., Parent, W., Wood, W., Michaud, C., Ford, C., Miller, S., Marchant, J., & Walker, R. (1987) *From school to competitive employment for young adults with mental retardation: Transition in practice.* Unpublished manuscript, Virginia Commonwealth University, Rehabilitation Research and Training Center, Richmond.

Wehman, P., & Pentecost, J. H. (1983). Facilitating employment for moderately and severely handicapped youth. *Education and Treatment of Children, 6*(11), 69–80.

Wehman, P., Renzaglia, A., & Bates, P. (1985). *Functional living skills for moderately and severely handicapped adults.* Austin, TX: PRO-ED.

Whitehead, C. W. (1979). Sheltered workshops in the decade ahead: Work wages, and welfare. In G. T. Bellamy, G. O'Connor, & O. C. Karan (Eds.), *Vocational rehabilitation of severely handicapped persons.* (71–84). Baltimore: University Park Press.

Whitehead, C. W., & Rhodes, S. (1985). *Guidelines for evaluating, reviewing, and enhancing employment-related services for people with developmen-*

tal disabilities. Washington, DC: National Association of Developmental Disabilities Council.

Wilcox, B., & Bellamy, G. T. (1982). *Design of high school programs for severely handicapped students*. Baltimore: Paul H. Brookes Publishing Co.

Wilcox, B., & Bellamy, G. T. (1987). *The activities catalog: An alternative curriculum for youth and adults with severe disabilities*. Baltimore: Paul H. Brookes Publishing Co.

Will, M. C. (1984a). Let us pause and reflect—but not too long. *Exceptional Children, 51,* 11–16.

Will, M. C. (1984b). *OSERS programming for the transition of youth with disabilities: Bridges from school to working life.* Washington, DC: Office of Special Education and Rehabilitative Services, U.S. Department of Education.

Wolfe, B. (1980). How the disabled fare in the labor market. *Monthly Labor Report: Research Summaries,* September, 48–52.

Zetlin, A., & Turner, J. L. (1985). Transition from adolescence to adulthood: Perspectives of the mentally retarded individuals and their families. *American Journal of Mental Deficiency, 89*(6), 570–579.

Index

Action plans, see Agreements,
    interagency
Adjustment, 29–48
    studies of vocational adjustment,
        32–38
    survey of, 42–48
Adjustment of Mentally Retarded
    Persons Survey, 42–48
Adult development centers,
    172–173
Adult services, 76–77
Agreements, interagency, 59–65,
    111–116
    sample, 116–130
        action plans, 59–65
        administrative considerations,
            128–129
        Consumer-Specific Intervention
            Time Recording Sheet,
            124–125
        cooperating agency liaisons,
            118–119
        exchange of information,
            126–127
        expected outcomes, 127–128
        individualized transition
            meetings, 119–122
        mission statement, 117–118
        supported employment
            services, 122–126
        three-way agreement, 129
    see also Interagency cooperation
Association for Retarded Citizens
    on-the-job training program,
        267–268

Career education, 132, 134–136
    see also Vocational training
Career Education Implementa-
    tion Incentive Act of 1977
    (PL 95-207), 132
Carl D. Perkins Vocational Edu-
    cational Act (PL 98-524),
    97–98, 205–206, 233, 237,
    262
Case management agencies, role in
    transition planning, 203–205
Chesterfield County Interagency
    Release of Information
    Authorization, 74, 120
Communication with parents, 96
Community adjustment, 3
Community-based instruction, 11,
    141–163
    see also Vocational training
Community services program
    effectiveness, 106–107, 111
    chart, 108–110
    see also Needs assessment
Competitive employment, 176–178,
    182
Consumer-Specific Intervention
    Time Recording Sheet,
    124–125
Curriculum, 8–9, 15–19, 138–142

Data collection in community-based
    training, 147–163
    Production Rate Recording Form,
        157

Data collection—*continued*
    Task Analysis Recording Sheet,
        153–154
    Work Regularity/Percent Time
        On-Task, 158–159
Developmental Disabilities Act of
    1984 (PL 98-527), 205, 262
Disabled adult clients, role in
    transition planning, 210

Education for All Handicapped
    Children Act (PL 94-142), 1,
    18, 99, 208, 245, 259
Education for Handicapped
    Children Amendments of
    1983 (PL 98-199), 4, 14, 57,
    232–233, 261
Educational and community
    integration, 9–10
Educational services approach to
    transition planning, 208–210
Employer resistance, 20–21
Employment
    incentive programs
        Association for Retarded
            Citizens, 267–268
        federal, 264–267
    information sources, 271–273
    opportunities, 165–167, 171–193
        choosing vocational
            alternatives, 192–193
        cost of unemployment, 168–171
        mobile work crews and
            enclaves, 187–191
        rationale for, 166–168
        small business option, 192
        supported employment,
            179–187
    options, 257–258
    programs in schools, 14–16
Employment Opportunities for
    Disabled Americans Act
    (PL 99-643), 205, 262
Enclaves, 187, 189–191

Family role in transition planning,
    206–208
Federal employment incentive
    programs, 264–267

Federal initiatives, 259–264
Federal legislation, 259–269
Federal priorities, 259–264
Federal role in transition, 4–5
Florida, transition programs in,
    241–243
Follow-up surveys, 30–48
    methodological and logistical
        problems of, 38–40
    reasons for, 30–32
    sample of, 41–48
    during 1970–1980, 32–34
    during 1980–1986, 34–38

Generic services, 2

Halpern model, 3
Handicapped Act Amendments of
    1986 (PL 99-457), 97

Illinois, transition programs in,
    229–241
Indiana, transition programs in,
    243–246
Individualized education programs,
    138–142
    see also Individualized transition
        plans
Individualized transition plans,
    12–14, 26–27, 70–96,
    195–196
    Cover Sheet for, 75
    exit meeting for, 70, 95–96
    goals of, 80–83, 86–87, 90–91
    implementation of, 70, 95
    initial meeting for, 70, 72–95
    samples of, 24–26, 84–85, 88–89,
        92–93
    team for, 65–68, 70–72
    updating of, 70, 95
    see also Individualized education
        programs; Transition plan-
        ning; Transition teams
Integrated settings, training in,
    141–163
    see also Vocational training
Interagency approach to transition
    planning, 210–215

Interagency cooperation, 13–14,
    16–17, 97–98, 195–215
  guidelines for interagency transi-
    tion planning, 58–59
  at local level, 50–68, 101–102,
    111–113
  models, 113–116
  at state level, 98–101
  see also Agreements, interagency

Job training, 268–270
  stations in industry, 133, 135, 137
  see also On-the-job training; Vo-
    cational training
Job Training Partnership Act
  (PL 97-300), 268–269

Liability, 22–23
Life-Centered Career Education Pro-
    gram, 136–137
Local core transition teams, 50–65,
    101–102
  development of, 50–55
  goals of, 54–55
  members of, 53–54

Media role in transition, 6–7
Medical services approach to transi-
    tion planning, 208–210
Mobile work crews, 187–191

Needs assessment, 55–62, 102
  sample chart for, 104–105
  sample issues for, 60–61
  sample questions for, 56–57
  see also Community services pro-
    gram effectiveness

Omnibus Reconciliation Act of 1981
    (PL 97-35), 205, 264
On-the-job training
  by Association for Retarded Cit-
    izens, 267–268
  by vocational rehabilitation agen-
    cies, 266–267
  see also Job training; Vocational
    training

Ongoing vocational services, see
  Supported employment

Paid job placements, 137
Parent role, 13, 19–20, 145,
    206–208, 253–255
Parents, communication with, 96
PL 92-223, 263
PL 94-142 (Education for All Handi-
    capped Children Act), 1, 18,
    99, 208, 245, 259
PL 95-207 (Career Education Imple-
    mentation Incentive Act of
    1977), 132
PL 96-265 (Social Security Dis-
    ability Amendments of 1980),
    263
PL 97-35 (Omnibus Reconciliation
    Act of 1981), 205, 264
PL 97-300 (Job Training Partnership
    Act), 268–269
PL 98-199 (Education for Handi-
    capped Children Amend-
    ments of 1983), 4, 14, 57,
    232–233, 261
PL 98-524 (Carl D. Perkins Voca-
    tional Education Act), 97–98,
    205–206, 233, 237, 262
PL 98-527 (Developmental Dis-
    abilities Act of 1984), 205,
    262
PL 99-457 (Handicapped Act
    Amendments of 1986), 97
PL 99-506 (Rehabilitation Act
    Amendments of 1986), 97,
    264
PL 99-643 (Employment Oppor-
    tunities for Disabled Ameri-
    cans Act), 205, 262
Production Rate Recording Form,
    157
Projects with Industry, 269–270
Public awareness, 23
Public resistance, 20–21

Rehabilitation Act Amendments of
    1986 (PL 99-506), 97, 264
Rehabilitation Act of 1973, 201–202
  1986 Amendments, 179, 201
Residential options, 257–258

School role in transition, 7–9
Services Referral Checklist, 94
Sheltered workshops, 173–176
Small business option, 192
Social Security Act, 205
  1965 Amendments, 263
  1972 Amendments, 263
  1974 Amendments, 263
Social Security Disability Amend-
    ments of 1980 (PL 96-265),
    263
Special education
  aid to vocational educators,
    17–20
  role in transition planning,
    198–201
Student role in transition planning,
    210
Supported employment, 2, 4–5,
    179–193
  local level programs, 217–228
  model for, 182–187
  sample interagency agreement for,
    116–130
  state level programs, 217–219,
    229–251

Targeted Jobs Tax Credit, 264–266
Task Analysis Recording Sheet,
    153–154
Three Stage Transition Model, 7–8,
    11
Time-limited services, 2–5
Transdisciplinary approach to tran-
    sition planning, 210–215
Transition, definition of, 2–3, 50
Transition planning, 11–16, 24–27,
    49–96, 195–215
  roles and responsibilities,
    197–210
  of case management agencies,
    203–205
  of disabled adult client, 210
  of educational and medical ser-
    vices, 208–210
  of parent and family, 206–208
  of special education, 198–201
  of student, 210
  of vocational education,
    205–206

of vocational rehabilitation,
    201–207
  sample interagency agreement for,
    116–130
  see also Individualized transition
    plans; Transition teams
Transition programs, 217–251
  at local level, 219–228
  at state level, 229–251
  in Florida, 241–243
  in Illinois, 229–241
  in Indiana, 243–246
  in Virginia, 219–228, 246–248
Transition teams, 195–210
  individualized transition plan
    teams, 65–68
  interagency transition teams,
    210–215
  local core transition teams,
    50–65, 101–102
  transdisciplinary teams, 210–215
Transitional employment, 178–179
Transportation, 22

Unemployment, 97, 165
  costs of, 168–171
U.S. Department of Education tran-
    sition model, 2–3

Virginia, transition programs in,
    219–228, 246–248
Vocational adjustment studies,
    postsecondary, 29–48
  during 1970–1980, 32–34
  during 1980–1986, 34–38
Vocational education
  role in transition planning,
    205–206
  special education aid to, 17–20
Vocational Education Act of 1963,
    205
  1968 Amendments to, 205
Vocational rehabilitation
  on-the-job training by, 266–267
  role in transition planning,
    201–203
Vocational training, 131, 133–135,
    141–163
  data collection, 147–163

Production Rate Recording
Form, 157
Task Analysis Recording Sheet,
153–154
Work Regularity/Percent Time
On-Task, 158–159
elementary school guidelines, 134
high school guidelines, 135
middle school guidelines,
134–135
Life-Centered Career Education
Program, 136–137
see also Career education; Community-based instruction; Integrated settings; Job training;
On-the-job training
Vocational training technology, role
of in transition, 5–6

Wehman model, 3, 7–8
Work experience, 133
Work Regularity/Percent Time On-
Task, 158–159
Workstudy, 133